TIME CAPSULE/1941

TIME CAPSULE/1941

A HISTORY OF THE YEAR CONDENSED FROM THE PAGES OF TIME

TIME-LIFE BOOKS, NEW YORK

TIME / **1941**

EDITOR *Henry R. Luce*
MANAGING EDITORS *Manfred Gottfried, Frank Norris,*
T. S. Matthews
ASSOCIATE EDITORS *Roy Alexander, Carlton J. Balliett Jr.,*
Robert Cantwell, Whittaker Chambers, Mary Fraser,
Laird S. Goldsborough, Walter Graebner, John Hersey,
David W. Hulburd Jr., Eliot Janeway, John K. Jessup,
John Stuart Martin, Sidney Olson, John Osborne,
Fanny Saul, Walter Stockly, Leon Svirsky, Dana Tasker,
Charles Wertenbaker

EDITOR *Maitland A. Edey*
EXECUTIVE EDITOR *Jerry Korn*
TEXT DIRECTOR *Martin Mann*
ART DIRECTOR *Sheldon Cotler*
CHIEF OF RESEARCH *Beatrice T. Dobie*

SERIES EDITOR *John Dille*
ASSISTANT EDITORS *John von Hartz, Jeffrey Tarter*
RESEARCHERS *Doris Kinney, Barbara Ballantine*
ASSISTANT ART DIRECTOR *Arnold Holeywell*
COPYREADER *Rosemarie Conefrey*

PUBLISHER *Rhett Austell*

COVER ILLUSTRATION *Lou Lomonaco*

EVENTS OF THE YEAR

FDR begins his third term
11

Congress passes the Lend-Lease Bill
35

Japanese planes bomb Pearl Harbor
67

The British Navy sinks the *Bismarck*
75

The Nazis invade Russia
91

Rudolf Hess, No. 3 Nazi, flies mysteriously to Britain
124

Champion Joe Louis defeats Buddy Baer, Billy Conn, Lou Nova
170, 171, 174

"The Hut-Sut Song" is on the hit parade
192

Sister Kenny's revolutionary treatment for polio
199

The deaths of novelists Fitzgerald, Joyce, Anderson, Woolf
224, 226, 227, 228

Editors' Note

December 7, 1941 will always be remembered as "the day the U.S. went to war." The fact is, as the news accounts now make clear, the nation was already thoroughly embroiled in the war—without really realizing it—long before the Japanese attack on Pearl Harbor. U.S. troops were moving to Iceland; U.S. ships were being sunk by Nazi torpedoes; U.S. aid was going to both Russia and Britain; U.S. industry was tooling up for "defense" long before that fateful Sunday, December 7.

In this volume, the first news of Pearl Harbor appears under the marginal date of December 15. The issue of TIME dated December 8 had already gone to press when the attack began. The first account of the attack shows up at the end of the War & Peace section on page 67. Follow-up reports on the fighting appear in the section labeled World War, starting on page 105.

■

TIME CAPSULE/1941 is one of a series of volumes, each adapted and condensed from a year's contents of TIME, the Weekly Newsmagazine. The words, except for a few connecting passages, are those of the magazine itself, and therefore reflect the flavor, the attitudes and the state of knowledge of the day—sometimes innocent, sometimes opinionated, sometimes prescient. The book is divided, like the magazine, into departments, and is organized so that each department forms a chronological chapter for the entire year. The dates in the margin are the issue dates of the magazine.

This is one of a series of volumes, each adapted and condensed from a year's contents of TIME, the Weekly Newsmagazine. The words, except for a few connecting passages, are those of the magazine itself, and therefore reflect the flavor, the attitudes and the state of knowledge of the day—sometimes innocent, sometimes opinionated, sometimes prescient. The book is divided, like the magazine, into departments, and is organized so that each department forms a chronological chapter for the entire year. The dates in the margin are the issue dates of the magazine.

NATIONAL AFFAIRS

The Presidency

Franklin Delano Roosevelt was starting an unprecedented third term in the White House. His New Deal measures had made him highly unpopular with many of the nation's businessmen and had aroused opposition even in the Democratic-controlled Congress. But in the fall of 1940 Roosevelt had defeated the Republican Presidential candidate, Wendell Willkie, by an overwhelming margin. With this new mandate he began to lead the U.S. away from its traditional isolationism and to align the nation more and more on the side of Great Britain and Russia in the war against Germany.

JAN. 6 **THE PRESIDENT SPEAKS:** The little oval room was hot. The score of frail, wobbly, gilt chairs were jammed close together on the deep scarlet carpet. Perspiring gently, the audience sat still, in some nervousness. In the front row, not grinning, was big, jug-eared Cinemactor Clark Gable in a chalk-stripe grey suit; his wife, Carole Lombard, in a funnel-like black hat with a veil, a simple black afternoon dress; Secretary of State Cordell Hull, as sombre as his dark suit; and the President's mother, Sara Roosevelt, in a grey-blue evening gown.

On the desk, its top drilled for microphone wires, were seven microphones, two glasses of water, two new sharp pencils, a notepad, an open package of Camels. The President came in five minutes before the broadcast, on his small rubber-tired wheel chair. Mr. Roosevelt, in a dark blue serge suit, a black bow tie, was in high good humor. In the room's warmth he mopped his big, tanned face from time to time with a large white handkerchief.

At 9:30 p.m. more than 500 radio stations in the U.S. were tuned to his desk. Attendance at movies dropped sharply. In barrooms, farmhouses, trains, planes and ships, people waited, listening. His words might mark a turning point in history.

As he began his 15th fireside chat the President spoke in

simple terms, clearly, gravely. He was deliberately trying to lead the nation as he had led it in 1933. More than once he talked down to his audience as he answered the questions men had been asking:

How great is the danger? Mr. Roosevelt said: "Never before . . . has our American civilization been in such danger as now."

Who is the enemy? The President pointed to the tripartite agreement of the Axis powers—Germany, Italy & Japan—in "the threat that if the United States interfered with or blocked . . . a program aimed at world control—they would unite in ultimate action against the United States."

What is the Nazi program? He said: ". . . to dominate all life and thought in their own country . . . to enslave the whole of Europe . . . to use the resources of Europe to dominate the rest of the world."

Why is this war a concern of the U.S.? Said the President: "If Great Britain goes down, all of us in the Americas would be living at the point of a gun. The vast resources and wealth of this Hemisphere constitute the most tempting loot in the world."

What's to be done? Arm, more and faster—more planes, tanks, guns, freighters. Required soon might be rationing of consumer and luxury goods. He concluded: "We must be the great arsenal of democracy."

FOR FOUR HUMAN FREEDOMS: The President leaned heavily JAN. 13 on the rostrum, threw open the big black leather binder, straightway began his message to the 77th Congress on the State of the Union:

"Armed defense of democratic existence is now being gallantly waged in four continents. . . . No realistic American can expect from a dictator's peace international generosity. . . . Such a peace would bring no security for us or for our neighbors."

Mr. Roosevelt spoke clearly as ever, but there was no lightness in his voice, no touch of humor. As he went on, his big head thrown back, his voice gained depth and strength and emotion:

"In the future days, which we seek to make secure, we look forward to a world founded upon four essential freedoms.

"The first is freedom of speech and expression—everywhere in the world.

"The second is freedom of every person to worship God in his own way—everywhere in the world.

"The third is freedom from want . . . everywhere in the world.

"The fourth is freedom from fear . . . anywhere in the world. . . .

"To that high concept there can be no end save victory."

Before the U.S. could serve as an arsenal of democracy, the President had to find a way to get around the Neutrality Act which banned military assistance to nations at war. One device to accomplish this was the Lend-Lease Bill, which empowered the President to disregard the neutrality provisions in the interests of national defense and to ship food and arms to nations already fighting the Axis without a formal declaration of war.

JAN. 20 **LEND-LEASE:** In Washington, President Roosevelt sent to Congress a bill whose vast powers made the crisis unmistakable. In effect a blank check for Congress's signature, the Lend-Lease Bill would give the Executive the power to obtain and transfer war supplies to Britain and her allies, was read to a startled Congress.

Yet there was less discussion of the bill than of President Roosevelt. The issues and charges of the campaign—the fear of dictatorship, the distrust of the Third Term, the charges that a continuation of the New Deal would mean a collectivized state—came back like echoes that blurred arguments before they were clearly heard.

Said distrustful Columnist Raymond Clapper: "When he is proposing to take power from Congress, Mr. Roosevelt is all eager for quick action. When it is for him to yield up some power, then the matter must be weighed very deliberately."

JAN. 27 **THIRD TERM BEGINS:** Inauguration Day, the sun rose on a city brave with flags. The sharp wind brought sounds that made people quicken their step—distant bands playing, far-off police sirens screaming faintly, the drone of planes high

overhead in wild-goose Vs. Along the route, sidewalk sales-
men did a brisk business hawking badges: "To Hell With
Hitler."

People came like an audience to the opera, dutifully, knowing that something fine would occur, that the main actors
would acquit themselves well in familiar roles. After repeating
the worn, full, old words of the oath, the President turned to
the crowd, waited a moment, and began his Third Inaugural
Address.

Said Mr. Roosevelt: "Democracy is not dying"; tyranny
and slavery are not "the wave of the future."

When he finished, he turned away, then turned back and
waved his top hat. At this familiar gesture the crowd cheered.

Suddenly the mood shifted; the mild, casual air of the inauguration gave way to a glimpse of the future. Armored cars
and soldiers on motorcycles began to stream by. Then three
tanks, more armored cars, 42 light tanks, eight truckloads of
anti-aircraft guns—the machines of war. The afternoon air
thickened and blued with gasoline fumes.

FAMILY MAN: The day after the inauguration for the Third FEB. 3
Term, President Roosevelt held his press conference as usual.
Only new note: he dodged unwelcome questions with a new
excuse—that he was too sleepy to answer, his children having
kept him up late.

ANSWER: When Wendell Willkie talked with President Roose- FEB. 17
velt before going to Britain, the President gave him a letter to
Winston Churchill. In a powerful speech last week Britain's
Prime Minister replied: "Put your confidence in us. Give us
your faith and your blessing, and under Providence all will be
well. We shall not fail or falter. We shall not weaken or tire.
Neither the sudden shock of battle nor the long-drawn trials
of vigilance and exertion will wear us down. Give us the tools
and we will finish the job."

"WATCH MRS. ROOSEVELT": In eight years the U.S. has had MARCH 3
plenty of time to put together a lifelike picture of Eleanor
Roosevelt. Some of the pieces were missing—part of the time
Mrs. Roosevelt was missing—but the outlines were clear: an
incredibly busy, indefatigable housekeeper who was forever

scrubbing out dark corners of her domain, worrying over the welfare of the poor people across the tracks, clucking disapproval of dust in Oklahoma and mud tracked into the living room by soil erosion. Some citizens were annoyed, some were puzzled.

President Roosevelt: "We must be the arsenal of democracy." Page 10.　　*Mrs. Roosevelt: the nation's busy housekeeper, clucking disapproval.*

Last week Mrs. Roosevelt warned housewives to start thinking about doing without new automobiles, aluminum kitchen utensils, etc. For once, Washington and Wall Street winced as one. *The Wall Street Journal* voiced a shadowy but growing fear: "Mrs. Roosevelt is increasingly active; watch her for tips on policies. Her discernible influence on the President is indirect but important."

Wall Streeters, already snowed under by dope-sheets, added *My Day* [a syndicated newspaper column by Mrs. Roosevelt] to their long list of required reading.

MARCH 17　**NINTH YEAR BEGINS:** At noon last Tuesday Franklin Roosevelt became the first man in U.S. history to serve as President for more than eight years. His head heavy with a cold, his natural buoyancy overlaid with the gravity of his ever heavier responsibility, he told reporters that the crisis today was greater in some ways than the crisis of 1933. His voice was low and tired.

DECISION: News from Washington was news for the whole MARCH world. The Lend-Lease Bill, granting military aid to Britain, had passed the House and the Senate. In 20 minutes it was delivered to the White House. Ten minutes later it had been signed by President Roosevelt, and had become law. Five minutes later the President approved a list of articles—what kind and to what amount he would not say—for immediate shipment abroad. U.S. flags were broken out in the shattered streets of London. All over the world the news and its import were heard and realized.

Later, at a crowded dinner of the White House Correspondents' Association, President Roosevelt spoke for 34 minutes, said:

"I remember, a quarter of a century ago . . . that the German Government received solemn assurances from their representatives that the people of America were disunited; that they cared more for peace at any price than for the preservation of ideals and freedom. . . . Let not dictators of Europe or Asia doubt our unanimity now. . . . May it be said of us in the days to come that our children and our children's children rise up and call us blessed."

REST: The Presidential yacht *Potomac*, armed for the first time MARCH with .50-calibre machine guns fore & aft, slipped out to sea from Port Everglades, Fla. with her two escorting destroyers, to undisclosed fishing grounds, to a period of rest and relaxation for the President. He needed it. The crises that were coming would require a reserve of strength through the spring.

NEWS AMONG NEWSMEN: The news was brought to the Pres- APRIL 14 ident as he sat at a banquet in the Willard Hotel. Secretary of State Cordell Hull adjusted his pince-nez, impassively handed a torn-off news-ticker scrap to Franklin Roosevelt. Russia and Yugoslavia had signed a non-aggression pact. While the President was speaking, another message arrived. Hitler had invaded Yugoslavia and Greece.

The headlines pounded with the rich, twisty Balkan names: Zagreb, Cattaro, Salonika, Ljubljana. But the President and his counselors had to watch the whole enormous scene in a world where the U.S. was a fulcrum, balancing Britain in the Western scale with Japanese-invaded Chungking in the East.

The grand strategy's whole great problem, and all the little problems, were bound up in ships. To supply even itself the U.S. must have more ships than it now has afloat. To supply Great Britain, Yugoslavia, Greece, Turkey, China, could mean a desperate bottleneck.

How did the President stand on the convoy question? Had he changed his mind about using U.S. warships to guard Britain-bound cargoes? He had repeatedly given the U.S. reason to believe he had no intention of using U.S. ships to convoy; recently he had remarked to a visitor: "But convoys mean shooting and shooting means war."

APRIL 21 **WAR WITHOUT FIGHTING:** Never before in World War II had Franklin Roosevelt acted so vigorously as last week, when the earth moved and the shock was felt in the White House.

To strengthen the British in the Battle of the Atlantic, the President gave ten 250-foot Coast Guard cutters; made an agreement with Danish Minister Henrik de Kauffmann allowing the U.S. to build bases in Greenland; declared the Red Sea —previously out of bounds under the Neutrality Act—open to U.S. shipping so that arms could be taken to ports of technically neutral Egypt; asked Congress for a seize-and-pay authority over all foreign shipping in U.S. harbors.

RITES OF SPRING: In the midst of a busy week of making-war-short-of-fighting, the President:

¶ Threw his usual eccentric sinker in tossing out the first ball of the new baseball season (Yanks beat the Nats, 3-0), leaving Woodrow Wilson's clear supremacy as a pitching President still unchallenged.

¶ Greeted 53,258 Washingtonians, including some damp, tear-streaked children, at the annual Easter egg-rolling lawn party, where the usual percentage still held: 1 to 1.3 mothers to each child.

APRIL 28 **ASSISTANT PRESIDENT:** The President last week formally placed his best friend, New Dealer Harry Hopkins, in charge of "the great task." Hopkins' job: executive secretary of the War Cabinet (Secretaries of State, War, Navy and Treasury) —in effect, Assistant President of the U.S. In 17 hastily cleared rooms in the magnificent white marble surroundings of the

Federal Reserve Building, Harry Hopkins and his staff of 35 men settled down to administer the Lend-Lease Act, spend $7,000,000,000, re-arm the democracies, and stop Hitler.

QUESTIONS AND ANSWERS: At a big Manhattan rally of the MAY 5 America First Committee, Colonel Charles A. Lindbergh asserted that:

¶ The majority of the U.S. people were opposed to U.S. participation in the war.

¶ The U.S. cannot win this war for England.

¶ "I have constantly advocated a negotiated peace."

¶ The U.S. has an independent destiny and should keep out of war.

A reporter asked President Roosevelt why Colonel Lindbergh had not been called to the colors. The President pondered, recalled that during the Civil War numerous people fought on both sides and that at the same time both sides did not call certain people to service who were Copperheads. Colonel Lindbergh pondered over the weekend, then submitted his resignation from the Army.

FIRST SINKING: According to unofficial reports reaching JUNE 16 Washington this week, the 4,999-ton *Robin Moor*, bound from New York to Cape Town with eight passengers and a crew of 35, was "torpedoed and sunk by a German submarine" in the South Atlantic May 21. If reports were correct, this was the first U.S. ship torpedoed in World War II. [The reports proved correct, but barely stirred public opinion because no lives were lost.]

DOOR BOLTED: Franklin Delano Roosevelt locked the barn JUNE 23 door last week and ordered a searching party out to look for the horse. The President with quick strokes of a pen affixed his signature to an order freezing all Axis assets in the U.S., along with those of all other European countries not yet frozen.

Ever since increasing U.S. aid to Britain began to show which way the wind was blowing, Axis interests in the U.S. have been in a frantic flurry of cleaning house, transferring cash and bank deposits to Latin-American nations, hiding stocks and bonds and patent rights in dummy accounts.

Only a fortnight back, Secretary of the Treasury Morgenthau, who for months had urged the President to take the step, virtually conceded that his freezing plan had been abandoned. He said it was too late: "The barn is empty. The horse is gone." Asked whether it was "a very big horse," Mr. Morgenthau sadly answered: "Well, it was larger than a Shetland pony."

JUNE 30 **WAR OF THE DINOSAURS:** It was 9:30 in the morning; Germany had declared war on Russia. President Roosevelt in his second-floor study in the White House faced the strangest and perhaps the most momentous turn of World War II. It might turn out to be the luckiest military break for the U.S. that the President could have hoped for.

Stalin had started the war by signing a non-aggression pact with Hitler which he thought would keep Russia safe, turning Hitler loose on the rest of the world to save his own skin. But this piece of smartness had now boomeranged.

Now the U.S. had gained at least a few precious days or weeks to push its arming, had found another great power besides Britain to keep Hitler occupied a little longer. Like two vast prehistoric monsters lifting themselves out of the swamp, half-blind and savage, the two great totalitarian powers of the world now tore at each other's throats.

THE ONRUSH: Within a week in swift moves and countermoves the U.S. had frozen German and Italian funds still left in this country, ordered out all Axis consuls, clamped down on Nazi propaganda agencies, and barricaded its borders against German and Italian travelers trying to get in or out. The final break in U.S.-Nazi diplomatic relations had not yet been made. But they were badly cracked.

JULY 14 **MR. ROOSEVELT'S WAR:** On the Fourth of July, as for 165 years past, fireworks softly zooped and swished, ending with a bang or a whimper. The President, lounging in seersucker trousers, a blue shirt open at the collar, tieless, told reporters at Hyde Park that he still hoped that the U.S. could stay out of the war. But he made it clear that his hope was not to be confused with belief: three days later Franklin Roosevelt moved the U.S. squarely into the Battle of the Atlantic by landing U.S. naval forces at Reykjavik, Iceland. From where they were, New York was 3,900 miles away, Berlin a mere 2,800 miles as the bomber flies. The Western Hemisphere had stretched.

That night, the President called seven Congressional leaders to a very secret conference at the White House. Sitting back of his big desk in his upstairs study, he frankly admitted that he had taken a serious step, but did not ask them to approve his act. As Commander in Chief of the armed forces and director of the nation's foreign policy he had become convinced that it was necessary to occupy Iceland in order properly to defend the U.S.

Even as the U.S. moved to extend its Atlantic defenses, the Japanese Empire was consolidating its hold on the Pacific. Japan's armies, already occupying much of China, seized French-ruled Indo-China, and were poised for attacks against the strategic Philippines and Netherlands East Indies.

THE LAST STEP TAKEN: President Roosevelt cracked down AUG. 4 on the Japanese move into Indo-China by freezing all Japanese assets (probably about $131,000,000) in the U.S., then folded the Philippine defense forces into the U.S. Army under the command of General Douglas MacArthur. The two acts were more than a warning to the Japanese of war to come— they amounted to a declaration of economic war with military war to follow soon unless the Japanese decided to reverse their course. The next major move on either side would mean war.

"HURRY UPKINS": Harry Hopkins, Franklin Roosevelt's AUG. 11 personal representative, was covering a lot of ground. Exactly three days after he made a radio speech in London, promising immediate aid to Russia, the skinny fellow who is called by London's pert cockneys "that there Mister Hurry Upkins" turned up at the Kremlin in person. He had two long talks with Joseph Stalin, repeated the President's offer to start war supplies flowing toward Russia at once. The Soviet Premier expressed his "heartfelt appreciation."

His first night in Moscow, Hopkins saw an air raid. He

stepped out on a balcony to watch the *Luftwaffe* come over. Next night the Nazis came again. This time Hopkins did not stop to see the fun: he went below for three hours until the raid was over. Three days after he arrived, Harry Hopkins was on his way back to London again, just as secretly as he came.

Harry Hopkins, "Assistant President," offers U.S. aid to Prime Minister Churchill. The British call him "Hurry Upkins."

AUG. 25   **HOME FROM THE SEA:** In the damp, disused, musty wharf shed at Rockland, Me. the 50 men stood and sat, impatient, griped, chilled: newsmen, cameramen, radiomen, technicians, bottleholders. They were the reception committee for Franklin Roosevelt, returning aboard the yacht *Potomac* from the greatest fishing trip that any President of the U.S. had ever undertaken.

The President brought back his half of a conference that had no parallel. The U.S., though not at war, had conferred through the head of its Government with Great Britain, a nation at war, on how Nazi Germany was to be defeated, had further agreed on control of the post-war world by the U.S. and Great Britain.

This extraordinary Roosevelt coup had all but ended in a bad press, for the newspapers of the U.S. were angry. They had been left out. The story of the meeting came to the U.S. press bit by bit, mostly from British sources.

The U.S. cruiser *Augusta* with its large escort of cruisers and destroyers, the British *Prince of Wales* with its own numerous escorts—together a fleet large enough to fight a major sea battle if an enemy appeared—rendezvoused on the North Atlantic coast. The place was almost certainly Newfoundland. At the first meeting Mr. Churchill boarded the *Augusta*, the eight brass buttons on his blue uniform slightly marred by the grey marks where he had hastily brushed away the little mound of silver grey cigar ash that collects on his stomach as he sits slouched down.

Except on Sunday, when the President crossed a short gangplank to attend services on the *Prince of Wales*, all the meetings took place on the *Augusta*. One person present later reported that Churchill was much moved as the chaplains carried on the service, as the British and U.S. crews sang *O God, Our Help in Ages Past*. Churchill finally said, gruffly: "I'm not a religious man. But I thank God that such a man as you is the head of your Government at a time like this." The chaplains led another song: *Onward, Christian Soldiers*. The President and Prime Minister sang lustily. But their voices were drowned in the drone of the patrol planes overhead.

What passed in the long sessions when the two sat together dredging, squeezing, milking each other's minds, only they know in full. They did hatch and execute on the spot two plans—a draft of war aims and an invitation to Stalin to confer on Russia's war needs. What else they planned, however, may pale into insignificance beside another thing that they accomplished: a meeting of minds. [They also signed a joint declaration of principles which came to be known as The Atlantic Charter. It stipulated, among other things, that Britain and the U.S. sought no territorial aggrandisement and "respect the right of all peoples to choose the form of government under which they will live."]

AS LINCOLN SAID . . .: The President talked a good war when SEPT. 1 he got back to Washington. Opening Volume One of Carl Sandburg's *Abraham Lincoln: The War Years* to page 553, he read the assembled newspapermen what the Emancipator said after one of the Civil War's bloodiest battles, Antietam: "I have no word of encouragement to give. The military situation is far from bright; and the country knows it as well as I do." Then to the U.S. press Mr. Roosevelt gave a free headline: "President Quotes Lincoln and Draws Parallel." Many a U.S. newspaper used the headline; and the New York (tabloid) *Daily Mirror* decided to give Mr. Roosevelt a check for a tyro head-writer's daily pay, sent him $5.94, deducting 6¢ for Social Security tax.

SEPT. 8 **DEADLOCK IN THE PACIFIC:** There was a change of atmosphere in Asia. One morning last week Japan's Ambassador to Washington, tall, one-eyed Admiral Nomura, called on President Roosevelt, wanted to discuss the "thoroughgoing settlement" of Japan's differences with the U.S. For 45 minutes Admiral Nomura worked his blandishments on the President, while Secretary of State Cordell Hull fingered his pince-nez ribbon. When the Admiral emerged, he flashed a smile at reporters, twirled a grey fedora in his brown hands. Back at his embassy, Admiral Nomura discovered he had walked off with Judge Hull's hat, left his own.

Where solemn words and warnings had failed to halt Japanese aggression in the Orient, strangling Japanese trade with the U.S. had prevailed. Tokyo was optimistic about a settlement now, hinted that a basic understanding had already been reached. But the crux of the matter is still Japan's invasion of China. If Japan will not get completely out of China, then there can be no thoroughgoing settlement unless the U.S. attempts a sell-out of China. No solution was in sight—but for the time being no blowup was in sight either.

SEPT. 15 **INCIDENT:** President Roosevelt got his incident—the incident he has been expecting ever since he stretched the Hemisphere patrol to Iceland. It happened this way:

Two hundred miles southwest of Reykjavik, U.S.S. *Greer* knifed through the cold and grey Atlantic, taking the mail to Iceland. Then suddenly it happened, the thing for which the whole U.S. Navy had waited breathlessly with infinite vigilance. The white wake of a torpedo was streaking toward the ship. The little destroyer lurched as her helm was put over, by the grace of God was not hit. For several hours the *Greer* quartered that sector of the sea, releasing depth charges at the slightest suspicion of any underwater object. The U.S. Navy was engaged. Apparently the U-boat escaped. [The Navy later recanted its tale of the *Greer*'s innocence, admitted that the destroyer had been aiding a British aerial patrol against the U-boat when attacked.]

"YOU SHALL GO NO FURTHER": The President addressed the SEPT. 22 world, carefully outlining the *Greer* incident. Said the President: "This was piracy."

The time had now come to tell the Nazi Government: "You shall go no further." He then pledged " . . . if German or Italian vessels of war enter the waters the protection of which is necessary for American defense, they do so at their own peril." Next morning the New York *Daily News* put the President's speech with absolute succinctness: SHOOT, F.D.R. TELLS NAVY. For the eighth time in its history, for the second time this century, the U.S. was at war—an undeclared war.

DESPERATE RUSSIA: As Hitler's pincers hooked their talons OCT. 20 toward Moscow, the eyes of the U.S. turned inevitably to the White House. In answer to that mute demand, the President this week announced that "everything possible is being done to send the material to Russia to help the brave defense which continues to be made"; earlier told Congressional leaders that Russian armies were far from defeat.

This was optimism. With Nazi troops now battering along the last hundred miles to Moscow, Russia's situation was patently desperate. Adolf Hitler was beating the last big, well-equipped army that opposed him on the continent of Europe.

VICTORY PROGRAM: To replace the old, merely enormous, OCT. 27 daily outmoded scheme of defense and supplies to U.S. Allies, the President readied a Brobdingnagian new program: to turn out by 1944, 125,000 airplanes, tens of thousands of tanks and guns of all kinds (cost: more than $100,000,-000,000)—to double not merely present production but plans for future production. The brave new word for the scheme: the Victory Program.

FIRST U.S. CASUALTIES: On the chilled hell's highway of the North Atlantic, the U.S. last week lost the illusion that it was not engaged in a shooting war.

The illusion faded when the U.S.S. *Kearny*, a crack destroyer scarcely a year in service, was torpedoed. The nation felt the dull visceral shock of reading its first casualty list of World War II: eleven "missing," two more injured, one critically, one seriously.

NOV. 3 **DECKS CLEARED:** The U.S. is at war with Germany. Franklin Roosevelt this week did not declare war—only Congress can do that. But he said plainly in a fighting speech: "We have wished to avoid shooting. But the shooting has started. And history has recorded who fired the first shot. . . . All that will matter is who fired the last shot."

The attack on the *Kearny* was no chance encounter, said the President. It was part of a long-range Nazi plan to drive U.S. shipping off the seas, then to dominate the Americas. "We Americans," said the President, "have cleared our decks and taken our battle stations. We stand ready in the defense of our nation. . . ."

NOV. 10 **WAR OF NERVES:** It was a war of nerves, a war fought in secrecy. President Roosevelt and Secretary of the Navy Knox were both asked: Has the U.S. struck back? Both refused to answer. Around the U.S., in rumors, stories, letters from sailors, there were reports that U.S. warships had sunk two submarines, three submarines, 16 submarines, 20. . . . There were practical reasons why the President did not turn the undeclared war into a declared war. One was political: no declaration of war could pass Congress. Another was that a declaration of war might bring in Japan.

NOV. 24 **SPECIAL ENVOY:** Last week Saburo Kurusu, Japan's special envoy, made his way across the wide U.S. of deserts, mountains, factories, farms, politics, confusion; at each step he could see reminders of the power of the U.S., must have known that in Washington it was estimated that the chances were 9-to-10 that Japan and the U.S. would go to war.

With Ambassador Nomura he called on Secretary of State Cordell Hull, remained 23 minutes, visited the White House. When he emerged, an hour and ten minutes later, a reporter asked Nomura if he felt the discussion was successful. Saburo Kurusu nudged Nomura into silence. The U.S. speculated.

Events in the Pacific were moving with blurring speed. The issue of TIME *dated December 8 had gone to press on Monday, December 1. Six days later, on Sunday, December 7, Japanese bombers over Pearl Harbor made much of the issue—but especially the following story—obsolete.*

BATTLE STATIONS: From Rangoon to Honolulu, every man DEC. 8 was at battle stations. And Franklin Roosevelt had to return to his. This was the last act of the drama.

The U.S. position had the simple clarity of a stone wall. One nervous twitch of a Japanese trigger finger, one jump in any direction, one overt act, might be enough. A vast array of armies, of navies, of air fleets were stretched now in the position of track runners, in the tension of the moment before the starter's gun.

Roosevelt and Secretary Hull had left one narrow bridge over the dreadful gulf of war. The Japanese could have peace with honor if they would agree to peace without empire.

But it was plain that Japan's answer was being given, not in words in Washington, but in troop movements in the Far East. Japanese troops were pouring into French Indo-China, threatening China's lifeline, the Burma Road.

Japanese Ambassador Nomura. He keeps silent on latest talks. Page 23.   *Japanese Envoy Saburo Kurusu. The chances of war were 9-to-10. Page 23.*

In Manila the U.S. air force was standing by; naval leaves were canceled. Leaves were canceled at Corregidor, the strong rock fortress guarding Manila Bay. All British and U.S. forces in the Far East were put on the alert.

Suddenly, the Japanese Cabinet instructed Envoy Kurusu and Ambassador Nomura to continue the talks. At least talking postponed war.

DEC. 15 **NATIONAL ORDEAL:** The Government and People of the United States declared war on the Japanese Empire at 4:10 p.m. Monday, Dec. 8, 1941. At dawn the day before, the Japanese had bombed the U.S. naval base at Pearl Harbor, savagely attacked the whole great U.S. island-bridge which stretches to the Orient. It was premeditated murder, masked by a toothy smile. The Nation had taken a heavy blow.

Instantly on the news from Pearl Harbor, President Roosevelt ordered the Army and Navy: "Fight Back!" The U.S., after 22 years and 25 days of peace, was at war.

All news from scenes of action was routed immediately to the White House, issued at once in bulletins to the press. The War Council was telephoned. The President called a Cabinet meeting for 8:30 p.m., a session with Congressional leaders for 9 p.m.

He had already finished the first draft of his war message. In the second-floor red-room study, he talked to the Cabinet, then brought in the Congressional leaders—among them, on his first visit to the White House in many a moon, aging, croak-voiced Senator Hiram Johnson of California, oldest of the Isolationists. The President was deadly serious. There was no smile. The lines in his face were deeper.

At noon next day the President sat back in the deep cushions of the big closed car, adjusted his big dark Navy cape. The gravel spattered from the driveway, the car moved off slowly toward the looming dome of the Capitol.

On each running board perched a Secret Service man. The President's car was flanked on both sides by open Secret Service cars, three men on each running board, four men inside. The men in the tonneaus held sawed-off riot guns. Those outside carried .38-caliber service revolvers. The Capitol was alive with police, Marines, plainclothesmen. The crowd spread the length of the Plaza, knotted here & there around portable radios.

The President moved slowly into the House of Representatives. Speaker Rayburn gave one smash of his heavy gavel, introduced the President in one sentence.

Mr. Roosevelt gripped the reading clerk's stand. He took a long, steady look at the Congress and the battery of floodlights, and began to read.

"Yesterday, Dec. 7, 1941—a date which will live in infamy —the United States of America was suddenly and deliberately attacked by naval and air forces of the Empire of Japan. . . ." He spoke of the Japanese treachery; then, his voice heavy, almost thick: "The attack yesterday on the Hawaiian Islands has caused severe damage to the American naval and military forces. . . very many American lives have been lost. . . ."

He outlined the long series of attacks: Malaya, Hong Kong, Guam, the Philippine Islands, Wake, Midway. The chamber was silent. When he said: "Always will our whole nation remember the character of the onslaught against us," the room roared with a cry of vengeance. "No matter how long it may take us to overcome this premeditated invasion," continued the President, "the American people in their righteous might will win through to absolute victory." At

All four Roosevelt sons are ready for war: Navy Ensign John, Air Corps Captain Elliott, Marine Captain James and Navy Ensign Franklin, Jr.

this, the biggest cheers of the day. "We will not only defend ourselves to the uttermost but will make it very certain that this form of treachery shall never again endanger us. . . . We will gain the inevitable triumph—so help us God. I ask that the Congress declare. . . a state of war."

DEC. 29 **SHAKE-UP:** The President of the U.S. last week gave the people of the U.S. satisfaction for Pearl Harbor. There was no public cry for a scapegoat, but long after the last blaze had been doused the nation wanted: 1) to know why the bombing attack had been permitted to happen; 2) to be reassured that it would not happen again.

The President removed the three commanders of Naval, Army and Air Forces in Hawaii and appointed as his new Commander of the Pacific Fleet a calm, frosty-faced, steel-blue-eyed Texan, Rear Admiral Chester William ("Cottonhead") Nimitz, one of the Navy's best strategists and administrators.

ROOSEVELTS AT WAR: All four of Eleanor Roosevelt's sons are in the service of their country. Cadaverous James Roosevelt, a captain of Marines, was ordered to the Fleet Marine Force at San Diego, will get active service at sea.

Chunky Captain Elliott Roosevelt of the Air Corps was ordered last week to join a reconnaissance squadron at Muroc, Calif.

Rangy Franklin Delano Roosevelt, Jr., an ensign in the U.S. Naval Reserve, is on duty with the North Atlantic patrol.

Tall, stringy John Aspinwall Roosevelt is now on duty with the Navy Supply Corps at San Diego.

The Cabinet

JAN. 13 **EMPEROR JONES:** If jobs were wives, Jesse Jones would be the patriarch of polygamists. He is as busy as the classic one-armed paperhanger. Primarily, he is Secretary of Commerce and Federal Loan Administrator. As such, he has charge of strategic war materials, loans to industry, financing the purchase of electrical and gas equipment, Federal housing mortgages, disaster loans, the Census, weights & measures, patents,

Secretary of Commerce Jesse Jones. *Secretary of State Cordell Hull: bur-*
He has a long list of jobs. Page 27. *ied in paper work. Page 30.*

steamboat inspection, the Export-Import Bank; he is either
the director or an ex officio member of so many boards and
commissions that there is no accurate count.

He is tough, shrewd, tricky. Power is his passion. In all the
U.S. today there is only one man whose power is greater:
Franklin Roosevelt, who can force Jones to resign at any
moment. Through the years of the New Deal he had become a patriarchal emperor, and his empire stretched beyond
all fences. He headed the RFC (Reconstruction Finance
Corporation) and was thus the greatest lender of all time
($9,146,735,055). Jones thinks borrowers are the salt of the
earth, the optimists, the builders, the men who take chances
and thus make the U.S. Little men and great peoples were
beholden to him, from China to Argentina, to the far corners of the British Empire. Had he not said: "Britain is a
good risk for a loan"? His solid, simple phrase had brought
assurance of a kind; it was an old-fashioned Yankee yard-
stick.

The self-made Texas titan suits Franklin Roosevelt's needs
(in the 1907 depression, when Houston was stagnant, Jesse
Jones began rebuilding it. Then he spread out, changed the
skylines of Fort Worth, Dallas, of Memphis and Nashville,
Tenn.). The President knows that Congress will give more to
Jones without debate than he can get after a fight. Jones's

knack of making profits while lending money to people and countries who can't borrow elsewhere suits Congress, and seems to prove: Democracy is a good risk.

JAN. 27 **GARNER LEAVES:** There is no ritual *Nunc Dimittis* for a departing Vice President of the U.S. Those who imagined that farewelling John Nance Garner might write one misread his bad-prosy character. Last week, when he attended his last Cabinet meeting, he was surrounded by reporters who hoped against hope that he might say something that might be interpreted as a last word. Never more in character, Statesman Garner squinted out a White House window at the foggy drizzle and grated: "It's a rough day out, isn't it?" When the inaugural bands blared forth, Mr. Garner, holding a borrowed silk hat, smilingly swore in new Vice President Henry Agard Wallace. Then, having regretted invitations to dinners, he took a last ride in the Vice President's car—to the station, where he entrained for Texas.

APRIL 28 **MADAM SECRETARY:** Chief criticism of Frances Cora ("Ma") Perkins when she first took office as Secretary of Labor eight years ago was that she wore skirts and a tricorn bonnet instead of trousers and a derby. First thing she did when she walked into her musty old office in Washington was to call for a dustcloth. Congressmen did not like her social worker's ways.

Through it all she has had the support of Franklin Roosevelt. She has administered many agencies of her department with fine, earnest competence. But in dealing with labor strife, almost from the start, Madam Secretary gave her critics their best excuse for attacking her. As the soft-coal tie-up stretched into its third week, with steel plants reporting that they were shutting down because of a coal shortage, Madam Perkins made appeals first to one side, then to the other. John L. Lewis refused point-blank to let his United Mine Workers go back to work until the Southern owners signed a contract. The Southerners refused to budge. Madam Perkins was frustrated. Forced to take over, Franklin Roosevelt this week urged mines and negotiations reopened. Perhaps the real cause of her failure to get results was that she did not wear a derby and smoke cigars. These days Washington wags crack:

The only reason she still holds office is that the President is too much of a gentleman to ask a lady for her seat.

NEW MANAGERS? If bad management was again carving over MAY 19
Democracy's door the bitter motto, "Too little & too late,"
immediate responsibility lay on the Roosevelt War Cabinet
—the Secretaries of State, War, Navy and Treasury. The
blazing exigencies of wartime have brought out their draw-
backs as managers and administrators of a war effort that
needs more dynamism.

¶ With grave, careworn Cordell Hull the reason is partly
age (69 years). Buried in the paper-shuffling details of his
mountainous task, he very often does not realize what goes
on in the intrigue-ridden old halls of the rococo Department.

¶ With Secretary of War Henry L. Stimson the reason is
both age and health. Now no cocktail party passes in the
District without a new anecdote about the Secretary's doz-
ing off in some important conference, of his inability to
work more than a few hours a day, of his valiant but losing
struggle to keep abreast of the demands of war in 1941.

¶ Secretary of the Navy Frank Knox is contrarily full of
vigor; but ice-cold appraisers praise only his muscles. When
he makes some such remark as "The U.S. will outproduce
Hitler in 90 days" his whole Department groans.

But if his managers were not the men to do the job, the
worst executive management could be traced to Franklin
Roosevelt. To solve his problem of management, the President never fires anybody, only creates new jobs and new
agencies, overlapping and ineffectual.

FITS AND STARTS: Duck-billed Harold Ickes, Secretary of the JULY 14
Interior, has emitted some strange noises, but his latest
squawk made U.S. motorists really jump. Secretary Ickes, now
U.S. Oil Tsar, threatened the arrest of "jack-rabbit" starters
who needlessly burn up gas for the sake of fast getaways, car
owners who fail to keep their old "oil-burner" crates tuned
up to efficient consumption.

HUNGER: Time & again he had trumpeted: "Food will win the JULY 21
war and write the peace." Now, as Secretary of Agriculture,
Claude Wickard has been charged by Franklin Roosevelt

with one vast responsibility: to feed the U.S. and Great Britain during the defense emergency and the war. He has gone beyond that charge already, to take the steps which he believes will put the U.S. in a position to write the peace.

To wage the war of food 48-year-old Indiana hog farmer Wickard has the most widely developed system of alarm in the history of the earth: his 101,000 agents can personally reach 6,000,000 farmers in the U.S. within 48 hours. And within this week or next, every one of them will be reached and told of the international emergency in food. They will be advised to change their crop plans from the five great domestic basic crops—cotton, wheat, corn, tobacco, rice—over to the produce the world needs more desperately—dairy products (milk, eggs, butter, cheese), pork (and lard), beef, fruits, vegetables.

Secretary of Interior Harold Ickes cracks down on drivers who waste gas.   *Secretary of Agriculture Claude Wickard: "Food will win the war."*

SEPT. 15 **NOBODY'S SWEETHEART:** When Harold Ickes is having a good, rich, wrathful week probably every man, woman and child in the U.S. is against him. Ickes is the gadfly of Conscience to the Administration. Every time the other New Dealers get fat, happy and optimistic, Harold bores in, stinging, squawking, kicking like a case of first-degree tantrums. This is his great service to the New Deal.

Ickes (the only Cabinet member who tiptoes about his Department turning off lights and running water) believes that when a policy has been laid down, it should be followed. When the Administration said: No-more-Business-as-Usual, when the President pledged the U.S. to become the "arsenal of Democracy," Ickes took it all literally. Then he watched the dinosaur of a defense program falter, swamp itself, stumble along from delay to delay, without plan or understanding or grim intent.

Ickes cannot watch any spectacle for more than a few minutes without comment, usually acidulous. First he chafed. Then his hackles rose. Finally he boiled over, blew his top. His basic point: the U.S. is going to run out of everything. Ickes ran out of aluminum months before Big Ed Stettinius' materials division saw any real problem. He ran out of steel in January, although the President, Economist Gano Dunn and Stettinius were still insisting in February that the U.S. had plenty of steel. In quick succession Harold Ickes then ran out of electric power, coal, transportation, railroad and shipping, and finally oil.

Fortnight ago Harold Ickes received his reward for having so long foreseen and so valiantly proclaimed the critical deficiencies in the U.S. defense program. He was left out of it. When Judge Samuel I. Rosenman waddled around getting advice for the President on defense reorganization he found unanimity on only one recommendation: keep Harold Ickes out of this. With the President's full approval, the Gadfly was then completely boxed off and shut out of the program.

IN MR. HULL'S OFFICE: Not until Pearl Harbor blew the lid DEC. 15 off diplomacy did the U.S. learn all the last-minute moves with which President Roosevelt and his Secretary of State tried to prevent war with Japan.

Conversations between the President and Japan's envoys, Saburo Kurusu and Admiral Nomura, had reached a stalemate when on Nov. 26 Secretary Hull gave the Japanese a memorandum for a general settlement of the Pacific's problems. Its terms:

¶ Withdrawal of all Japanese troops and naval forces from China and Indo-China.

¶ Recognition by Japan of Chiang Kai-shek's Chinese National Government.

❡ A new trade agreement between the U.S. and Japan.

❡ Removal of all restrictions on U.S. funds in Japan, Japanese funds in the U.S.

❡ An agreement to stabilize the yen with the dollar.

❡ An invitation to Japan to change sides, join the U.S., Britain, The Netherlands, Russia, Thailand and China in a non-aggressive settlement.

While Mr. Hull and the President waited for Japan's reply, ominous reports of Japanese troop movements in French Indo-China began to pour in on Washington. At week's end President Roosevelt dispatched a personal message to Emperor Hirohito.

Next day was Sunday. At one o'clock that afternoon (it was 7:30 a.m. in Hawaii) a telephone rang at the State Department. Japan's envoys had a communication for Secretary Hull. Mr. Hull arranged to see them at 1:45. At 2:05 the two impassive envoys stalked in, twenty minutes late. Mr. Hull kept them waiting another 15 minutes for good measure.

At the precise moment that Mr. Hull received them, the news was being received at the White House that Japan had attacked Hawaii. Courtly Mr. Hull took the document which Admiral Nomura gave him, adjusted his spectacles, began to read.

It was the Japanese answer to Mr. Hull's memorandum, a flat rejection of the U.S. proposals and an incredible farrago of self-justification and abuse. Wrote the Japanese: "Ever since the China affair broke out, owing to the failure on the part of China to comprehend Japan's true intentions, the Japanese Government has striven for the restoration of peace. . . . On the other hand, the American Government, always holding fast to theories in disregard of realities, and refusing to yield an inch on its impractical principles, caused undue delay in the negotiations. . . . An attitude such as ignores realities and imposes one's selfish views on others will scarcely serve the purpose of facilitating the consummation of negotiations. . . . Therefore. . . the Japanese Government regrets it cannot accept the proposal."

Cordell Hull's eyes began to blaze as he read this document. He looked up at Japan's nervous envoys. What Mr. Hull was quoted as saying by the State Department was this: "In all my 50 years of public service I have never seen a document that was more crowded with infamous falsehoods and distortions—infamous falsehoods and distortions on a scale so huge that I never imagined until today that any government on this planet was capable of uttering them."

Saburo Kurusu and Admiral Nomura walked out, pale and quiet. Whether they had been cat's paws or knowing agents of Japanese "diplomacy," their job was done. They had played a useful delaying action, helped pave the way for a treacherous attack. [Disclosures after the war made it clear that both Kurusu and Nomura were aware of a Japanese plan to attack the U.S. But both maintained to their deaths that they were ignorant of the details and did not know that the attack was being launched in the midst of their negotiations.]

The Congress

REBIRTH: The 76th Congress finally died last week. Minutes JAN. 13 later, the 77th Congress rose from its predecessor's ashes. The phoenix nest where this political rebirth occurred looked not unlike a bird cage, thanks to a network of steel girders, erected temporarily to hold up the aged and rickety Congressional roof.

The Senate made the transition from old to new with little more ceremony than the thump-thump of Vice President John Garner's ivory gavel. (Garner would preside until Vice President-elect Wallace is inaugurated Jan. 20.) There were five more Republican Senators than there had been a year ago—28 in all.

The House, as usual, resembled a street scene more than a legislative body. In a constant babble-bedlam, members took the oath and went through the routine of organizing. On one side of the centre aisle sat 162 Republicans, two less than last year; on the other, 268 Democrats.

NO. 1776: The President's lend-lease plan was introduced as JAN. 20 Bill No. 1776, entitled "A Bill to Further Promote the Defense of the United States, and For Other Purposes." The historic number, the majestic vagueness of the language were symptomatic. No bill like it had ever been introduced. Under the bill, powers would go to Franklin Roosevelt such as no American has ever before even asked for.

In short: almost anything is a defense article, if the President says so; any defense article may be released for export to any country he names; terms and conditions for all such loans, sales, etc. may be any he approves.

Congressional reaction to the bill was more like a reflex. Members who saw that the British Fleet could use New York and Norfolk as repair harbors at U.S. expense jumped like cats from a hot stove. There was immediate general agreement that the bill would pass—with perhaps slight modification—by overwhelming majorities, in from three to six weeks.

JAN. 27   **MATTER OF FAITH**: Behind the horseshoe desk, puffing reflective pipes, cigarets, or gnawing at cigars, sat 23 members of the 25-man House Foreign Affairs Committee; in the middle of the curve crouched little Sol Bloom, chairman, looking like a Neanderthal man dressed up in clothes. Before his committee was the Lend-Lease Bill, H.R. 1776.

Into the room came the first witness, a slender man whose shoulders stooped with 69 years, striding gravely in a worn, shiny blue serge suit, his hair silvery-white, his face pale as candle wax, his brown eyes a little sharp under his salt-and-pepper eyebrows. Little Sol Bloom scrambled down from his eminence to be photographed with Secretary of State Cordell Hull. Mr. Hull sat down, began to read his prepared statement, restated the Administration's foreign policy. Finished, Hull politely parried questions from furious, bulbous Republican Isolationist George Holden Tinkham. Typical Tinkham "question": "You say all international law should be dispensed with?"

Typical Hull finesse: "My door has been open for eight years and you've never darkened it in quest of information."

Tinkham: "We're supposed to be neutral."

Hull: "We aren't going to let [neutrality] chloroform us into inactivity."

FEB. 17   **260-TO-165**: The House passed the Lend-Lease Bill. The vote by parties—*For*, 236 Democrats, 24 Republicans; *Against*, 135 Republicans, 25 Democrats, 3 Progressives, 1 Farmer-Laborite, 1 American Laborite.

Canny little Speaker Sam Rayburn had done a shrewd job. The bill passed with only face-saving amendments (e.g., setting a five-year limit on delivery), put in to salve Congressmen frightened by dictatorship-bogies.

The bill was halfway through Congress. In the Senate, where the Senate Foreign Relations Committee was concluding hearings, the victory vote margin might be greater.

IN TOGAS CLAD: Last week the Senate tried its level best to MARCH act like a body of statesmen. Debate on the Lend-Lease Bill opened on a plane so high that many Senators felt a little difficulty in breathing. Crowded galleries, hoping for an old-fashioned quick-&-dirty scrap, with plenty of rabbit punches, were disappointed. The Senate wrapped the toga of dignity and dullness about its collective paunch and gamely strove for classic words.

Here & there in the long groundswell of words a whitecap showed. When Washington's eloquent little Senator Homer Bone asked the question that invariably has cornered interventionists before—what is worse than war?—Republican Senator Warren Austin of Vermont answered: "I say that a world enslaved to Hitler is worse than war, and worse than death. A country whose boys will not go out to fight to save Christianity in the world and to save the principle of freedom from ruthless destruction by a fiend—well, we do not find such boys in America."

The galleries roared applause. Bone sat down. The debate went on. Majority Leader Alben Barkley of Kentucky calculated that the opposition would scrape barrel-bottom in a few days.

PEACEMONGERS: Lend-Lease opponents, ready for glorious MARCH martyrdom, with headlines and pictures, knew the bill would pass without substantial amendment. Yet they hammered nightly on the radio, appealing to U.S. mothers to write their Congressmen, protesting against the Bill. Some mothers did. The group known as the "Mothers' Crusade Against Bill 1776" did more: they staged a sit-down strike before the door of bantam, spitfire Senator Carter Glass of Virginia, who is ready to declare war on Hitler any time. Glass straightaway invited the G-Men to investigate the Mothers, added tartly:

"It would be pertinent to inquire whether they are mothers. For the sake of the race, I devoutly hope not."

MARCH 24 **STEP IN THE DARK:** By last week each side had exhausted its arguments, and 60-to-31 the Senate passed the Lend-Lease Bill—taking a great step in the dark. Almost immediately, the President signed the Bill into law, asked Congress to confer with him about appropriations.

Senator Warren Austin: "A world enslaved to Hitler is worse than death."   *Representative Robert Rich. He shouts "April Fool" in the House. Page 38.*

APRIL 14 **GOOD CLEAN FUN:** Representative Robert Fleming Rich, a Republican from Woolrich, Pa., needs only a plug hat to look like the drawings of Mr. Prohibition. Off the floor of the House he is stuffed to the brisket with charity for one & all. On the floor, he is a terrible tempered Mr. Bang. Each day he arrives for work in a state of condensed fury. Moment the House convenes and the prayer is over, Mr. Rich, bursting with wrath, demands the attention of the House, then explodes. His constant subject is the national debt, his constant refrain, "Where are we going to get the money?" The House has become so used to Mr. Rich that members often join in the chorus, roaring in unison: "Where are we going to get the money?"

One day last week, Mr. Rich, grimmer than ever, rose as usual and demanded 60 seconds of the House's time. Members groaned. Grinning fiendishly, Mr. Rich shouted: "April Fool!" He sat down to tumultuous applause.

A CHECK FOR MR. JONES: Last week Jesse Jones asked the JUNE 9 House to countersign a blank check already drawn for him by the Senate. The provisions of the new RFC bill were staggering. If passed, Jones could:

1) Set up any corporation which the President thinks necessary to "expedite the defense program."

2) Lend money (with the President's approval) to any foreign government, so long as the loan was secured.

3) Increase RFC's lending capacity by $1,500,000,000.

To some the prospect of turning Mr. Jones loose with all this money sounded like the finishing blow to U.S. free enterprise. Under the new law, RFC will be able to set up in any business at all—in competition with existing enterprises. Kewpie-faced Representative Jesse Wolcott shouted to the House: "This bill would . . . make it possible to establish a Fascist state in the U.S." Many a U.S. citizen agreed with Representative Hamilton Fish that Jesse Jones could be trusted not to misuse his powers in this great emergency. But others looked beyond the emergency and shivered.

THE LAST GAVEL: The Speaker's gavel pounded the desk. JUNE 16 Cried the Speaker: "The time of the gentleman from New York has expired!" But thin, grim Representative Mike Edelstein, fighting mad, talked on.

He was replying to Mississippi's fuzzy-headed Representative John Rankin, No. 1 Jew-baiter of the House, who had just told a deathly-still audience: "Wall Street and a little group of our international Jewish brethren are still attempting to harass the President . . . into plunging us into the European war, unprepared."

New York's Edelstein, most popular of the six Jews in the House, jumped to his feet. Cried Mike Edelstein: "Hitler started out by speaking about 'Jewish brethren.' . . . I deplore the idea that . . . men in this House . . . attempt to use the Jews as their scapegoat. I say it is un-American. . . ."

The Speaker's gavel banged in vain as Mike Edelstein had his say. Then Edelstein walked down the well of the House, out through the swinging glass doors into the Speaker's lobby and slumped suddenly against a door. Congressmen and attendants came running. They were too late to help; Michael Edelstein's heart had stopped. The time of the gentleman from New York had expired.

JULY 21 **JOINT RETURNS:** The U.S. taxpayer is willing to swallow a camel-sized defense tax, but a gnat-sized affront will still make him gag. Such a gnat was the rule requiring husbands & wives to file joint returns, in the proposed 1941 tax bill, thereby raising $323,000,000 in extra revenue. Many a woman felt that the rule raised a long-laid bogey: the notion that a wife's property belongs to her husband.

Said Wendell Willkie: "That's a proposal out of the dark ages. It would set the cause of emancipation of women back 500 years." Wrote scholarly Columnist Arthur Krock in *The New York Times*: "It puts a premium on divorce, celibacy, a lower birthrate and a mercenary attitude toward the estate of marriage." Wrote one letter-writer to the *Times*: "Such discrimination is immoral as well as unmoral, for it allots a premium . . . to living in sin."

AUG. 11 **TREMBLING HANDS:** As Franklin Roosevelt this week boarded the Presidential yacht *Potomac* for a cruise, he had no more to say about the impending tax bill. He left it in the trembling hands of Congress.

Only one of the President's points on which a fight was expected in the House was the committee proposal to make joint husband and wife returns mandatory. Congressmen feared its impact on the women's vote, thought wives might imagine that it somehow abridged their rights. When they marshaled their forces in the House this week, they obliterated the joint-returns proposal like a *Panzer* division going through a troop of Girl Scouts. They did not even stop to fill the $323,000,000 gap where joint returns had been. Instead, they rolled on, passed the rest of the bill as it stood, left the mopping up to the Senate.

AUG. 18 **OUT ON THE LIMB:** Is there a national emergency or is there not? With fear & trembling the House confronted this question—in the form of a bill to extend the service of draftees in the Army.

If the U.S. actually were in danger, the bill would pass like a shot. If no danger could be clearly demonstrated, the bill might fail, the half-baked U.S. Army would lose its half-baked soldiers, would have to start from the beginning again with raw recruits. The Senate had already passed a bill extending service for 18 months; but the Senate had not answered the big question. Isolationist after isolationist had stood up and shouted that he wanted to be shown. California's old irreconcilable, Senator Hiram Johnson, shouted in a throbbing voice: "I will not subscribe to the doctrine that you must be a Stalinite to be an American. . . . Good God! Did we ever sink so low before as to choose one cutthroat out of two? This man was Hitler's ally. . . . Now we furnish him with weapons which may be turned upon us."

Editorial writers throughout the land pointed out that Congress was getting itself out on a creaky limb. If Russia were suddenly to go down before the Nazis, just as the U.S. Army was broken up, Hitler would have all of Europe and a big chunk of Asia and the U.S. would be armed only with the tongues of its Congressmen.

STATE OF MIND: The eyes of the world were on the House as AUG. 25 the draft bill came finally to a vote. The 20 other American republics watched; the President watched from his sea conference with Winston Churchill; Adolf Hitler's representatives and Emperor Hirohito's observers waited. If the draft extension bill failed to pass, most of the half-trained U.S. Army would slowly dissolve as draftees and guardsmen went home. The nation would have to start again building and training another army.

The roll call began; 45 minutes of grinding suspense as the clerk growled out the 432 names, listened for an answer, repeated the vote. The jammed galleries seemed hung over the rails. The little tally meter of Tally Clerk Hans Jorgensen registered 204 aye votes, 201 nay votes. (Twenty-seven were not voting.) Hubbub boiled about the rostrum. Lean, dyspeptic Democrat Andrew L. Somers of New York, hoping to beat the bill, changed his vote from Aye to No. The Chair took hold. Whacking the gavel block like a smith at the forge, Speaker Sam Rayburn announced the vote: 203-to-202.

The closeness of the vote was partly due to the fact that

Minority Leader Joseph Martin had agreed with the most Isolationist hate-Rooseveliers in his party to swing the Republicans almost solidly into opposition. His decision seemed dubious political wisdom. A large part of the press hammered at the 202 Congressmen; even the most Isolationist newspapers wasted no space and ink defending their vote, merely changed the subject.

OCT. 27 **ARMS & THE MERCHANT MARINE:** Little, egg-bald Speaker Sam Rayburn, cello-mellow with satisfaction, last week saw one of his predictions come true: that members, after a month's vacation listening to the folks back home, would return to Washington with less isolationist notions. Sure enough, the chastened House passed a second Lend-Lease appropriation: 328-to-67.

Last week the House also voted on the next move of the President's Thousand-and-One-Steps-to-War policy: repeal of the Neutrality Act's Section 6, which forbids U.S. merchant ships to have any armament greater than a captain's pistol or a harpoon gun. On the morning the bill came to a vote, Sam Rayburn got a further break: the U.S.S. *Kearny* was torpedoed. After one day and one hour's debate, the House passed the bill: 259-to-138. [The bill went on to the Senate, which in a rush of enthusiasm added its own amendments that meant virtual repeal of the act.]

NOV. 24 **HOUR OF DECISION:** The question before the House: Should it concur in the Senate amendments? If it did, the Neutrality Act would be gutted like a caught trout, the U.S. would return to its historic principle—abandoned for the last four years—of freedom of the seas. If the House did not concur? Hardly a man dared guess at the consequences. But the immediate effect would plainly be a Dunkirk for U.S. foreign policy.

The clerk's voice boomed: "Allen of Illinois!" "No!" "Allen of Louisiana!" "Yes!" The count seesawed, nip & tuck. Not until the "Ws" were reached could Rayburn be sure. He announced the vote at 4:25, in a hushed House: "212 ayes to 194 nays." The bill was passed. A shift of ten votes would have killed it. Of 159 Republicans, 137 had voted against repeal.

This week, with the bill's signing, trained Navy gun crews will go aboard many a merchant ship, where the ready guns are quickly fixed on the already-prepared gun mounts. The ships will begin to move into the horizon, headed for England and Russia, will dock at Liverpool, London, Archangel—or perhaps with Davy Jones.

VOTE FOR WAR: In the packed, still House chamber stood the DEC. 15 men & women of the House of Representatives, the Senate, the Supreme Court, the Cabinet, all of the U.S. Government under one skylight roof. Below the great flat-hung Stars & Stripes stood Vice-President Henry Agard Wallace, Speaker Sam Rayburn, President Franklin Delano Roosevelt.

The President spoke briefly to the joint session, outlining Japanese aggression, and asked Congress for a declaration of war.

The President left the House. Members began roaring impatiently: "Vote! Vote! Vote!" The Speaker gaveled for order. The Senate left, promptly passed the declaration of war, 82-to-0. (There were 13 absentees, Washington-bound by train and plane, and one vacancy.)

The House received with a whoop the identical Senate bill, adopted it as a substitute. The vote: 388-to-1.

The lone dissenter was Miss Jeannette Rankin, Montana Republican, grey-haired pacifist who also voted, with many a tear, against the declaration of war on April 6, 1917. This time Miss Rankin, to whose pleas for recognition the Speaker was conveniently deaf, mostly sat, with a bewildered smile, muttering over & over to all those who pleaded with her to change her vote: This might be a Roosevelt trick. How do we know Hawaii has been bombed? Remember the *Kearny*! I don't believe it. In Montana, Republicans raged, cried shame.

ROUTINE DECLARATION: President Roosevelt sent to Con- DEC. 22 gress a 136-word message that took less than two minutes to read: "The long-known and the long-expected has thus taken place...." This was his only I-told-you-so to all the isolationists who had so long insisted that nothing of the sort would ever take place.

That morning (Dec. 11, 1941) Adolf Hitler and Benito Mussolini had done some routine ranting, had roared some routine lies, had returned to their routine aggression—after declaring war on the U.S.

With a single speech, without one wasted word, the Senate voted war with Germany, 88-to-0, war with Italy 90-to-0. The House voted war with Germany, 393-to-0. (In both House votes, Republican Pacifist Jeannette Rankin cinched her footnote place in history piping "Present"—a refusal to vote.) After the declaration of war with Germany was passed, the House galleries held up the second roll call by noisily tromping out. War with Italy (399-to-0) wasn't worth sitting for.

The President's message had been read at about 12:30 p.m.; by 3:06 p.m. he had the two declarations. Thus, as it must to all good peoples, war with the Nazis came to the U.S.

Labor

JAN. 27 **C.I.O. FACES DEFENSE:** To the U.S. it had become a matter of great concern that the men and machinery that make steel should keep going. Let there be no strikes. Preventive measures had already been pondered, including legislation flatly outlawing strikes. But any plan would depend on the attitude of labor. And the most important attitude in labor was the one taken by a tall, grey-haired citizen of Pittsburgh named Philip Murray.

Head of the Steel Workers Organizing Committee, vice president of the United Mine Workers, and president of the C.I.O., Murray is boss of the majority of workers in key industries of defense. Though he speaks with a Scot's burr, actually he is an Irishman out of the coal pits. An Irish mother bore him in Scotland. When the family emigrated to the U.S., he went down into the mines of Pennsylvania. In 1912, Murray climbed out of the mines for good when he was elected a member of the U.M.W.'s executive board.

Andrew Carnegie and his Pinkerton rowdies had crushed the union in a murderous fracas at Homestead in 1892. Corporations enlisted even their clergy in their war against the unions. Cried the Rev. P. Molyneux, of Braddock, Pa. in 1919: "That's the only way you can reason with these people: knock them down."

After 1929, corporations laid off workers, staggered work, cut wages. Desperation walked the steel towns. That was the bloodied territory which Murray and his Steel Workers Organizing Committee invaded. U.S. Steel signed a contract and the bars were down. But the die-hards of "Little Steel" (Bethlehem, Youngstown, Republic, National) held out, still do. Murray is determined that Little Steel shall not hold out forever. He now demands: "Do we want to hear the same story in 1940-41? Total war means total defense. This is possible only with the full cooperation and participation of labor. . . . Labor demands that industry get on with the job by getting on with labor."

NOTHING SERIOUS: A crisis on the labor front—the gravest MARCH 10 since the defense program began—had the Office of Production Management scared stiff last week.

Outside Bethlehem Steel Co.'s Lackawanna plant, in freezing weather, Polish, Negro and native-born steelworkers angrily marched in a picket line, on strike. Inside, one by one, open-hearth furnaces shut down, production dwindled, came almost to a standstill.

What scared OPM was that the strike might spread from Buffalo to other Bethlehem plants—Pottstown, Lebanon, Johnstown, the big parent plant at Bethlehem itself. In danger of disruption or complete stoppage was work on a $1,500,000,000 Government contract.

While striking workers fought the Buffalo police, OPM's double-headed boss Knudsenhillman (William Knudsen and Sidney Hillman acting together) took a deep breath, summoned Bethlehem spokesmen and union heads to Washington.

Bethlehem, under President Eugene Grace, had doggedly resisted C.I.O's Steel Workers Organizing Committee from the start. Doggedly, Bethlehem spokesmen rejected S.W.O.C.'s terms for ending the Lackawanna strike. When the company threatened to demand that the militia be called out, Knudsen leaned across the table, shook a long finger, declared, "That would be pure murder." Hour after hour the conferees wrestled and wrangled. Near midnight, Knudsen and Hillman called in newsmen, in weary triumph announced the terms of a truce. At the Lackawanna plant, workers accepted the terms with a whoop. Said Van A. Bittner, regional director and chief organizer of the strike: "This is. . . the first time on a large scale that our union has been able to get any sort of agreement from Bethlehem." No one believed that Bethlehem had surrendered, but it was a notable truce: thirty-nine hours after the strike began, steel was beginning to roll again in Lackawanna.

MARCH 17 **MODEL T TYCOON:** Henry Ford, the most famed tycoon alive, was up a tree this week. The old coon had been treed before, but this time not only Organized Labor but the U.S. Government was after him. C.I.O.'s tough young United Automobile Workers had given formal notice of their intent to strike Ford's River Rouge, Highland Park and Lincoln plants. In Dearborn, Mich., in the vast River Rouge plant, mounted policemen patrolled the grounds. There was no trouble yet, but no one could say when there might be.

Mr. Ford had either to deal with the union or fight the fight of his life.

Both sides were adamant. U.A.W. was confident that it had the strength to cripple Ford's production, if not stop it completely. And Henry Ford seemed determined not to budge from his lifelong position. Said he: "We do not intend to submit to any union, and those who belong to one are being fooled. . . . The men in our plants are satisfied generally with wages and conditions. Occasionally agitators try to keep our employes stirred up, but the men know they will be treated fairly by the company, without outside intervention."

Most of the limbs on Henry Ford's tree have been lopped off—one of the last ones by the Supreme Court, which cleared the way for union organizers at Ford. About the only limb left was delay. Said Ford's hard-fisted right-hand man, Harry Bennett [Bennett was in charge of plant security and labor relations]: "If the NLRB orders an election, of course we will hold one, because Mr. Ford will observe the law. C.I.O. will win it, of course, because it always wins these farcical elections, and we will bargain with it because the law says so. We will bargain until Hell freezes over, but they won't get anything."

Michigan Governor Van Wagoner proclaimed that the public interest was involved. It certainly was. At River Rouge, men were beating ploughshares into swords—$122,000,000 worth. Greatest preparation of all was centered around the building for making airplane engines. Another project: a technique of seam welding and gang riveting which would make possible the mass production of airplane fuselages. If there was a strike, all this would cease.

"Labor-union organizers," says Henry Ford, "are the worst thing that ever struck the earth." Until recently, Ford has paid and publicized the highest wage, and the Ford method of keeping organizers out of the plants has been simple and direct: hit them first. Harry Bennett got a cracked head in a fight outside the Rouge plant in 1932, in which four jobless marchers were killed. Brutally beaten by Ford agents were two other men who are now in the very front rank of U.A.W. —Richard Frankensteen and Walter Reuther.

It was nothing new for Henry Ford to be in the midst of conflict. From time to time he had given the world the benefit of his experience: "If you will study the history of almost any criminal, you will find he is an inveterate cigaret smoker. ... An army or navy is a tool for the protection of misguided, inefficient, destructive Wall Street. . . . A man learns something even by being hanged."

PROBLEM CORKED: Just before he went on vacation last week MARCH 31 President Roosevelt gingerly stuck a cork in his most explosive problem: the rising number of labor disputes and stoppages in defense work—and the rising protest over them. The cork: a new National Defense Mediation Board, composed of four businessmen, four labormen, three representatives of "the public." But critics called the board a clumsy compromise in a situation which, they felt, called for something tough and full of teeth.

SHOWDOWN AT FORD: Last week, for the first time in history, APRIL 14 Henry Ford's main plant at Dearborn was shut by a strike. The whole production flow of Ford was dammed. There was no serious violence until 200 non-striking Negroes, who had remained inside the beleaguered plant, made a sortie through Gate 4 armed with iron pipes, bolts, razors, knives and charged the pickets. Hot & heavy was the battle until the attackers withdrew, fled back inside. Finally the company agreed to negotiate tentatively, the union agreed to remove the barricades and send maintenance men inside to bank fires, keep them going. Company officials charged that dies and tools needed in aircraft production had been destroyed.

Strikers fight non-strikers at a Ford plant. For the first time in its history, Ford deals with a union.

APRIL 21   **PRAYER ANSWERED:** Peace, as it must eventually to all disputants, came last week to Henry Ford and his striking workers. For the first time in his long career, Henry Ford had agreed to negotiate with a labor union. Ford agreed to reinstate five of the men whose dismissals precipitated the walkout. The union agreed to leave the cases of three others in arbitration. Both sides agreed to cooperate in a National Labor Relations Board election to determine finally whether C.I.O. or A.F. of L. had a majority in the plant and was entitled to be certified as exclusive bargaining agent. Breathed Michigan's Governor Van Wagoner: "Our prayers for peace have been answered."

JUNE 2   **LABOR'S DAY:** Last week C.I.O. had something to crow about. After a four-and-a-half-year campaign, every major auto manufacturer was now CIOrganized. Some 80,000 Ford workers were given the chance to decide whether they wanted C.I.O. or A.F. of L. to represent them. Result: only a little more than 2% voted for no union at all; nearly 70% voted for C.I.O. Growled Ford's Harry Bennett: "A great victory for the Communist Party."

SHOWDOWN: Having tolerated strikes in defense industry for JUNE 16
many months—until the public was fed up and Congress indignant—Franklin Roosevelt either had to put up or curl up.
The three strikes which put him in that spot were in the logging camps of the Northwest, in San Francisco shipyards, at
North American Aviation in Inglewood, Calif. In each case
strikers had arrogantly defied the Federal Government. In
each case responsible labor leaders repudiated the strike. So
finally the President spanked. From the White House came
an order to reopen North American's plant. If necessary, the
plant would be put under Army operation. C.I.O. President
Philip Murray sent an emissary to beg the workers to get back
to work; but he was booed off the platform. Warned a defiant local union leader: "Armed forces will not break our
strike. Bombers can't be made with bayonets."

Finally the President made good his threat. A few hours
after two battalions of troops had taken over, workers were
streaming through the gates and limited production had been
resumed.

But in the logging camps, local strike leader O.M.
("Mickey") Orton was still defying both the government and
the C.I.O. leadership. Surly, sandy-haired Mickey Orton, who
has frequently been accused of leftist sympathies, had the support of few labor leaders. Best he could produce was a tele-
gram from Harry Bridges, West Coast longshoremen's chief,
who was in the midst of a deportation hearing on charges of
being a Communist himself. [Bridges was later cleared of
these charges by the U.S. Supreme Court.] Bridges wired
"wholehearted support."

THE MIND OF MR. LEWIS: The big man strides ponderously AUG. 4
up and down the big, dark-paneled office, his wide feet sinking heavily in the broadloom carpet. John Llewellyn Lewis
is thinking. Now his pale thick hands are clasped behind him;
now they jam in great fists in his pockets. Deep in his heavy
chops he grips a cigar the size of an auto's gearshift, and like
a gearshift the cigar slides slickly from point to point along
the wide mouth. A mountain in a white suit, the 61-year-old
labor leader strolls and ponders.

He hates the New Deal. He hates Franklin Roosevelt. He
thinks the President has betrayed labor. He believes that the

U.S.'s first concern should be domestic affairs. He has no faith in Roosevelt's foreign policy, and his opposition makes him an isolationist. He believes that the defense program is being tragically bungled, with an inefficiency that fairly invites graft and waste.

He is against Hitler. But he does not share the usual horror at the possibility of a Hitler victory. He has an almost fanatical hope that the Russian army will beat the Germans. For one thing, a Russian victory would defeat Hitler and expose the Roosevelt emergency in the U.S. as unnecessary. Such were the thoughts last week of this big man, gnawing his great cigar, storing up the Biblically powerful invective of which he is a master, and biding his time.

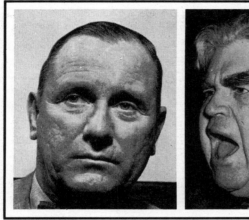 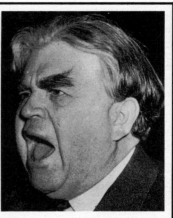

Harry Bennett: "A victory for the Communist Party." Page 47.   *John L. Lewis. He hates the New Deal. He hates Franklin Roosevelt.*

NOV. 3 **LEWIS' GREAT DEFIANCE:** In one of the loudest and brashest performances of his career, John L. Lewis this week defied the President of the U.S. All his long, pent-up hatred of Franklin Roosevelt boiling over, John Lewis, like an angry, ranting, old-style tragedian, flatly rejected requests made in the name of his country.

After Lewis had decreed a strike of 53,000 miners in the soft-coal fields, after the President had made two mild pleas for peace, Lewis summoned newsmen to hear his great defiance. Pale face glistening in the floodlights, he mugged for

cameramen with evident satisfaction. Behind him stood three aides, two of them chomping gum. Waggling his eyebrows, in sonorous, sneering, ironic tones, he intoned his letter:
    "Sir,
    "Your letter at hand. . . ."
Denying that the defense program would be impaired, reasserting the loyalty of his miners, Lewis said that if the President was going to restrain him, "then, sir, I submit that you should use the same power to restrain my adversary, who is an agent of capital. My adversary is a rich man named Morgan, who lives in New York." It was J.P. Morgan, member of the Board of U.S. Steel, declared Lewis, who determined the policy of the mine operators. (Sniffed Banker Morgan: "What utter rubbish!")

As for calling off the strike—in his own brand of inflated English, Mr. Lewis told the President of the U.S. to go jump in the lake.

At week's end, Franklin Roosevelt sat down and wrote a second plea to the man who had chosen to put his personal feuds above the welfare of the country. No immediate answer came from proud, peculiar Mr. Lewis. The Roosevelt patience was at last exhausted.

That evening, broadcasting to the nation, the President clipped Mr. Lewis a glancing blow on his jutting jaw, declared: "Our national will must speak from every assembly line—yes, from every coal mine. . . . It cannot be hampered by the selfish obstruction of a small but dangerous minority of industrial managers . . . [or] by the selfish obstruction of a small but dangerous minority of labor leaders who are a menace to the true cause of labor itself, as well as to the nation as a whole."

HIP AND THIGH: John L. Lewis' defiance of the President NOV. 10 jarred the whole U.S. From left & right, commentators smote him hip and thigh. Cried the pinko *New Republic*: "The magnificent megalomania of John L. Lewis has reached its apogee." The cartoonists took their pens and demolished him. Reports of a survey taken among union members themselves should have given Labor Leader Lewis pause. Workers voted 56% in favor of forbidding defense strikes; only 39% were opposed; 5% undecided.

NOV. 24 **UNION v. THE U.S.:** The facts were simple. Lewis' Mine Workers have a closed shop for 350,000 miners in the bituminous commercial coal mines, but the "captive" mines (those owned by the steel companies to produce coal for their own use) are not closed shops—though they are 95% union-organized. As the present union contract with the captive mines expired, Lewis threatened to strike the 53,000 captive coal miners unless the closed shop was granted. Last week the contract expired, the miners went out.

Franklin Roosevelt, the Great White Father of Labor, is also President of the U.S. He summoned the disputants to the White House, told them off in language that had the forceful clarity of a long-suffering man boundlessly irked. Then he said something that many a U.S. citizen had never expected to hear from him: "I tell you frankly that the Government of the United States will not order, nor will Congress pass legislation ordering a so-called closed shop."

Next day, Lewis walked up one flight of the Wardman Park Hotel in Washington to Suite 200-B, where steel operators Fairless, Purnell and Grace awaited him. Reporters knew that Frank Purnell of Youngstown Sheet & Tube Co. and Ben Fairless (of U.S. Steel) were inclined to sign with Lewis. But Lewis is Eugene Grace's devil (Grace is President of Bethlehem Steel Corp.) and vice versa. They have a long record of hatred, these two—the smooth, hard-boiled man whose income has averaged about $600,000 a year for 23 years and the huge, hard-boiled man who had seldom been down a mine in the last 20 years but lives luxuriously on $25,000 a year and perquisites squeezed out of the $35-a-week earnings of 400,000 very poor men. The sessions went on and on. No agreement. At midnight on Saturday, the miners officially went on strike. The miners didn't want to strike. They never do. But they had faith in John Lewis. They know the old, old response; when the union chief roars: "No contract—?" they sing out "No work!"

DEC. 1 **ROARING LION, COOING DOVE:** For six days, while John Lewis curled his long lip in scorn over every Presidential appeal for some kind of settlement of the captive mines walkout, his pallid-faced miners obeyed his orders, roamed the drab hills, picketed gates, shot and were shot at, and made the strike all that John Lewis could have demanded. They not only walked out of the captive mines, they struck at mines already under contract. One by one, in the nation's industrial center, open hearths were banked. At one plant alone, the strike cost some 200,000 miners a week's wages and cost the U.S. some 30,000 tons of steel (enough for 3,000 light tanks or 30 destroyers).

Then John Lewis unexpectedly gave in, agreed to submit the dispute to arbitration. Observers wondered why this roaring lion had suddenly begun to coo like a sucking dove. Some suggested a possible reason: Mr. Lewis had good reason to suppose that the arbitration board—which included John L. Lewis himself—would decide in Mr. Lewis' favor. [It did, on the night of December 7, 1941.] To Labor Leader Lewis it was a big and gratifyingly noisy success. To the U.S. it was time wasted that could never be bought back. Most people hoped John L. Lewis would now get off the front page and stay off.

DEC. 7, 1941: It was Sunday midday, clear and sunny, when DEC. 15 the flash came that the Japanese had attacked Hawaii. What would the people, the 132,000,000, say in the face of the mightiest event of their time?

What they said—tens of thousands of them—was: "Why, the yellow bastards!"

A steelworker said: "We'll stamp their front teeth in."

John L. Lewis: "When the nation is attacked every American must rally to its support. . . . All other considerations become insignificant."

National Defense

FLYING INFANTRY: First army to try parachute soldiers was JAN. 6 the U.S. Army, which had dropped the first troops in history in 1928, then abandoned the whole business as unpractical. Last week, with a good start toward regaining lost ground, the Army had its first full parachute battalion in training. At Fort Benning, Ga. the 501st Parachute Battalion was going through jumps from dummy airplanes, exercises in combat tactics, bruising training in tumbling and other roughhouse, good for jumpers. Trained to pack and maintain their own 'chutes, Benning's jumpers go over the side armed, like Germans, with pistol and a bag of grenades. The rest of their fighting equipment, from rifles to light mortars and folding bicycles, is dropped separately. [By the end of World War II, the U.S. had five airborne divisions in action—including the famed 101st which fought the Battle of the Bulge.]

The Army's first parachute battalion loads up. The soldiers jump with only pistols and grenades. The heavier weapons are dropped later.

MARTIN'S MIRACLE: Day in & day out last week a stubwinged, twin-motored monoplane darted off the Glenn L. Martin Airport near Baltimore, cut the sky at 340-360 m.p.h., landed for checkups by Martin engineers and Army Air Corps observers. It was one of the Army's (and the Royal Air Force's) latest and best bets for air war: the Martin B-26 medium bomber. From two electrically twirled turrets and from fuselage blisters a dozen machine guns bristled. It also had leakproofed fuel tanks, armored cockpits.

Glenn Martin has a $131,000,000 order for about 1,000 B-26s, last week had the first 20-odd moving rapidly along his assembly line. The best news of his plane last week was not its performance (1,000-mile range, 3,000 to 4,000 lb. of bombs) but the fact that it was approved. "Never mind about further testing," said Major General Henry H. ("Hap") Arnold, the Air Corps' Deputy Chief of Staff. "You start sending us the planes as fast as you can and don't stop until we say when."

PRODUCTION: Four months ago the site of the Detroit Tank JAN. 27 Arsenal was a farm, turning brown and sere under a hazy autumn sun. During the summer Mobilization Director Big Bill Knudsen had called bulky K.T. Keller, president of Chrysler Corp., and asked him, as one motormaker to another: Could Chrysler build the Army a medium tank? K.T. said, Sure. Could he see one to get an idea what it was like?

Four days later, K.T. and a few technicians were looking over a medium tank (one of about 200 now on hand, mostly out of date). Day after, he was back in Detroit with 186 pounds of blueprints of an improved 25-tonner. To work on the blueprints went 197 Chryslermen, led by Staff Master Mechanic Edward J. Hunt. They worked seven days a week, had things in shape by Aug. 15, when Chrysler and the U.S. Army finally signed the contract. It called for a $20,000,000 arsenal to be built by Chrysler (Chrysler's fee:$1), an initial order of 1,000 tanks at $33,500 apiece. The new M-3 tank will be more powerful than anything the U.S. Army has ever had, as good as anything the Germans have, and maybe better.

PLANES FROM DETROIT: The U.S. public last week got its FEB. 3 answer to the big question: When, and on what scale, was the automobile industry going to turn its mass-production genius into the job of building airplanes for national defense? Fortnight ago, Ford and Chrysler announced that they would help. Last week the rest of the answer came from General Motors. The Big Three will not turn out complete planes in Detroit, but will build airplane sub-assemblies, ship them to four midwest and southwest plants, there to be put together by aircraft mechanics. General Motors' choice of an airplane to build was the Army's speedy B-25, a slim, two-engined bomber made by big North American Aviation. Ford will build the four-motored B-24 bomber. Chrysler's pick was Glenn Martin's new B-26. Detroit has already prepared to build engines to fly the bombers. Ford is building Pratt & Whitney engines. Buick will build a plant to do the same. Studebaker will build Wrights.

U.S. officials were hoping to set a production total of 33,000 planes by July, 1942. The U.S. had loafed in its armament race. Should Britain be defeated the Axis will outnumber the U.S. on the sea and in the air.

MORE CURLS: Up in Oklahoma City went the draft number of Ivan Barzella Heiderich, 33. Farmer Heiderich, who shuns barbers like boll weevils, showed up with golden curls down to his shoulders, full of worry that the Army would snip them off. His explanation: "When I was a little boy I had beautiful curls and my mother wouldn't cut them. . . . You might say it's gotten to be a hobby with me." The draft board decided that Mr. Heiderich was more useful as farmer than soldier, sent him home to grow more crops, more curls.

EYE, LEG: Twelve per cent of all draftees accepted by local draft boards have been rejected by the U.S. Army for physical defects. Recently an Army induction officer found a Chicago draftee with a glass eye. Growled the disgusted medico: "Some of these days one of these boys is going to come in here with a wooden leg."

Last week James Brown, 25, appeared before the wary induction officer. Brown's draft board had given him a clean bill of health except for the notation: "Enlarged tonsils." Told to strip, he took his trousers off, revealed an artificial leg.

MAY 5   **HOW'S IT COMING?:** Last week the U.S. people got two reports on the state of their new Army. One was from Chief of Staff George Catlett Marshall. The other was from Brigadier General Harry Lewis Twaddle, who last week took over the General Staff division (G-3) in charge of Army operations, organization and training. (Besides General Twaddle, the nearly 30,000 regular officers in the professional establishments include: Rear Admiral Felix Xerxes Gygax, Ensign Strong Boozer, Lieut. Jud F. Yoho, Lieut. Clarence Clapsaddle.)

Gist of both reports: the Army is over the hump. It is far better off than was the U.S. Army of 1917. It will soon be the first Army-in-being, ready to fight, which the U.S. has ever had before entering a war. Said General Twaddle:"We have created a fighting army in less than a year. By June 30, 1941. . . we will have 27 divisions in being. . . . We will likewise have four armored divisions. We had none a year ago."

When Senator Harry Truman asked whether the divisions had their equipment now, General Twaddle answered: "No, sir. . . . Only a few are ready to move into the theater of operations." Senator Truman observed that General Twaddle's "fighting army" was by no means ready to fight last week. General Twaddle agreed.

YOUNG EYES: U.S. pilots of fighting age and temper—mostly MAY 12 young lieutenants under 25—are going to Great Britain as observers. When they finish their tours abroad, they will know something firsthand about air fighting in modern war. Already, according to a British account, one U.S. observer who took a British Spitfire up for a trial round found a Messerschmitt on his tail, had to shoot it down to save his own skin.

THE OTHER GUY: Said Master Sergeant P. Hitler, of the 101st JUNE 2 Military Police Battalion at Fort Dix, N.J.: "Sure, that's my name. Let the other guy change his."

TEST IN THE FIELD: North of Tennessee's meandering Duck JUNE 23 River, where rolling meadows and woods break sharply into commanding hills, 55,000 U.S. fighting men last week worked at war. A few weeks before, frank General George Marshall had said that the U.S. Army was still in the high-school stage. In Lieut. General Ben Lear's Second Army, three divisions were far enough along in their courses to be sent to the Tennessee laboratory to show what they had learned, and study further in the hard school of field maneuver.

Last week they met in mimic battle. It was a realistic, competent job of battle craft. Supply functioned without a major hitch. Motorcycle dispatch riders, powdered with dust, clattered into well-hidden command posts with battle messages that got prompt handling.

There were also plenty of deficiencies, and none knew them better than burly, barrel-voiced General Ben Lear. Most annoying were shortages of equipment, trucks, radio equipment, .50-caliber machine guns, mortars. Throughout the maneuver area many a crew worked, deadly serious and full of ginger, around a log that represented a mortar or a gun.

YOO-HOO! Along busy Central Avenue, on the outskirts of JULY 21 Memphis, Tenn., rolled 80 trucks of the 110th Quartermaster Regiment, making slow progress through Sunday traffic. In the cabs and on the hard seats sat 350 soldiers, ties discarded, collars open under a blistering sun. After the manner of the U.S. soldier, Model 1941, or the Roman soldier, B.C. 100, they were also making merry by waving at girls, shouting boisterous pleasantries at civilians. They had a right to be cheerful, they had just finished more than a month's hard work in the Second Army maneuvers, and done a good, cheerful job of it.

Past the first tee of the Memphis Country Club the convoy moved at a snail's pace. Along the walk bordering the course strolled a group of girls in shorts. From the trucks came a drumfire of soldiers' shouts—"Yoo-Hoo-o-o"—"Hi, baby"—a fanfare of whistling.

On the first tee, hard by the street, a leathery-faced golfer was getting ready to tee off. "Fore," shouted a soldier. The golfer turned and glared at the trucks. Thereupon the soldiers let him have it: "Hey, buddy, do you need a caddy?" The man on the tee jumped a three-foot fence, stalked to the convoy. A command car in the column jerked to a stop, and its officers piled out to face an Awful Fact. The golfer was Lieut. General Ben Lear, commander of the Second Army, director of the maneuvers from which the 110th had just emerged.

Ben Lear was a first sergeant before he was an officer, and what he had to tell the 110th's officers sizzled with first sergeant's wrath. When all the burning words had been said,

Farmer Heiderich's draft board sends him home to grow curls. Page 55.

General Ben Lear hates to hear soldiers yell "Yoo-Hoo."

Ben Lear told the convoy to move on, that it would hear from him after it got back to its home station at Camp Robinson, 145 miles away.

The men of the 110th know Ben Lear (in uniform) as a ranker who lives close to his troops, a rugged soldier, a great believer in spit-and-polish. They know and generally approve his dislike of sloppy soldiers. They know him, too, as a commander too much preoccupied with small details. But tough and touchy as Ben Lear is, no soldier of the 110th was prepared for the tough touch that awaited them when they pulled in at Camp Robinson toward sundown. The General's order: to return at once to Memphis and stand by. They were to get mass punishment, the innocent with the guilty.

Toward midnight the trucks were loaded again and the convoy was off. To rest tired drivers, it stopped three hours on the way, resumed the journey by dawn. Before noon the 110th had pitched tents on Memphis airport, was waiting for the lightning to strike. It struck soon. To the airport came Ben Lear in person, read the riot act again—"disgrace to the Army . . . loose conduct and rowdyism . . . breach of discipline." Then he announced sentence. After a night's rest, the 110th would head home. And on the way every man in the outfit must march 15 miles.

Next day, the hottest day in two years (97°), the trucks rumbled off, let all but the drivers out. Five miles ahead the drivers stopped, got out, started to march. Through the morning and afternoon, the trucks were leapfrogged until everybody had had his dose. The stragglers and heat-stricken took emergency treatment from a dentist and a sanitary officer who were also being disciplined. The rest ate plenty of salt against the heat, filled their canteens silently at wayside towns while the citizenry eyed them with sympathy.

But the 110th's Battalion took the whole business as soldiers should. When civilians were not around, they laughed and kidded, tried to improvise on an old song—"General Lear he missed his putt, Parley Voo—. . ." They did not seem to feel that they had disgraced the Army.

Neither did some Congressmen, who roundly trounced Ben Lear. Missouri's isolationist Senator Bennett Champ Clark called Ben Lear "a superannuated old goat, who ought to retire." The controversy spread like a heat wave. Mothers demanded Ben Lear's removal. It was the first time U.S. citizens had had a chance to make a song & dance out of anything connected with World War II, and they made the most of it. They saw nothing wrong with yoo-hooing, and proceeded to tell the Army so, with many a yoo-hoo.

But in the Army a general is always right. In the view of professional officers, Ben Lear was not dishing out punishment as a champion of U.S. womanhood, nor because a soldier threw him off his golf game. He saw a breach of discipline, and smacked it good & proper. That he smacked it harder than was good & proper was—in a professional's view —beside the point.

Meanwhile, at a bathing-beauty revue at the El Paso (Tex.) Country Club, brimstony Major General Innis Palmer Swift, commander of Fort Bliss (and one of the judges) watched the girls prance by, and owlishly hooted "Yoo-Hoo."

AUG. 4   **DEMOTED PROMOTION:** Field Marshal Douglas MacArthur, Military Adviser to the Philippine Commonwealth, had just taken a demotion in rank. As he stood at a window in his penthouse apartment atop the swank Manila Hotel, looking out on the bay, on the brooding fortress of Corregidor, he was (for practical purposes) no longer a field marshal or the four-starred general he had been when he retired three and a half years ago from the U.S. Army. His Commander in Chief had just called him back to that Army in reduced but impressive rank as a three star lieutenant general.

General MacArthur was not downcast at this technical demotion, and he had no reason to be. For he had also been made commander of the U.S. Army Forces in the Far East.

From Hyde Park, N.Y., Franklin Roosevelt issued an order that threw Douglas MacArthur's new-trained and untried Philippine Army, reputedly of 150,000 officers and men, into the U.S. Army. A supplemental order also put Douglas MacArthur, once the youngest (50) Chief of Staff the U.S. Army ever had, in command of the whole works—Philippine Army, U.S. regulars and Philippine Scouts, the Army's Philippine Air Force.

BRIDGE TO THE ORIENT: On a tiny Pacific island huddled within the circumference of a broken coral ring, a detachment of white-clad U.S. sailors last week went through a time-honored ceremony. The bugles blared "To the Colors," the flag was run up, the watch posted. The Navy's new station on the Midway Islands, first pier in the tenuous 5,860-mile water bridge between Pearl Harbor and the Philippines, was in commission.

From Midway's dredged-out central lagoon (landing place for Hawaii-bound Pan Am Clippers) the largest Navy seaplane tenders can mother a fleet of patrol bombers, ranging as far north as Alaska's Aleutian chain, south to Pago Pago, west to the edges of Japan itself.

Beyond Wake Island, the bridge passes through the Japanese mandated islands. Since the early 30's Japan has worked hard building up air bases in this cluster of hundreds of islands. On Yap, on Palau, on more other islands than Navymen like to think about, she has stored fuel, erected air and submarine bases. Yet the Navy is fairly well off with its own Pacific defenses, can cover the Pacific against any surprise attack. Once its reconnaissance pilots have located the enemy, the job is up to the bombers, and to the Pacific and Asiatic Fleets, which are now spread from Hawaii to Manila in a pattern that no Navy man will reveal. [Midway never fell to the Japanese; Wake Island fell on December 23, 1941.]

JEEP O' MY HEART: The Jeep, a stubby, bouncy 2,200-lb. cross- NOV. 3 breed between the half-ton command car and the motor-tricycle, is as ugly as a bull pup. But after a year and a half of service it has been recognized as an unexpected and unique success. Lieut. Colonel Ingomar M. Oseth, the Army's No. 1 Jeep expert, said last week: "Transportation in the U.S. Army is at least 50% superior to that of any other army in the world, and the Jeep can grab a big share of the glory." It has no trouble pulling light field pieces, can skitter along a road at 60 m.p.h. Designed to replace motorcycles and sidecars for reconnaissance work, it can go anywhere a cycle can, and a lot of places a cycle can't. It can be used as a troop carrier (three men easily, six with crowding), weapon carrier (machine guns, 37-mm. anti-tank guns, mortars), communications truck (to mount radios and carry wire). It has been successfully carried in transport planes and it is planned to try dropping it from a plane with a giant parachute.

War & Peace

JAN. 6 **THE WHIRLPOOL:** All the world watched the U.S. Whirlpool, to see what river might flow out of its settling. France had fallen before it knew what the war was about; England, taken suddenly by the throat, hadn't had time to figure things out. The U.S., under the impression that there was still time and room to make up its mind, was arguing along as it always had: in straggling, disputative, disorderly democracy.

Nearly everybody, it seemed, wanted to aid Britain, but nearly everybody also wanted to stay out of war. (According to Pollster Gallup's figures, 60% of U.S. voters now want to aid Britain even at risk of war. Only 12% wanted to go to war deliberately.)

FEB. 17 **EIGHTEEN DAYS:** *I feel that I am walking through history.*
— Wendell Willkie
Last week Wendell Willkie [who was defeated for President in 1940] returned to the U.S. from the British Isles and the war. Extremely tired, his white shirt rumpled, his grey herringbone suit needing pressing, the returning traveler greeted his son, kissed his wife, and said: "I'm glad to be home."

Behind him lay one of the most extraordinary journeys in U.S. history. In 18 days he had traveled 14,000 miles. He had talked with four Prime Ministers, twelve Cabinet members, one King, one Archbishop, innumerable soldiers, dock workers, charwomen, bricklayers, shopkeepers. While bombs dropped outside, he listened to a debate in the House of Commons. Everywhere his reception was tumultuous.

The Wendell Willkie who returned from Britain measured his words. He said he had found no trace of defeatism, observed that "the free people of the U.S. should be prayerfully thankful that they are not living as the free people of Britain are compelled to live, with sleepless nights of apprehension and days of fear for what may happen on the morrow."

FEB. 24 **LET THEM FIGHT:** While debate on the Lend-Lease Bill rolled on, many a U.S. citizen raised shrill anti-war cries. To the ingenuous mechanic's mind of Henry Ford, the logical course was for the U.S. to help the nations destroy each other. Mr.

Wendell Willkie in Britain: "I feel I am walking through history." Page 61.   *Charles Lindbergh. The hero of the '20s is a top isolationist of the '40s.*

Ford suggested that the U.S. give both England and the Axis powers "the tools to keep on fighting until they both collapse." Said he: "There is no righteousness in either cause. . . . When both nations finally collapse, then the U.S. can play the role for which it has the strength and the ability."

PASSAGE TO INDIA: More than halfway across the Pacific, MARCH 3 over 8,000 miles from Washington, D.C., 1,400 miles from Tokyo, the island of Guam lies midway in the passage to India. About 50 miles away, visible on a clear day, lies the mysterious, Japanese-controlled island of Rota that Pan American clippers are forbidden to fly over. Two years ago, a $52,000,000 naval authorization bill contained an item of $5,000,000 for harbor improvements at Guam. Congressmen raged against this item—their theme: it might offend Japan, cause war. The item was stricken from the bill. Last week, in a bigger naval appropriation bill, there was an item of $4,700,000—principally bombproofing and dredging of the harbor—for Guam. This time there was no such debate, no such delay. The authorization went through with one lone *Nay* registered against it: the methodical *Nay* of New York's left-wing Vito Marcantonio, who has voted against almost every bill for U.S. defense.

APRIL 28 **ISOLATIONISTS:** At an America First rally in Chicago, mention of Churchill drew boos from the 10,000-person audience. When Colonel Charles Lindbergh, most popular and highly respected U.S. isolationist, said that England was in a desperate situation, her shipping losses serious, "her cities devastated by bombs," he was stopped—and embarrassed—by applause.

JUNE 23 **ON THE HIGH SEAS:** It was 4 o'clock in the morning, a grey dawn on a grey sea, when the *Robin Moor* first saw the signal lights blinking. They signaled: "Send over a boat." The captain came up on the bridge in his pajamas. A boat was lowered and four seamen rowed the chief officer through the lifting dawn toward the long, low shape awash in the water, a mile and a half away.

The submarine was a Nazi U-boat with the word *Lorricke* or *Lorickke* and a picture of a "laughing cow" painted on her conning tower. The *Robin Moor*'s mate clambered aboard, met her captain on the deck. Ten minutes later the mate was back. Said he: "They're going to let us have it."

The submarine's commander gave the *Robin Moor* half an hour to abandon ship. The eight passengers (three women, one child) were roused. Three more boats were lowered. As the sun rose, after the boats were in the water, the submarine fired a torpedo into the *Robin Moor* amidships, shelled her for 23 minutes. She went wearily down by the stern.

The submarine circled about the captain's boat. A Nazi sailor gave the men four tins of ersatz bread, two tins of butter. Said the Nazi commander: "I'm sorry, but you were carrying supplies to my country's enemy." He promised to radio the *Robin Moor*'s position. Then he slid away into the sea.

Thus, one morning last month, 750 miles off the British port of Freetown, Africa, the U.S. freighter *Robin Moor* met her end. She carried no munitions, no material of a military character. On her side, the U.S. ensign was clearly painted.

For five days, through torrential rains, high seas and blazing sun, the four life-boats stayed together. Then they separated, headed into a fresh wind toward the Brazilian coast. Late on the 18th day after the *Robin Moor* went down, one of the boats sighted a ship on the horizon. The men signaled across the water with flashlights. A ship halted, picked them up. For seven days the U.S. believed that the rest of the passengers and crew were lost. Then came word from Capetown that they had been rescued by a British ship bound for Africa.

Nazi spokesmen in Berlin defiantly intended to continue such sinkings. Henceforth the U.S. would either have to recall its ships from the ocean or enforce its right to the free use of the seas.

NAME CHANGE: The Charlotte, N.C. City Council changed JUNE 30 the name of Lindbergh Drive to Avon Terrace.

STOCKING RUN: U.S. women, who are credited with having AUG. 11 the shapeliest legs in the world, last week faced the horrifying knowledge that soon they would have to go silk-stockingless. Raw-silk imports from Japan had ended.

Skeptical of substitutes, correctly assuming that there would not be enough nylon stockings to go around, women stormed stores. One department store executive, reporting on the mob at the gates, declared: "When you opened the doors at 9:30 they fell flat on their faces."

What would U.S. women do without silk stockings? Some predicted that they might copy their English sisters, paint their bare legs stocking color. A hopeful note in the panicky bedlam was a report of a new stocking made of cotton mesh which "wears like iron" and "looks very sheer."

MITE: The poor people of Booger Hollow, Ark., deep in the OCT. 6 Ozark Mountains, had taken years & years to save $75 toward building a community house. Last week they invested the $75 in defense bonds, reported the matter to Secretary of War Henry L. Stimson. Said they: "What good is a community house without freedom?"

THE U.S. NAVY FINDS TROUBLE: On the chilled hell's high- OCT. 27 way of the North Atlantic, the U.S. last week lost the illusion that it was not engaged in a shooting war. The illusion faded when the U.S.S. *Kearny* (rhymes with Blarney), a crack destroyer scarcely a year in service, was torpedoed. But the illusion did not disappear until the nation felt the dull visceral shock of reading its first casualty list of World War II, reading of its own men "The next of kin have been notified."

The U.S. Navy's North Atlantic Patrol which has expected trouble ever since the occupation of Iceland, has been actively looking for trouble since Franklin Roosevelt's "shoot on sight" speech of Sept. 11.

First news of the *Kearny*'s brush was brief; her skipper wanted no German raider to spot him through radio messages. Net of his message: the *Kearny*, torpedoed 350 miles southwest of Iceland, was proceeding to port under her own power. Two days later came a few more details. The *Kearny* had got to Iceland. The U.S. public had assumed that there were no casualties. Now it learned that eleven of the crew were "missing," presumably trapped in a ruptured water-tight compartment. Barring a miracle, they were dead. Ten more of the *Kearny*'s crew were injured, two of them seriously. Navy men had waited with foreboding. They knew that when a torpedo hits a destroyer, somebody usually dies.

NOV. 10 **A SURVIVOR TALKS:** The true story of the U.S.S. *Kearny* was told from a hospital cot in Iceland by Ensign Henry Lyman of Ponkapog, Mass.:

The *Kearny* was on escort duty, westbound. She received a signal to leave her convoy and go to the assistance of another convoy, which was being attacked by U-boats. The scattered convoy reformed and sailed into what Ensign Lyman called "as black a night as I've ever seen." Out of the blackness came a second submarine assault.

"They started to fire torpedoes and we dropped depth charges to drive them off. The submarines were probably on the surface with their decks awash and their engines cut, so we couldn't hear them. One tanker was afire and sinking. Somehow a U-boat had maneuvered between the *Kearny* and the convoy. She went after us.

"The U-boat fired three torpedoes at us. The third hit us on the starboard side at the forward engine room." Ensign Lyman heard a terrible roar as the warhead bit through the *Kearny*'s armor. The explosion killed seven men stationed in the forward boiler room. Its force ripped up through the deck, knocked the forward stack back and broke the siren cord so that its shrill yowl could not be shut off. Four other men disappeared, probably blown overboard.

"We couldn't hear a damned thing on the bridge because of the siren. . . . We had no compass working and the helmsman steered by watching the flag to see which way the wind was blowing." Thanks to her construction and the tenacity of her men, the *Kearny* limped to port. "If I am torpedoed again," said Ensign Lyman, "I hope I have this crew with me."

CHANGE OF HEART: In a survey made for the interventionist NOV. 17 Continental Congress for Freedom held in Washington last month, 59 Nebraska editors and publishers reported that their communities were now overwhelmingly in favor of the Administration's foreign policy, substantially in favor of Neutrality Act repeal. Said one editor: "The so-called 'Isolationist Midwest' exists only in the minds of Congressmen who have failed to keep abreast of a great surge of public opinion during recent months."

"AND SHOOTING MEANS WAR": W. Averell Harriman, U.S. DEC. 1 Lend-Lease Coordinator, told Britain in a broadcast this week what the U.S. wanted to know: "Our Navy is shooting Germans—German submarines and aircraft at sea."

THE U.S. FLAG GOES DOWN: *The photograph above, the first clear picture of the U.S. flag going down in World War II, was taken by James E. Earle, second assistant engineer of the freighter "Lehigh," sunk on Sunday, October 19, while voyaging to Africa to pick up manganese ore. The "Lehigh" was the tenth U.S. merchantman to be sunk by a German sub.*

DEC. 15 **TRAGEDY AT HONOLULU:** The U.S. Navy was caught with its pants down. Within one tragic hour—before the war had really begun—the U.S. appeared to have suffered greater naval losses than in the whole of World War I.

Days may pass before the full facts become known, but in the scanty news that came through from Hawaii in the first 36 hours of the war was every indication that the Navy had been taken completely by surprise in the early part of a lazy Sunday morning. Although the Japanese attackers had certainly been approaching for several days, the Navy apparently had no news of either airplane carriers sneaking up or of submarines fanning out around Hawaii. Not till the first bombs began to fall was an alarm given. And when the blow fell the air force at Pearl Harbor was apparently not ready to offer effective opposition to the attackers.

In fine homes on the heights above the city, in beach shacks near Waikiki, in the congested district around the Punchbowl, assorted Japanese, Chinese, Portuguese, Filipinos, Hawaiians and *kamaainas* (long-settled whites) were taking their ease. In the shallow waters lapping Fort De Russy, where sentries walked post along a retaining wall, a few Japanese and Hawaiians waded about, looking for fish to spear. In Army posts all over Oahu, soldiers were dawdling into a typical idle Sunday. Aboard the ships of the Fleet at Pearl Harbor, life was going along at a saunter. Downtown nothing stirred save an occasional bus. The clock on the Aloha Tower read 7:55.

The Japs came in from the southeast over Diamond Head. They could have been U.S. planes shuttling westward from San Diego. Civilians' estimates of their numbers ranged from 50 to 150 [the actual number, given by the Japanese after the war was 360]. They whined over Waikiki, over the candy-pink bulk of the Royal Hawaiian Hotel. All that they met as they came in was a tiny private plane in which Lawyer Ray Buduick was out for a Sunday morning ride. They riddled the lawyer's plane with machine-gun bullets, but the lawyer succeeded in making a safe landing. By the time he did, bombs were thudding all around the city.

Torpedoes launched from bombers tore at the dreadnoughts in Pearl Harbor. Dive-bombers swooped down on the Army's Hickam and Wheeler Fields. Shortly after the attack began, radio warnings were broadcast. But people who heard them were skeptical until explosions wrenched the guts of Honolulu. All the way from Pacific Heights down to the center of town the planes soared, leaving a wake of destruction.

With anti-aircraft guns popping and U.S. pursuits headed aloft, pajama-clad citizens piled out of bed to dash downtown or head for the hills where they could get a good view. Few of them were panicky, many were nonchalant. Shouted one man as he dashed past a CBS observer: "The mainland papers will exaggerate this."

When the first ghastly day was over, Honolulu began to reckon up the score. It was one to make the U.S. Navy and Army shudder. Of the 200,000 inhabitants of Oahu, 1,500 were dead, 1,500 others injured. Not all the civilian casualties occurred in Honolulu. The raiders plunged upon the town of Wahiawa, where there is a large island reservoir, sprayed bullets on people in the streets. Behind the Wahiawa courthouse a Japanese plane crashed in flames.

Heaviest military toll was at Hickam Field, where hundreds were killed and injured when bombs hit the great barracks and bombs were reported to have destroyed several hangars full of planes.

HAVOC AT HONOLULU: Secretary of the Navy Frank Knox DEC. 22 announced the official reckoning of the damage, which he flew to Honolulu to get.

The limited extent of U.S. materiel losses was most heartening, made complete liars out of the Japanese High Command. Lost:

¶ The 26-year-old battleship *Arizona*, by a bomb that "litterally passed down through the smokestack."

¶ The ancient *Utah*, a target-training ship long out of combatant service. Atop the *Utah* was a steel platform for sandbags (as crew protection) when she was doing duty as a moving target for bombing novices. The attacking Japanese, thinking her an aircraft carrier, subjected her to repeated, withering attack.

¶ Three destroyers, the *Cassin*, *Shaw* and *Downes*.

¶ The mine layer *Oglala*, an old passenger ship converted during World War I.

¶ Other damage ranged from "ships which have already been repaired, and are ready for sea, or which have gone to sea, to a few ships which will take from a week to several months to repair." In the last category Secretary Knox placed the battleship *Oklahoma*, launched March 23, 1914, which capsized. ¶ Harbor approaches received little damage, and the vast spread of oil storage tanks was unscathed.

The Japanese, said Frank Knox, lost two of their little-known, tiny two-man submarines (one sunk, one captured), one full-sized sub and 41 aircraft, including those shot down and those forced down for lack of fuel.

"The United States Services were not on the alert against the surprise air attack on Hawaii," said Knox. "This fact calls for a formal investigation which will be initiated immediately by the President."

Up-to-date Navy casualty figures dwarfed previous unofficial estimates: officers (including Rear Admiral Isaac Campbell Kidd, commanding a battleship division), 91 dead, 20 wounded; enlisted men, 2,638 dead, 636 wounded. Army losses: 168 killed in action; 223 wounded; 26 missing. A Japanese fifth column, "the most effective actually in this war since Norway," knew the sites of all defenses, the comings & goings of the various patrols.

To the Japanese the Secretary issued a taunting challenge: "The essential fact is that the Japanese purpose was to knock out the United States before the war began. . . . In this purpose the Japanese failed. . . . The entire balance of the Pacific Fleet with its aircraft carriers, its heavy cruisers, its light cruisers, its destroyers and submarines are uninjured and are all at sea seeking contact with the enemy."

ROUNDUP: The zealous authorities in Norfolk, Va. did not even wait to hear from the FBI. At the news of Pearl Harbor, they rounded up every Japanese they could, clapped them in jail.

From coast to coast, FBI men swooped on Axis nationals. In the Canal Zone hundreds of Japanese aliens were interned. By week's end 1,370 Japs, 1,002 Germans and 169 Italians had been arrested.

The 1,124,000 citizens of Germany, Italy and Japan who live in the U.S. are potentially the biggest fifth column in the world. Said Attorney General Francis Biddle: "So long as the aliens in this country conduct themselves in accordance with law, they need fear no interference by the Department of Justice."

All suspicious aliens will receive hearings before they are interned. Some may be paroled if found harmless, the rest will go to detention camps. They will be considerably more comfortable than they would be at home. At the camps are warm barracks, playing fields, good food. Chef at one camp where 1,000 or so agents of the Duce are already held is Orlando Figini, who managed the restaurant in the Italian Village at the New York World's Fair.

Not half so happy were thousands of enemy aliens who did not fall into the FBI dragnet last week. In Los Angeles a 61-year-old Japanese, Takematsu Izumi, a resident of California since 1896, swallowed poison when he heard that Japan had attacked Hawaii.

Unhappy too were *Nisei*, the 79,642 native-born citizens of the U.S. who are descendants of Japanese. Said a young *Nisei* with yellow skin, slant eyes, and a college education: "Over there I'd be a coolie. Over here I have enough money to own a car, I can talk to any man. Over here, by God, we believe enough in what we have to fight Japan." But panic was in his heart. Would other U.S. citizens know the difference?

Not all of them would. At Ann Arbor, Mich., a young Filipino marched into a police station, asked politely: "Now can I shoot the first Japanese I see?" In Nashville, Tennessee's Department of Conservation put in a request for 6,000,000 licenses to hunt Japs at a fee of $2 each. The purchasing department vetoed the requisition, with the note: "Open season on 'Japs'—no license required." [When the war was over, and the hysteria had passed, it was generally agreed that the nation had acted hastily in its treatment of aliens, and that the vast majority of them were loyal to the U.S.]

WORLD WAR

As World War II entered its second year, the Axis was trium-
phant everywhere. Norway, the Netherlands, Belgium and France
had fallen to the Nazis. London and other British cities were
enduring the fierce bombing raids and fire storms of the Battle
of Britain; a German invasion was expected any day. At sea,
Hitler's subs were sinking supply ships in an attempt to starve
out the beleaguered British.

In June Hitler broke his non-aggression pact with Stalin and
launched a massive attack against the Soviet Union. German
troops were threatening Moscow by the end of the year.

Japan, which had attacked Manchuria in 1932 and had start-
ed to overrun China in 1934, had joined the German-Italian
Axis in September 1940. On the first Sunday of December
1941, Japanese forces attacked Pearl Harbor and British
bases in Asia.

To keep all these battles in proper perspective, this section
has been arranged in five separate chapters, each bearing the
heading under which the battle was reported in TIME: *The*
Battle of Britain, The Southern Theatre (i.e. Africa and the
Middle East), The Eastern Front (the Balkans), Germany v.
Russia and War in the Pacific.

Battle of Britain

JAN. 6   **MIST & MYSTERY:** Heavy mists hung over northwest Europe
last week and so did heavy suspense. The most terrific military force in the world, the German Army, had been idle for
six months and on Christmas Eve its commander, Field Marshal Walther von Brauchitsch, visited camps on the Channel
coast. Near the long-range guns which sporadically hurl shells
into England, he told his men: "The Channel will protect
England only so long as it suits us." The British Army and

Royal Air Force took no chances. As soon as the Christmas truce was over, Germany's "invasion ports" were thunderously plastered with bombs night after night, from Norway to lower France.

While the Nazis' other plans matured, the *Luftwaffe* returned to its central task with a freshly furious fire-raid on London. Hundreds of huge blazes severely taxed the courage of London's thousands of firemen and volunteers. The Guildhall and other ancient monuments went down in avalanches and up in flames.

It was the most dangerous conflagration in modern history —and London's water pressure was low.

LULLABLITZ: The dead calm in night bombings of Britain FEB. 10 which began fortnight ago continued last week, until British nerves strained for bombs. The *Daily Express* called the pause a "Lullablitz." U.S. military men indicated that they now believed an attempted invasion of Britain might be no further than 60 days away. One German remarked last week: "We'll take England by employing the same method we used in taking Eben Emael"—the key Belgian fort which was subdued by treachery, flame, bombs, parachutists, gliders, above all, by surprise.

WAITING: By last week the Lullablitz had lasted nearly a FEB. 24 month. More jittery in their breathing spell than they had been under their worst plastering, the British tried to guess what was cooking. Whatever was up, the R.A.F.'s growing invasion-busting offensive was out to stop it before it got started. Escorted by fast Hurricanes and Spitfires, Blenheims of the Bomber Command struck in broad daylight at docks and shipping in Antwerp, Dunkirk, Boulogne, Calais. At night even stronger formations coventrized [the cathedral city of Coventry was bombed into rubble on November 14, 1940] Hanover, pouring explosives and incendiaries into factories and oil stores.

BLACK WEEK: From a German newsman aboard a German surface raider came an "eyewitness story" which, if true, revealed one of the most devastating attacks British shipping had yet suffered. "Tuesday we encountered an armed English merchantman. This vessel was sunk by several well-aimed salvos and soon only floating oranges marked the spot. . . . Soon after sunrise Wednesday we saw three tiny shadows. Then we saw five, then six, then eight, and then more and more. We fired a salvo of medium calibre shells. A fireball went up from a hit vessel. Another turned aflame. On the place where still another vessel had sunk only a long, smoking flame was visible. We reached the end of the convoy and turned and once more passed it. Altogether, 14 vessels of 82,000 tons have been sunk. Only one ship remained. The commander of our ships ordered 'cease firing.' The last ship was permitted to participate in the rescue work and take the shipwrecked crews aboard."

MARCH 17 **AT SEA:** A speech with the sound of history about it was made before Parliament last week by the First Lord of the Admiralty, a man who more than any other knows to what extent Britannia rules the waves. What he said about merchant shipping was a chilling mouthful. First Lord Albert Victor Alexander warned his people that they were now witnessing "The Battle of the Atlantic."

The whole coast of Europe was now German. The shipbuilding facilities of the whole Continent were now German. Germany now had (with the Italians) at least 300 U-boats, and more being readied. Last week the Germans were out in force with a new tactic which was the fruit of winter experiments: hunting in packs. In one recent case, nine simultaneous torpedo explosions gave a convoy its first warning of attack.

"They lose more subs that way," said one survivor. "But we lose more ships. The Jerries seem to feel it's worth it."

NIGHT OUT: The orchestra at London's Café de Paris gaily played *Oh, Johnny, Oh Johnny, How You Can Love!* At the tables handsome flying Johnnies, naval Jacks in full dress, guardsmen and just plain civies sat making conversational love. Sirens had sounded, but to those in the cabaret, leave time seemed too dear to squander underground. Then the hit came. What had been a nightclub became a nightmare: heaps of wreckage crushing the heaps of dead and maimed, a shambles of silver slippers, broken magnums, torn sheet music, dented saxophones. But some of the carefree young survived. They dragged themselves out, went with their bruises and grime to a West End hotel. They washed up. They went to the hotel ballroom and ordered food and drinks. They asked the bandleader for a number they will never forget: *Oh, Johnny, Oh, Johnny, How You Can Love!*

WAR'S WORST RAID: When the alarm came, no one in Lon- APRIL 28 don took it particularly seriously. Just another nuisance raid, most people thought. A few fire bombs began falling. People drove to watch fires for a lark. Then the flares began to float down—long graceful chain flares, star flares, flaming onions. From all directions the planes began to dive-bomb, lower than usual. This, the citizenry suddenly realized, was a return visit for a big fire-raid the R.A.F. had bestowed on Berlin the week before; this would be bad.

Wherever they were—on roofs dousing incendiaries, in basements trying to forget—Londoners could hear the terrible falling bombs, like ripping muslin at a distance; and then the thuds. Some tried to read; most turned their radios off, because it was intolerable only to half hear the bomb each thought had his initials on it.

The raid continued for eight hours, until 4:50 a.m. Everyone hurried to bed for a few hours of bottomless sleep before getting up to work. London was defiantly gay the next morning. The women had on their cockiest spring hats, the men their brightest ties. Amid the shoveling of shattered glass were sounds of phonographs.

END OF THE BISMARCK: Aerial reconnaissance warned the JUNE 2 British last Thursday that the 35,000-ton German battleship *Bismarck* and her escort, the cruiser *Prinz Eugen*, had left the Norwegian port of Bergen for a dash for the open sea to raid the Atlantic convoys. Powerful units were at once mobilized to intercept them. At dawn Saturday, the *Bismarck* was engaged by Britain's largest warship, the 42,100-ton *Hood* and Britain's newest and mightiest, the *Prince of Wales*.

The *Hood* was blown to bits by a lucky hit on her powder magazine at a range of more than 13 miles. In the battle the *Bismarck* was slowed down by a hit on her bow. She was still further slowed by an aerial torpedo which struck her that afternoon.

In the fog and darkness Saturday night, the British warships lost contact with the raider, but a long-range scouting plane (a twin-engine American-built Catalina flying boat) spotted her again Sunday noon making for the French ports. Monday afternoon she was attacked by wave after wave of fleet-based bombers and planes from the *Ark Royal*. Two torpedoes struck her, apparently affecting the steering of the ship. Said First Lord of the Admiralty A.V. Alexander: "She continued making uncontrollable circles in the sea, in which condition she was attacked by our flotillas with two more torpedoes which brought her virtually to a standstill." This Tuesday morning the *Bismarck* was attacked by British pursuing battleships, including the *Prince of Wales*. It was not until some seven or eight hours later that the coup de grâce was delivered. The German fleet now includes only three capital ships. These are the *Bismarck*'s sister ship, the *Tirpitz* [which was sunk in 1944], and two 26,000-tonners, the *Gneisenau* [sunk in 1945] and the *Scharnhorst* [sunk in 1943].

In London a victim is pulled from the rubble as the Nazi bombing continues.   *Wing Commander Bader lost his legs, but the R.A.F. dropped him new ones.*

OCT. 6 **LEGS BY DAY:** The night the legs arrived everyone had a big time. When the Germans captured R.A.F. Wing Commander Douglas Bader, D.S.O., they had been amazed at the gallantry of this boy, with no legs of his own (he had lost them earlier in a crash), whose duralumin pair were crushed when his plane was shot down. They had (according to last week's version of the tale) offered the R.A.F. a two-hour local armistice to come over with a spare pair and drop them unmolested on a Netherlands field. The R.A.F. had refused, saying it would drop bombs and the legs at the same time. It did.

The Germans ducked the bombs, picked up the legs, turned them over to Douglas Bader and gave him a *gemütlich* party. Everyone had a bit to drink. Pilot Bader did wonderful feats on his tin limbs—danced, ran, turned somersaults. After that Douglas Bader was just another prisoner—until he used his new legs in a new way. One morning his warders found knotted sheets hanging from the window of his empty prison room. They found Bader four days and 100 miles later, walking toward the coast. Since that time, the Germans have taken Douglas Bader's agile legs away from him every night and locked them up.

DOWN THE RABBIT HOLE: From the German prison camp NOV. 10 designated as *Stalag XX*, a British soldier wrote to his small daughter:

In a burrow like a bunny father has his little lair,
Sleeps and eats and reads and lazes, sometimes coming up
*   for air;*
Puts his head beneath a trickle when he wants to have a wash,
Bumping into other bunnies cause there's something of a
*   squash,*
Every morning he is counted, every midday he is fed,
And they lock him in his burrow when it's time to go to bed.
If he wants to go out walking, lots of beefy men with guns
Say they'd like to come out with him just, you see, in case
*   he runs.*
Many, many times I've wondered what it would be like to go
Down dark, damp and draughty tunnels like a bunny—now
*   I know!*

Rx FOR RAIDS: By an old Scottish woman: "When the air- NOV. 24 raid warning sounds, I take the Bible from the shelf and read the Twenty-Third Psalm. Then I put up a wee bit prayer. Then I take a wee drap o' whiskey to steady my nerves. Then I get in bed and pull up the covers. And then I tell Hitler to go to hell."

The Southern Theatre

Shortly before the fall of France in June 1940, Mussolini had entered the war. He sent his troops marching from Libya into Egypt to attack British positions there and threaten the Suez Canal. By December 1940, the British had thrown the Italian forces out of Egypt and in January 1941, were pressing them hard in Libya. But then the Germans took over the African campaign, with General Erwin Rommel in command of the Nazi troops. From then on the fortunes of war in North Africa seesawed back and forth until the final defeat of Rommel by British forces under Field Marshal Montgomery in May 1943.

JAN. 13 **FALL OF BARDIA:** At dusk the British bombers began to thunder in from the east. Out in the Libyan desert the Australians lay hidden with their tanks. Offshore the main body of the Mediterranean Fleet was steaming into position.

The besieged Italians had never seen anything like it. Incendiaries and explosives touched off fires that lit the whole town, a rain of bombs gouged out pillboxes and machine guns. Then, at dawn on Jan. 3, backed by the R.A.F. and a barrage of heavy artillery, the Australians struck—big, husky, uncontrollable men who took the war as a vast, rowdy picnic. Their big tanks raced forward through clouds of sand, followed by waves of soldiers shouting out the chorus from *The Wizard of Oz.* By noon they had driven a gaping wedge into the Italian defenses 12,000 yards wide, 3,000 yards deep.

At nightfall, the Royal Navy began its part. In toward shore slipped the monitor *Terror.* Her big 15-inchers opened up, started chewing at the cliffs where Italian batteries were dug in. Within two hours the main line of the battle fleet had started pumping a stream of shells into the shore batteries.

By dawn on Jan. 4 the Italians could reply only with intermittent fire. At sunset the Italian flag was hauled down from the Bardia Government House; that night the estimate of Italian prisoners taken was boosted to 30,000.

FEB. 17 **FALL OF BENGASI:** Far faster than even the sanguine British had imagined possible, eastern Libya had collapsed. In exact-

WAR IN THE BALKANS AND AFRICA: *On January 20, the publication date of this map, Bulgaria looms as the main center of attention. Italian troops are being pushed out of Greece into Albania by Greek troops. German armies forming up in Bulgaria would soon attack Greece, and by late April Athens would fall to the Axis. Meanwhile, British troops in Libya have just recaptured Bardia from the Italians and are proceeding along the coast toward Tobruch and Bengasi. Bengasi fell to the British in February, but in April German units led by Nazi General Erwin Rommel recaptured Bardia and Bengasi from the British. An Australian garrison held out against the Nazis in Tobruch. The British-held island of Crete fell to German paratroopers in May.*

ly two months Italy's colonial ambition of 15 years had collapsed like a pricked balloon. The Italians could not run fast enough last week. While the main Australian force chased them along the coast, a mechanized force branched across the hump of Cyrenaica to form a pincer's jaw straddling the highway to Tripoli.

With the Australians relentlessly behind them, the Italians who reached Bengasi did not pause even for a last sentimental look at the white houses, the long rows of mimosa. They beat it to the south in headlong flight—only to come smack up against the southern jaw of the pincer. With claustrophobic fury, they threw tanks, field guns, even suicide troops with gasoline bombs, against the British ring of mobile steel. But the British held, and soon the Italians gave up.

MARCH 3   **CAUTION & SKILL:** General Sir Archibald Percival Wavell, commander of British troops in Africa, spent two months planning his campaign against the Italians. He studied desert warfare in all its phases. He memorized topography and used exhaustive British researches on sand. He even used the Bible as a military handbook. From Gideon, who fought on the scarred plain of Armageddon, he says he learned principles of night attack. On the use of mechanized equipment in the rainy season, he took the warning of Elijah: "Prepare thy chariot and get thee down, that the rain stop thee not."

The campaign itself brought out General Wavell's great military qualities. He showed that he knows, as so few generals do, when *not* to stop. "The troops, having beaten the enemy," he says, "will want to rest. They must be given as objectives, not those you think they will reach, but the farthest they could possibly reach."

The Australians, to whom this enthusiasm was second nature, roared into Bardia singing:

> *Once a jolly swagman camped by a billabong*
> *Under the shade of a coolibah tree.*
> *And he sang as he watched and waited till his billy boiled:*
> *"You'll come a-waltzing Matilda with me."*

APRIL 14   **SEESAW IN AFRICA:** The London *Times* divulged to its readers last week "a disagreeable surprise." Bengasi had fallen into Axis hands again.

The real Axis commander in Libya was now no Italian. It was Lieut. General Erwin Rommel, a *Panzer* expert whose appointment to Libya must have maddened the Italians: he distinguished himself against them in World War I. General Rommel apparently used one mechanized division in his giant raid, and by outflanking tactics took several outposts.

The British nowhere put up real resistance, claimed they evacuated Bengasi without losing a man. The British were evidently perfectly willing to cede territory, since in desert warfare, as in sea warfare, the destruction of enemy fighting units is the only thing that counts.

THE OTHER WAY IN LIBYA: Under a brilliant moon the APRIL 21 desert looked like a plain of salt. Across it three British staff cars sped. Soon they overtook a lorry convoy, which had halted to remove some anti-tank blocks. At this point a lone Nazi on a motorcycle appeared at the convoy's rear. An armed guard stuck his head out from the rear lorry's tarpaulin. The Nazi tommy-gunned him. A few more Germans came up on motorcycles, covered the staff cars before the officers realized what was happening. Thus were captured last week two top-flight British generals who had played a major part in the British advance. The loss of the generals was almost as bad news as the misfortune in which they were lost— a six-day Nazi advance from Bengasi right into Egypt.

With complete recklessness, the Germans charged past the British forces, straight on to Bardia, and took it. In ten days the Germans recovered ground which the British had taken eight weeks to cover. Once again the Suez Canal—keystone of all British operations in the eastern Mediterranean—was in grave danger, and the British began to get panicky.

CRETE AGAINST THE SKIES: Even the antiquity of the place JUNE 2 and its traditions seemed braced against the expected. Cretans reminded themselves that the greatest god of them all, Zeus, had spent his boyhood on Mount Ida; that an air attack on Crete would be flying in the face of classical omen, for it was from Crete that incautious Icarus flew to man's first crash landing.

Last week the expected Germans came. Soldiers said later the scene was like a bad dream: flares shedding their unnatural light, *Stukas* making their unnatural shriek. The big, Messerschmitt 110s came in to strafe. Some time after midnight about 100 Junkers and Focke-Wulf transport planes swept in over Crete's western end. Some disgorged men wearing leather jackets, crash helmets, kneepads and pistols, with two little boxes of iron and chocolate rations strapped to their chests. Planes in the center of the formations dropped rifles, sub-machine guns, machine guns, light mortars and ammunition. At the first hints of dawn, new waves of transport planes came in with more parachutists. This time the planes towed gliders.

By the third day the Nazis had achieved air supremacy. An R.A.F. bulletin announced that all fighter aircraft had been withdrawn, explained: "Experience in this war has already proved that it is impossible to develop satisfactory fighter defense from a few comparatively ill-equipped airports if these are subjected to high-scale enemy air attack."

JUNE 9 **WORSE THAN GREECE:** Crete was lost. The factor of defeat was the *Luftwaffe*. All day long dive-bombers and strafers kept the British immobilized under cover. Anything which moved—man, woman, child, tank, gun, sheep, cow—was strafed until it stopped moving. The only time the British could attack was by night, and even then the *Luftwaffe* dropped flares and death.

One of the shortest battles of the war was fought in Syria, a small Mediterranean country which was under a mandate to Vichy France. To forestall the possibility that France might turn Syria over to Germany—which would have allowed the Nazis to encircle Turkey, get access to the oil fields of nearby Iraq and threaten the Suez Canal—a mixed force of British and Free French troops marched into Syria early in June.

JUNE 23 **MIXED SHOW:** The first eight days of the British-Free French drive for Vichy-held Syria were a weird combination of Blitz and bicker, glad-handing and heavy punching, push-over and furious resistance. Opposing Frenchmen kissed or killed each other. But at week's end General Sir Henry Maitland Wilson, the mixed show's producer, could look at his opening week with some satisfaction. Sidon fell after three days of bloodshed; Australian troops pressed on up to the outskirts of Beirut. Damascus was threatened by three Allied columns.

ACRE PACT: Even the date mocked General Henri Fernand JULY 21 Dentz, for it was Bastille Day. The five-week Syrian War was over. As he took up the pen at an H-shaped conference table in Acre, Palestine, General Dentz's throat must have worked. Last year he signed Paris away to the conquering Nazis. Now, as Vichy's High Commissioner to the Levant States, he sighed, then signed Syria away to the conquering British and, even worse, to the conquering Free French.

WRONG RAID: "Italian planes successfully raided Gibraltar and all machines returned to Italy safely after sinking three British destroyers and leaving half of the Rock in flames following a petrol dump explosion."

Mightily surprised were Gibraltar residents, who had seen neither planes nor bombs, to hear this announcement over the Rome radio. Not surprised, but mad clear through, were the people of La Linea, just over the Spanish boundary, when they tuned it in. Early the same morning unidentified planes had swooped over the Spanish town, bombed several houses to bits, killed eight of the townspeople, wounded 19.

Since La Linea had no destroyers to sink or petrol dumps to burn, for once the world had a gauge of the accuracy of Italian Air Force communiqués.

WHAT WAR LOOKS LIKE: Desert warfare is like naval war- DEC. 8 fare, as Winston Churchill has said. Herewith a composite picture of a day in Libya last week, as described by British correspondents on the spot:

The escarpment is empty. It is a plateau covered with scrub and occasional boulders and here and there it is cut by dry stream-beds called wadis. On the horizon a low-lying cloud appears and grows. It is a column of dust, signalling a column of vehicles. They clank to a stop and lie scattered. Men crawl out, stretch, make repairs, crawl back in.

Another column of dust peels from the skyline. The supply trucks of the first column withdraw. The tanks fall into for-

British vehicles churn across the North African desert. Amid the thick clouds of dust, sometimes friend hits friend.

mation, face the approaching column. The first cannon flashes. Then the two formations gambit and answer with feints, approaches, withdrawals which seem as tentative and formal as a minuet. Then they begin to mix it up.

Suddenly the whole field is a melee. Low-lying British tanks, flying their proud little regimental pennants, crisscross with the darker Nazi vehicles, each marked with great white crosses. Tanks suddenly buckle into twisted masses. Shells crash in all directions; sometimes friend hits friend.

In the murk new forms rush. Supply vehicles, naked of protection, dart squarely into the mix-up, make contact with tanks which have run out of fuel or ammunition, and, if they are not crumpled, bounce out again. Ambulance crews run about hunting wounded men.

Suddenly all the tanks of one adversary wheel out of the fight. The other tanks also go off to a rendezvous. Now the escarpment is strewn with broken, burning vehicles, the guts of trucks, upended smoldering airplanes. A lost truck stops and asks a wounded man where a certain regiment's headquarters have gone. "Can't say," comes a Tommy's reply. "I'm a stranger 'ere myself."

DEC. 15 **DUST IN THE COGS:** All the King's tanks and all the King's men ranging across the Libyan desert had not succeeded, in three weeks of renewed fighting, in achieving a single major aim of British strategy. The one apparent success, the relief of long-besieged Tobruk, was last week negated by the Germans, who cut the relieving corridor with their main tank forces.

The British situation was not all black. Although General Erwin Rommel's *Panzer* divisions turned out to have stores vastly greater than the British had counted on, it still appeared that the Axis powers had great problems in logistics. The British Navy last week said it had stopped 60% of all enemy supplies destined for all ports in Africa. A British raiding force presumably still straddled the Axis supply roads. The only steady flow of Axis supplies came by plane and night. But this time the R.A.F. was dominant, and British soldiers were spared the nightmare of swastikas screaming down the sky.

FIGHT TO A FINISH: New York *Times* Correspondent Joseph DEC. 29
M. Levy wrote from Cairo last week: "The British armored forces and infantry units have broken the Axis line west of el-Gazala and have sent the Germans reeling backward in headlong retreat." In one of the biggest battles of the Desert campaign, the British cut the el-Mechili-el Tmimi road and started their advance. This was apparently the beginning of the end. With British reports putting some British units far south of Bengasi, Rommel seemed to be facing disaster. This week the British hoped they were entering the last round of the Rommel fight.

Eastern Front

Hitler began his campaign against the Balkans by moving troops into Rumania in the fall of 1940 "to protect the oil fields from the British." At the same time Mussolini invaded Greece. But the small Greek army, aided by British troops and planes, fought so gallantly that the Italians were thrown back— and in the spring of 1941 Hitler had to send German troops into Greece and Yugoslavia through Bulgaria to rescue his Axis partner from catastrophe.

JAN. 6 **ON THE MOVE:** The German army was definitely on the move. Men and materiel moved in great numbers over the state railways of occupied Hungary. As many as 25 trains a day rolled into Rumania, long strings of flat cars loaded with every kind of tank and cannon. Box cars by the hundreds with seals on the doors rolled too, containing—some estimators said—enough soldiers to bring Hitler's strength in the Balkans up to 600,000. These troops began settling themselves in camps along the ice-filled Danube's left bank.

Soviet Russia, vapid monster in the East, emitted troubled grunts but nothing more. But there were reports that 30 crack Soviet divisions had arrived in Soviet Bessarabia to counter Hitler's army. With grim significance, German sources intimated that Rumania was unable to govern herself, that the time was at hand for the Nazis to assume complete military and political control. Bulgaria, vital pawn in the giants' chess game, entered an uneasy new year. King Boris III had told Adolf Hitler that, rather than see German troops in his peasant kingdom, he would abdicate. Last week he retired 27 high Army officers who had demanded that Bulgaria join the Axis. With the arrival of the first Nazi units at the frontier, Bulgarian resolution seemed less firm, and foreign observers believed that under pressure the Government might concede the "futility" of armed resistance.

JAN. 20 **"THE ONLY NEUTRAL":** Now that the strategy of war has put Bulgaria on the spot, King Boris, man of peace, is the focus of manifold pressures. He rules over a nation of Slavs. His blood is mostly French. His wife is a daughter of the King of Italy. Tsar Nicholas II of Russia was his godfather. Recently someone asked the King what Bulgaria's foreign policy was. Boris answered: "My ministers are pro-German, my wife is pro-Italian, my people are pro-Russian—I am the only neutral in the country."

FEB. 24 **HITLER GETS IT:** When Adolf Hitler wants something he gets it. Last week he had the Balkans convinced that the kill was imminent. Bulgaria, in the midst of terrible fear of being overrun by the Nazi Army, looked about and began to realize that it was already overrun. Bulgarians thought they saw Germans everywhere. They saw Germans in ski clothes leave

Sofia hotels early every morning in automobiles. They saw Germans in civilian overcoats driving through the countryside by the truckload. They saw Germans shoring up bridges, building up the shoulders of highways, stocking airfields with gasoline.

At week's end, Bulgaria's people learned two sickening truths. The Government came right out and said that the Nazis intended to march their army across the land to attack Greece—and there was nothing to be done about it. The British Minister to Bulgaria answered this with a curt announcement: "If the Germans occupy Bulgaria and make it a base against our ally, obviously we shall have to . . . take whatever measures the situation requires,"—i.e., Britain would make war on Bulgaria, and nothing could be done about that either.

SPRING IS HERE: The long awaited Armageddon in south- MARCH 10 eastern Europe approached so fast last week that all but the troops involved were left behind the rush of events. It was spring—the season of past German invasions of Austria, Czecho-Slovakia, Denmark and Norway. One day the only Nazis in Bulgaria were a few scattered thousands in mufti. Next day Bulgarian roads were jammed with mechanized Nazi columns.

The conquest was as efficiently formulaic as most of Adolf Hitler's. With 600,000 Nazi troops across the northern border in Rumania, Bulgaria was hardly in a position to say no. The occupation was advertised to the Bulgarian public, thousands of whom are violently anti-Nazi and pro-Russian, by squadrons of Nazi bombers and fighters roaring low over Sofia's roofs. Except for their ear-splitting drone the city was quiet, and along the sunny boulevards many shopkeepers unfurled the swastika. As the shrewder Balkan politicos remarked, it was all a foregone conclusion.

GREEK GIANTS: The stuff that myths are made of was being MARCH spun out in Greece last week. The Greeks spoke and acted like a race of giants 20 feet tall, hurlers of thunderbolts, crushers of men. Far from being daunted by the noisy threat which was giving Germany victory after bloodless victory in the Balkans, the Government declared: "Greece has shown in the most definite way that any idea of armistice would find her disdainfully hostile." The heart was still fiercely hot in Greece's Army; it launched a violent attack along the entire central section of the Albanian Front, and within 48 hours announced the capture of positions which the Italians had spent months fortifying.

MARCH 24 **A GIDDY MOMENT:** In Belgrade, key to the whole Balkan tangle for the moment, there was a strange gaiety last week. The most reliable index of Yugoslavia's enthusiasm is the amount of glass that gets broken. In Belgrade champagne bottles, having uttered their pops and spilled their bubbles, smashed against walls. Glasses, having been touched in toasts, crashed into fireplaces. Siphon bottles, mirrors, windows were broken in greatest good humor.

No one seemed to know exactly what the celebrations were about. But probably the celebrants were happy because they suddenly realized Yugoslavia's fleeting power. For a giddy moment, Yugoslavia was the most powerful nation in Europe. For an hour, Yugoslavia was stopping Hitler. The Yugoslavs realized that until Hitler was sure of them, he preferred to undertake no new adventure in the Balkans. He could scarcely afford to attack Greece from Bulgaria alone—through what the Yugoslavs could make a deathtrap, the Struma River Valley. He would have to be sure first of the Yugoslav flank.

MARCH 31 **HITLER AT THE FRONTIER:** There is a Serbian proverb, from the time of the Turks, which says that when Serbia is threatened the peasants pick up their guns and sing. Serbia's peasants marched and sang last week. Everywhere across Yugoslavia they sang the new song:

> *Listen, girl I love,*
> *Hitler has come to our frontier,*
> *But the Serbs are ready with their guns*
> *To see how many ribs the Germans have.*

If Yugoslavia would not join the Axis outright, Hitler would be reasonable. He would settle for the right to use Yugoslav railways for "supply trains." Yugoslavia's youthful Regent Prince Paul last week worked night and day to reor-

King Boris of Bulgaria: "I am the   *Prince Paul of Yugoslavia (right)*
only neutral in the country." Page 85.   *handed his country over to Hitler (left).*

ganize his cabinet to win its acceptance of German demands.

Finally Prince Paul had his pro-Axis Cabinet and fresh jets of steam shot up from a special train as it chuffed out of Belgrade's station on a clear track for Vienna, where Premier Dragisha Cvetkovitch and Foreign Minister Aleksandar Cincar-Markovitch were ready to sign on Hitler's dotted line. Yugoslavia had fallen to the Axis.

FREEDOM TAKES A BASTION: At 1 o'clock in the morning APRIL 7 of March 27, 1941, grey-green tanks [of the Yugoslav Army] began lumbering through the streets of Belgrade, going slowly so as to make as little noise as possible. Behind them were the anti-tank units and machine-gun crews. Along the roads and at every strategic spot in Belgrade the tanks and guns took their positions.

At 2 a.m. a patrol of soldiers, commanded by an Air Corps officer, appeared at the hilltop home of Premier Cvetkovitch, who had signed the Axis pact in Vienna scarcely 48 hours before. A guard stood before the door. "The Premier cannot be disturbed," said the guard.

The officer said: "Nevertheless disturb him." The guard raised his rifle, but the officer was quicker with his revolver. "Stand aside," he said.

To Premier Cvetkovitch the officer simply said: "Come."

The Premier dressed and went with the patrol to General Staff Headquarters. Soon other members of the Cabinet arrived. When all were there General Dusan Simovitch, the Air Corps Chief, told the Ministers that the Army required their resignations. Less than 60 minutes after they had been aroused from their beds the Cabinet had resigned.

At sunrise, 17-year-old Peter Karageorgevitch [the son of King Alexander, who was assassinated in 1934] proclaimed himself King Peter II, issued a proclamation:

"Serbs, Croats, Slovenes! In this moment so grave for our people I have decided to take the royal power into my hands. . . . The Regents have resigned. . . . I have charged General Simovitch with the formation of a new Government. . . . The Army and Navy are at my orders."

While the people sang with joy in the streets, General Simovitch worked. Whether Yugoslavia could continue to exist as one nation was in doubt, and that was a risk the tall, grave-eyed General took when he staged his coup. To reach the Greeks, Hitler would now have to fight the Serbs in their own mountains or risk exposing his flank. Either course would be hazardous. At week's end Premier General Simovitch sternly demanded of his people that they stand fast and "if destiny so orders it, give their lives for the good of their homes, their fatherland and King."

APRIL 21 **WEAKNESS DEFIES STRENGTH:** More than ever, Nazi speed was the shocking thing. Everyone thought that Belgrade, lying in an open plain, would fall. But not even the gloomiest super-realists believed that the whole strategic Vardar Valley, protected by formidable hills, would lie under Nazi treads in two days or that Albania could be reached in six.

General Simovitch's 21 Yugoslav airfields were pocked, his hangars burned, his fuel dumps blasted. The Yugoslav army was cut in pieces, but was still in being, in divided units operating as colossal guerrilla parties in the Serbian hills.

Devout Greek soldiers, before they manned their guns on the Thracian front, asked for the last sacrament. They were not only resigned to death; many expected it. In many forts they fought until every man was wiped out. In one fort they abandoned the upper works, retired underground, and conked Nazis one by one as they tried to enter.

HAPPY BIRTHDAY: The railway car, resting on a siding under APRIL 28 the shadow of a Balkan mountain, was set as usual for Adolf Hitler's morning conference with his advisers. Assembled were all the biggest of the bigs: Goering, Goebbels, Ribbentrop, Himmler, Hess. They were gathered together to congratulate Adolf Hitler on his 52nd birthday.

Hitler, with soldierly simplicity, accepted the good wishes of his good friends, stared for a moment at the maps of slaughter spread out on the table, retired to peruse the latest military reports. They were almost universally favorable to his cause.

The Yugoslavs were out of the war. They had capitulated after just twelve days of resistance. In Greece the Allied lines had been repeatedly pushed back. Eventually weight told. The same British, Australian and New Zealand troops, five divisions at most, fought day after day, while the Germans rotated 40 divisions, constantly feeding fresh troops into the battle. At some points Adolf Hitler's infantry troops had attacked in old-fashioned, 1918-style, suicidal mass, but at a price. According to Greek accounts, "Adolf Hitler's Own" SS (Elite Guard), magnificent hand-picked lads of 19 and 20, bore the brunt of the slaughter.

Thus did Adolf Hitler celebrate. At least one of his birthday tributes, a couplet composed by Britain's wit, A.P. Herbert, was not good news:

> *Napoleon died at fifty-two*
> *And, Adolf Hitler, so may you.*

SWASTIKA IN ATHENS: German motorcyclists, then truck MAY 5 troops, then tank crews coasted unopposed into Athens. The swastika, trade-mark of totalitarianism, was planted on the Acropolis. The Battle of the Balkans was over.

Germany v. Russia

After the conquest of Greece, Germany was free to attack Russia. On June 22, 150 Axis divisions began a massive assault against the Soviet Union along a 2,000-mile front from Bessarabia to Finland.

JUNE 30 **WORLD OR RUIN:** "German People! National Socialists! Weighted down with heavy cares . . . the hour has now come when at last I can speak frankly. . . ." Thus, with bad grammar, did Adolf Hitler begin a proclamation that ended with a declaration of war against the largest country and the largest army in the world. Hitler did one supreme service to the world: he made clear his intentions to all who might still doubt them. He was declaring war upon the world. For with Russia's Armies defeated, Germany could turn all her power against the British Isles. With Russia conquered, Turkey would be gobbled up; the entire Middle East and India would be opened to German attack; not only Suez, but Africa, would be outflanked; China would be surrounded; the seas would be opened; the Western Hemisphere would be encircled by enemies.

The irony of the new attack was that smart Joseph Stalin had outsmarted himself. Russia, whose pact with Germany enabled Hitler to start the war, now felt the full fury of the war. Before it ended, either Stalin or Hitler would no longer be a great dictator.

HOW LONG FOR RUSSIA?: With every detail worked out, even to the designation of the trees behind which propaganda broadcasters could crouch, the veteran German Army took on its hugest job. Though bigger potential armies (10,000,000 Russians, 9,000,000 Germans) had never fought on a bigger potential front, the weathered Germans began fighting Russia just as they had opened against all the other opponents, with apparent calm, with obvious savvy.

They opened with blows which had become familiar even to the civilians of the world. The airmen executed "rolling attacks" on Russian concentrations, materiel dumps, communications. Other bombers blitzed cities. Engineers built bridges. Infantry advanced fluidly.

The Russian defensive remained to be developed. Remembering how they beat Napoleon, the Russians have the option of using the size of their country as a weapon to wear down the enemy. They have a childlike, Oriental faith in the unanswerable power of machinery, and have equipped their divisions to the ears. Each division has an unusually high percentage of tanks. But the one thing that might save the Rus-

EARLY GERMAN ADVANCES AGAINST RUSSIA: *This map, which appeared in the July 14 issue of* TIME, *shows the progress of the Nazi advance across Russia less than a month after Hitler declared war. German troops, pouring into the Soviet Union along a front extending from Finland in the north to Hungary and Rumania in the south, have moved as far as 350 miles into Russian territory in some sectors and have captured the major city of Minsk. The long string of Russian fortifications shown on the map, known as the Stalin Line, has slowed the German advance. But Leningrad on the northern flank and Odessa in the south would soon be under German siege. The city of Smolensk, just west of Moscow, fell in July, and by October 14 the German armies were within 60 miles of Moscow itself.*

sians was genius of generalship. The Germans have some pretty seasoned generals. To beat them was the staggering task of Commander in Chief Marshal Semion Timoshenko, a hero of the Soviet invasion of Finland. Tough, stone-bald, peasant-born Timoshenko first fought against the Germans as a Czarist draftee in 1915, since then has risen in Stalin's favor—and replaced many a general who had been executed on Stalin's orders—by proven military ability.

JULY 14 **GUERRILLA MOSQUITOES:** The initial Nazi torrent, catching the Russians with their rubbers off, had swept ahead breathtakingly. But in the second week the Germans came up against ferocity and tenacity everywhere. Said Stalin: "In occupied regions conditions must be made unbearable for the enemy. . . . In case of a forced retreat of Red Army units, all rolling stock must be evacuated; to the enemy must not be left a single . . . pound of grain nor a gallon of fuel."

Before Joseph Stalin's words were out of his mouth the commands were being carried out. German supply trains met strange accidents. German columns fell into ambush. Even the Russian mosquitoes from the endless Pripet Marshes conspired in guerrilla activity. The Russians amazed the Nazis with their fanatical courage. When German anti-tank guns made a sieve of a Soviet tank turret in Minsk, the brown dinosaur-like monster came, firing in all directions. In the end the tank burned, and inside it the Russian crew.

AUG. 4 **NO BLITZ OBLIGE:** For a whole week the German *Krieg* had been without *Blitz*, a lightning war without the lightning. German propaganda reporters complained that the enemy, even when surrounded, fought with "stupid Asiatic courage." The obvious fact was that the German *Panzer* divisions, although they had sliced through the Russian lines in a dozen places, had divided but not crushed the Russian Army before Moscow. They bit off hunks, but the vast Russian hunks were too large to swallow without chewing. The chewing job had to be done by the German infantry that followed the *Panzers*. That meant the German losses were probably considerable.

Meantime it was hard to tell whether the German *Panzer* divisions that had pierced the Russian lines had cut off Russian Armies or been cut off by them. It was a strange battle, fought not with the opposing armies lined up facing each other like two football teams, but with sizable units of both armies mixing it up in all directions like players on a basketball court.

JOE'S BAD BOY: Jacob was never much. Papa Djugashvili (who later called himself Stalin) used to try to toughen up little Jacob's lungs by blowing pipe smoke in his face. So Jacob took up smoking before he was ten; and his father had to beat him for that. Papa Joe tried to make an engineer of Jacob, but Jacob was a lazy fellow. Finally he disappeared into the Army. Last week the Germans announced that *Panzer* forces had captured Jacob, son of Joseph Stalin. They were very proud of the feat, and issued pictures of the wonderful heir. But all they had was a boy with a hangdog look, who was never much.

Jacob Stalin, Joseph's bad boy, is captured by the Germans.

Marshal Timoshenko takes charge of the southern front. Page 98.

ON THE UKRAINE FRONT: "The German forces," Herr Hitler AUG. 18 wrote last week, "now stand ready to continue with a new phase of operations"—a great effort to clean up the Ukraine. Cleaning up the Ukraine is no afternoon tea party. But Adolf Hitler must have it, must grasp its steelworks, its great Dnieper dam, its rich black dirt which pushes up abundance and covers coal and iron. Early results were claimed.

AUG. 25 **LESS THAN ONE TWENTIETH:** To divert the home folks, the German news agency D.N.B. estimated that the German Armies had occupied 388,185 square miles. This, the estimators said, was more than twice the area of old Germany. They failed to add that it was less than one-twentieth of Russia.

LAST WISH: The Moscow radio in its best button-nosed deadpan last week reported that the following story was current among German soldiers: Adolf Hitler, visiting the Eastern Front, asked a soldier what his last wish would be if a Russian shell should land near him.

"I would wish," the soldier answered, "that my Fuehrer stood beside me."

GREATEST BATTLE OF ALL: The Germans claimed they had entered Smolensk on July 16. Last week, 29 days later, the Russians admitted they had evacuated it. In that month, in and around that dying city, had been fought the greatest pitched battle of World War II, perhaps of all time.

Russian defenses were disposed not in lines, but in densely packed islands of troops, gun emplacements and even fortresses. The system was calculated to canalize enemy attack into defiles covered by cross fire from several islands at once. Germans had to abandon the fundamental pattern of Blitzkrieg—cutting as if with a knife through one strategic spot and then encircling—instead dug in with five parallel prongs. Each pair of prongs had to reduce island after island between them.

TROJAN WHORES: A Russian dispatch from the front last week claimed that the Germans, unable to force a crossing of an unnamed river, brought up a large number of prostitutes from Hamburg, undressed them, sent them wading in the river opposite the strongest Russian defenses. Simultaneously, the story went, the Germans tried a crossing at another place. The strong Red Army men, said the dispatch, "were not fooled."

SEPT. 22 **NAPOLEON TO HITLER:** Napoleon Bonaparte started for Moscow on June 24, 1812. Adolf Hitler started on June 22, 1941.

Napoleon, whose fastest unit was the horse, reached Moscow on Sept. 14. This week, on Sept. 14, Hitler, whose fastest unit is the plane, was fighting Russian counter-attacks some 200 miles from Moscow. Napoleon stayed in Moscow for nearly six weeks, suffered cold and defeat in the frigid Russian winter, was back in Paris by Dec. 18.

Last week Adolf Hitler ordered the requisitioning of all skis, ski poles and snow-shoes in Germany, all furs suitable for military wear.

TWO SIEGES: Last week at opposite ends of the Russian Front the German Army besieged two Russian cities:

¶ Lionhearted Leningrad: All day long-range Nazi cannon, skulking in ash-colored Karelian soil, cracked high explosives into Leningrad's defenses. All night the ugly "black beetles" of the *Luftwaffe's* smart Richtofen Squadron dealt out destruction, until the night glowed red with fire and death.

¶ Bloody Odessa: For five weeks the Rumanians have laid siege to the Black Sea port of Odessa. Locked within the city, whose present population is 605,000, is part of bogey-mustachioed Marshal Semion Budenny's Southern Army. The Russians claim to have killed thousands of General Antonescu's Rumanians [who were fighting as German allies]. Every now and then, they say, a placard reading "Cease Fire and Take Away Your Dead" has to be hoisted.

TWO-THIRDS OF THE UKRAINE: Kiev, cradle of Russia and SEPT. 29 capital of the Ukraine, a city decorated with bluffs, monuments and ancient legends, fell to the Germans after withstanding encirclement and assault for four weeks. This city of 850,000 souls was the first of the major German objectives to go. But even more serious was the destruction of vast amounts of materiel and the encirclement of a large Russian force—250,000, the Germans said.

All of the industrial area of the central Ukraine was now lost to the Russians, and the invader pressed on for the vital Donets basin, where most of Russia's coal and much of its remaining industry lie. The new Nazi plunge was alarming. It made Adolf Hitler's avowed aim of reaching the Volga by winter seem a possibility. If he did, it would not mean Russia's inevitable surrender any more than an invader's reaching the Mississippi would mean inevitable U.S. surrender. But it would mean that the easiest route for U.S. and British aid to Russia—via the Middle East and the Caucasus—was gone. Adolf Hitler would once again have succeeded in dividing his deadly enemies.

175,000,000 FACES: The faces of Russians were drawn last week. It was not terror that made their lips tight, their eyes tired; not despair, not resignation. It was the awful waiting. When would the glorious Red Armies win? For years one had watched tanks clanking through the streets, and outside the villages had seen the parachutes pouring down like crazy cotton snowflakes; one had accumulated tremendous faith in this power. But this power had been pushed back, now, deep into Russia. When would the marshals, who wear gold stars studded with diamonds, show their worth to the men who have never had any badge but mud? When would winter come? It would make a big difference.

Faces of the Russian people: When would their glorious Red armies win? When would the Allies send help? When would winter come?

Even if the Red defenses could by sheer will power hurl back the enemy, Russia would have to start building all over again. And if the defenses failed, then there was nothing to look forward to but a world beyond imagining, in which a face was not even a face unless it was German.

THERE ARE SMILES . . .: Wrote a German propaganda re- OCT. 6
porter at the front last week: "The smile is precious and difficult to preserve in all wars, but especially difficult in this war
in the East. It withers, it dies in the head. It suffocates in the
dust and the pathless mud. . . . There are also moments and
hours when the smile completely freezes, because this country,
under a curse, suddenly leers at us with frosty demonism."

FIRST: One afternoon last week the first silent flake of snow
fell on Moscow.

NEW COMMANDS: Joseph Stalin shuffled his High Command NOV. 3
last week. By doing so, he admitted that Russia had suffered
grim defeat. By the way he did it, he served notice that his
country was by no means finished.

He moved his best field general, Marshal Semion Timoshenko, to the area of worst disaster—down south, where the
Germans threatened to cut Russia off from its oil and from
its greatest remaining industrial centers. To stem the German
wave before Moscow, Stalin assigned General of the Army
Georgy Konstantinovitch Zhukov. General Zhukov has energy to throw away. As commander at Kiev, he used to ride
20 miles before breakfast, then work twelve hours straight.
He fenced with his aides till they were bleary-eyed.

Marshal Klimenti Voroshilov from Leningrad and Marshal
Semion Budenny from the south were given a new job, the
clearest signal yet that Russia will fight to the last snowball:
to form great new armies from raw conscripts, armies to take
their stand beyond the Volga, beyond the Urals. The new
armies will be ill-equipped, ill-trained, ill-fortified. But they
would not be formed if the Russians did not intend to fight.

WINTER COMES: This week German civilians went to their
cinemas and saw newsreels of winter on the Russian front.
They saw carloads of woolen socks and greatcoats rolling to
the front through snow-covered countryside. They saw German kitchen police getting water by chopping holes in ice,
German greaseballs sweeping snow off the wings of planes.

Winter had come. In the far north it had come with sub-
zero weather that made gun barrels so cold they burned flesh.
Around Leningrad it had come in great fogs, sleet and cold

Winter comes to the Russian front: German troops and supply wagons struggle against a cold that feeds on human marrow.

which fed on human marrow. Near Moscow it came in snow and wind howling in the forests. In the south it came in torrents of snow as wet and heavy as soaked cotton.

DEC. 8 **DEATH ON THE APPROACHES:** When the Germans launched their second and supposedly final attack on Moscow a fortnight ago, Berlin military spokesmen called it a "do-or-die" drive. It was commanded by Field Marshal Fedor von Bock, a gaunt, steely general who, because he loves to lecture his men on the glory of dying for the Fatherland, is called *der Sterber* (the Dier).

The approaches to Moscow make a first-class military cemetery. The land is mostly flat, some of it gently rolling. This terrain is decorated with superb internal communications—railroads, truck highways and numberless small roads—which favor the defender. Moscow teems with busses, trucks and cars available for urgent transport. The city itself is a super-deathtrap. It is huge, a maze of irregularly winding streets. It is remarkably self-sufficient.

But Moscow's greatest death-dealing weapon is its life. And last week Moscow's 8,000,000 had this stern order from their Government: "To retreat one more step is a crime none shall forgive. Stop the enemy. Beat him out of his positions. This is an order which is not to be broken."

RED ARMY FORWARD: Moscow was again the capital of Rus- DEC. 22
sia this week. As the Government moved back from its hide-
away in Samara, the Russians told the world their story of
the Battle of Moscow.

An overwhelming German offensive begun on Oct. 2 had
cracked the city's defenses wide open. On Oct. 15 and 16 the
Russians had considered the capital lost. Then came the organization of fresh reserves and civilian defenders.

On Nov. 16 Field Marshal von Bock, indifferent to the
cost-in-blood, flung his armored divisions against Moscow
for a second time. By Dec. 6 the cold of winter hit his soldiers
and the Russians counter-attacked.

By the end of last week, Bock's northern army was driven
back, his southern army was withdrawing rapidly under fero-
cious hammering. The Soviet cavalry was harassing the
Germans in retreat. Since Nov. 16, said the Russians, 85,000
Germans had been killed.

Farther south in the Ukraine, Marshal Timoshenko was
driving the Germans farther back from the oil of the Caucasus. About Leningrad, Red banners moved forward too.
An offensive for the relief of the city was under way.

It was too early to assess the action. Perhaps the Germans
were withdrawing to a line, well-prepared in their rear, where
they might rest through the frightening winter cold. At the
very least, this was a Russian success, for the German retreat was costly.

In Moscow's snow-clad streets celebrating infantrymen in
fleece-lined leather coats and yellow fur hoods, provincial
troops in worn quilted jackets and spiked woolen forage caps,
Cossack officers in capes, spurred knee boots and high As-
trakhans would not reason with their joy. In the street a grinning, drink-happy young man suddenly seized New York
Times Correspondent Cyrus Sulzberger by the arm, exclaimed
in joy and wonderment: "It is Moscow! Here we are in Moscow!"

It was a scant two months and two weeks since Adolf Hitler had announced to the German nation: "I say that this
enemy is already smashed and will never rise again." [This
was as close as Hitler ever got to Moscow; he continued to make
gains in other sectors, but in April 1945, the Russians finished
off the battle in the streets of Berlin.]

The Far East

As early as February 1940 Japan had sent an ultimatum to French Indo-China demanding military facilities there. After the defeat of France, the Vichy government granted Japan permission to establish a few bases on Indo-China. Then, taking advantage of a border dispute between Thailand and French Indo-China, the Japanese appointed themselves mediators in early 1941 and thus gained a foothold in both countries for further military action against China.

FEB. 3 **CHIANG AND THE COMMUNISTS:** Japan is not fighting a united nation in China, but a restless coalition of Nationalists and Communists. Without the help of the Communist armies Generalissimo Chiang Kai-shek cannot hope to defeat Japan. So Chiang has had to follow a flexuous policy of giving the Communists enough arms, money and freedom of action to keep them fighting against Japan, but not enough to let them maneuver themselves into a commanding position in South China. What has kept the Communists fighting for Chiang is the fact that they fear Japan more than they fear Chiang Kai-shek.

Chiang Kai-shek has a dilemma: to beat Japan he must help the Reds.　　*General MacArthur: "My message is one of serenity." Page 106.*

MEDIATION; IT'S WONDERFUL: The war between Thailand FEB. 10 and French Indo-China ended last week. The victor was Japan. Nobody had asked Japan to mediate the quarrel, which had gone on intermittently since October. When Tokyo's offer was not immediately accepted, Japan became insistent, threatening. Nipponese war lords insisted that, as "the most stabilizing power in the Far East," Japan alone had the right to settle oriental differences. Under duress Vichy, then Thailand, accepted.

Before either country could present a claim or grievance, Japan handed both a bill for her services as mediator—to be paid in advance. She demanded: a virtual monopoly over Indo-China's production of rice, rubber and coal; military garrisons along the Chinese frontier; airbases throughout Indo-China; a naval base in the Gulf of Siam for 15 battleships, cruisers and other craft. Unless the terms were accepted on the spot, it was intimated, naval units would go into action and invasion of both countries would follow.

The delegates signed.

EXTENSION OF HEAVEN: Japan's grave-faced Emperor Hiro- FEB. 24 hito last week wrapped himself in a silken robe and stepped into the innermost sanctuary of the Imperial Palace to celebrate the ascension to the throne 2,601 years ago of his lineal ancestor, the great Emperor Jimmu. There was a striking difference between the two ceremonies: whereas Jimmu had given thanks to the Sun Goddess *after* his conquest of Central Japan, Hirohito, the Son of Heaven, prayed *before* Japan's conquest of southern Asia, which Japan and her enemies alike agree must be this year or never.

In Australia Acting Prime Minister Arthur William Fadden, a man who does not scare easily, called a meeting of the Advisory War Council and issued a warning to the country: "The war has moved into a new stage of the utmost gravity." London also believed that Japan was on the warpath.

Japan's eventual objective, as Japan has made clear long since, is an Asiatic empire embracing an area as great as North and South America. Standing in the way of Japan's grand objective are the Chinese Army, the land forces of British, Dutch and U.S. possessions, the British and U.S. navies.

JUNE 9 **WIDER BOUNDARIES:** Japan's proposed "New Order in Asia" has been steadily increasing in scope. At first it was to include only North China, but gradually the conception has expanded to embrace all of China, then "Greater East Asia," then "Oceania."

During a recent Diet session Japan's spouting little Foreign Minister Yosuka Matsuoka seemed to assign to the Asia of the future its widest boundaries yet. Said he: "We Japanese have a heaven-sent right to settle in some part of the United States [that is] climatically healthful and enjoyable."

JUNE 16 **DEATH IN THE DARKNESS:** Chungking is a rocky, corrugated tongue of land sticking out at the junction of the swift-flowing Kialing and Yangtze rivers. One evening last week, as the moon painted the rivers silver to guide the invading Japanese planes once more to their mark, the tongue squirmed in pain as never before. Under the silent city, waiting for the bombers in the world's largest dugout (estimated capacity: 30,000), hundreds of Chinese died. They died not of bombs but of suffocation, in mad frenzy, as they clawed and tore at each other to fight their way to fresh air. In one of the longest (five hours) raids in Chungking's three years of experience, the ventilation system had failed. Last official count of the dead: 461—a full half-season's toll in a single evening.

In 1941 a U.S. aviation colonel, Claire Chennault, went to China to organize a volunteer group of American airmen that came to be called The Flying Tigers. The colonel soon became a general, and his feats, and the feats of his young pilots, became a legend of the war.

JUNE 23 **"CONVOYS" TO CHINA:** China's only unblockaded supply route for U.S. goods is the Burma Road. Since the Japanese occupation of French Indo-China last January the Road has been within 350 miles of Japanese airfields. The best way to keep U.S. supplies running over the Burma Road is to keep Japanese planes away from it. The Chinese fighter Air Force is practically nonexistent. Only solution, therefore: air patrols by U.S. planes flown by U.S. fighter pilots.

Last week 100 Curtiss P-40 planes had reached Burma. For the past few months tall, bronzed American airmen have been quietly slipping away from U.S. ports, making their way to Asia. These pilots were not just a crew of barnstormers turned war-stormers. They had been, until recently, crack U.S. military pilots. To take on this combat job they had been allowed to resign their posts, enlist in the Chinese Air Force on the understanding that their U.S. Army seniority would not be affected. Another somewhat whimsical technical understanding is that they will not "take the offensive" against the Japanese Air Force, but will merely defend the Road.

When this "convoy" system has been set up, Chinese troops would be able to take advantage of their long seasoning and go on the offensive, and U.S. pilots would get a little seasoning against the day when they may have to go on the defensive.

U.S. MOVES IN: Groggy from typhoid and cholera inocula- JUNE 30 tions, but bubbling with enthusiasm at the prospect of the toughest job of a tough career, rawboned, hulking, strike-breaking Dan Arnstein was en route from San Francisco to China.

Product of the violence of Chicago's stockyard district, a onetime professional football player, a taxi driver in his youth, Dan Arnstein had pounded his way up until he owned and operated the Terminal Taxicab System of New York. Harry Hopkins had assigned him—at $1 a year—to one of the most important posts on the world democratic front: reorganization of trucking on the Burma Road. Mr. Arnstein's chief regret: he could not take his taxi drivers with him to Burma. Moaned he: "Half the boys wanted to quit and go with me; the boys don't want to get paid for it—all they want is the excitement."

BLACK HOLE OF CHUNGKING: The official version and offi- JULY 7 cial death figure of Chungking's air-raid-shelter disaster were horribly revised last week. Not 461 people died by suffocation and mutual trampling inside this black hole, but 4,000.

Hundreds of people had left Chungking's monster downtown dugout for fresh air between raiding waves; a sudden attack alarm frightened them back. They clogged the shelter's narrow twisting entrance. Guards lost their heads, locked the milling mass in, vanished. The fatal crush near the exit shut off air, suffocated those behind. Next noon soldiers were still hauling out corpses. It was the worst tragedy in the history of China's second city.

NOV. 10 **SPY:** U.S. Navy officers in Honolulu chuckled mightily last week over a Japanese submarine's periscope upped furtively in Hawaiian waters. U.S. naval units had spotted the spying craft, could have sunk it at will. Consensus: The sub saw nothing of value.

But New York *Times* Correspondent Hallett Abend paid unwilling tribute to Nipponese ingenuity. Said he: "Other semi-hostile Japanese naval actions have been openly conducted . . . always keeping 2,000 yards beyond the utmost range of American coast-defense batteries. The only disturbing feature of this phase of Japanese naval activity is how Japanese espionage agents have so accurately learned the extreme shooting range of the shore batteries. . . ."

Following the attack on Pearl Harbor (page 67), the war exploded all across the Pacific. The Japanese attacked the British possessions of Malaya and Hong Kong, U.S. installations in the Philippines, and the U.S.-controlled islands of Guam, Midway and Wake. The early reports from the area—as the following excerpts from TIME'S *coverage show—were filled with a false optimism that did not disappear until after the first of the new year.*

DEC. 15 **FORT BY FORT, PORT BY PORT:** The first crashing blows were so widespread that it looked as if the Japanese were trying to realize their "Heaven-sent," Hell-patented ambition of dominating the Pacific all at one fell shock. Actually they had no such crazy plan. They had, instead, a pattern of attack for a first move which was brilliant, thorough, audacious, and apparently successful.

After the first assault on Pearl Harbor, Guam, Wake, Midway, the soft little links between Hawaii and the Philippines were quickly neutralized. Two small British islands, Nauru and Ocean, just south of the Japanese-mandated Marshall Islands, were taken.

By the time the morning had pushed westward from Hawaii to the Philippines, Lieut. General Douglas MacArthur had been hauled out of bed and told of the attack. Manila snapped to attention. General MacArthur said: "Every possible defense measure is being undertaken. My message is one of serenity and confidence."

HEROIC STORY: A recruit seaman at Pearl Harbor is credited DEC. 22 with the first blow against the enemy. General Quarters had not yet sounded when he fought off an attacking plane single-handed with a machine gun. A battleship captain had his stomach laid open by a shrapnel burst as he went from conning tower to bridge to direct his ship's fight. He fell to the deck, disdained attempts to lift him to safety, continued to command until the bridge went up in flames. When a brig door blew open, a seaman confined for misconduct dashed to his post at an anti-aircraft gun. One tough sailor, unable to find a mount for a heavy machine gun, fired the weapon from his arms.

A moored aircraft tender, blazing under repeated attacks, downed a Japanese plane on her own decks. Simultaneously her captain spotted a midget submarine's shadow within yards of his vessel. Hits were immediately scored. The tender then shot down a second plane. Almost without exception officers and men exhibited quick thinking, coolness, coordination.

THE PHILIPPINES STAND: The Philippines were ready. For days before the war began, the guns had been manned and the planes had stood alert. After a week of heavy bombing, of fierce scraps on Luzon beach-heads, of dogfights among black bursts of ack-ack, the Philippines stood fast. The Jap had done a decently good job of bombing; had smashed up some buildings, some airplanes. But the Army's Far Eastern Commander, lean, brilliant Lieut. General Douglas MacArthur and his grizzled Navy side-kick, Admiral Tommy Hart, had been waiting with their knives out.

At Clark Field, 50 miles northwest of Manila, the gun crews had finished their noonday Monday dinner when the

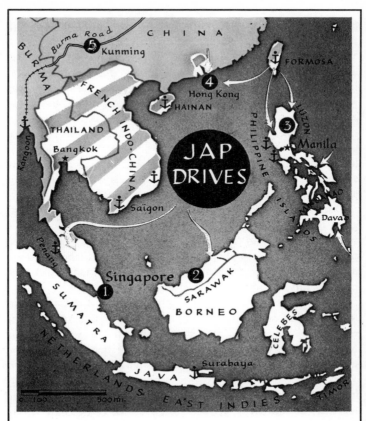

JAPANESE STRATEGY: *By the end of December, using Formosa as a base of operations, Japanese troops are besieging the city of Hong Kong (which would fall December 25), invading the Philippine Islands (Corregidor would fall on May 6, 1942), and making landings in Borneo and Malaya to outflank the vital fortress of Singapore (which would fall on February 15, 1942). Some of the attacks were launched from Indo-China, which the Japanese occupied in mid-1941.*

Jap struck. "I just yelled to the fellows to stay low, keep calm and keep firing," one of the gunners said later. "None of us were really excited after the first few minutes. . . . We just said: 'Get those bastards out of the air,' and we kept at it till we knew we'd run them off."

Little soldiers in mushroom helmets were soon assaulting the beaches and U.S. soldiers were meeting them. The Jap put down troops at Aparri, whence a road leads to Manila 260 miles south. He established a flying field, landed planes. Soon the invader was catching hell. U.S. pilots raided his field. Ground troops slashed savagely at his landing party. But he still kept his hold on Aparri this week. At Vigan there was another landing party. From Douglas MacArthur's terse communiqués it appeared it was under control.

On Lingayen Gulf the Jap tried to land 154 motorboats of soldiers. To stop them MacArthur interposed a division of his pride & joy, the new Philippine Army. It sank most of the Jap boats, routed the others. After three days of fighting, not a Japanese soldier reached shore alive.

Over the sea, heroic Captain Colin Kelly jumped the pagoda-topped battleship *Haruna*, sent her down with three bomb hits. Early in the week Army flyers sank a Jap transport, damaged two others. Later MacArthur had better news: his flyers had sunk three more. For reinforcements and supply, the Jap was apparently not doing too well.

This week an officer suggested to General MacArthur that the U.S. flag on Army headquarters was a fine marker for raiding airmen, suggested it be brought down. Said Douglas MacArthur: "Take every precaution for protection of the headquarters, but let's keep the flag flying."

STAND AT WAKE: Beyond the International Date Line, where it is always tomorrow, Wake lifts itself in three desolate sandy specks in the midst of a watery nowhere. A Clipper stop on Pan Am's famed Pacific run, it was defended by a tiny band of U.S. Marines who had been there since the first day of war, beating off attack after attack. Somehow they managed to sink a Jap cruiser and a destroyer. They knocked down two enemy planes.

Farther west, at Guam, the part-Marine, part-Navy garrison had been subdued by the Japanese. Guam, long denied the sinews of defense by a strangely bemused Congress, could have met no other fate. But east of Wake, on Midway, Marines also stood fast. They sent out no news beyond the fact that they were still hanging on.

THE WAY TO SINGAPORE: To U.S. homebodies, the field where U.S. soldiers were giving their lives seemed the most urgent. But to the Allied strategists, there was no more important battlefield than Malaya. On that battlefield Singapore was at stake. At Singapore the future of the Allies in Asia was at stake. As everywhere, the Japanese made a spectacular beginning in Malaya. First they attacked Malaya's east coast to reduce the principal British airdrome and get a foothold for air attack. They succeeded in this aim, and the British admitted falling back in the face of another assault on the neck of Thailand. As for the defenses of Singapore itself, the British had, as yet, no qualms.

YAMAMOTO v. THE DRAGON: A humble wireless set trembled last week with quasi-divine vibrations as the Son of Heaven himself sent Admiral Isoroku Yamamoto, Commander in Chief of the Combined Imperial Fleets, congratulations for the daring execution of a brilliant treachery. Congratulations from Emperor Hirohito fix upon their recipient an incredible joy; but also a certain uneasiness. This is because they not only bestow praise; they also adjure the congratulatee to continue the good work—or else.

This will not be easy. Though he has depleted the forces arrayed against him, Admiral Yamamoto knows that his enemies' regenerative powers may soon seem as formidable as those of the mythical dragon which, when his tail was cut off, grew not only a new tail on his body but a new body on his tail. Isoroku Yamamoto is not fighting U.S. production. It is his job to consume the product. If he can consume it fast enough, he will have accomplished his mission. He must drive away, or preferably destroy, the white man's bridge to Asia: his fleets.

Admiral Yamamoto's men, used to negotiating the rip tides and foul weathers of their islands, are fine navigators. They service their ships smartly. They submit to living conditions at which U.S. soldiers would mutiny. The Admiral is an adversary who does not want underrating. His name means Base of a Mountain, and the Admiral is solid. He is deliberate, positive, aggressive. His passion for winning has made him the bridge, poker and chess champion of the Japanese Navy. Once an American asked him how he learned bridge so quickly. He explained: "If I can keep 5,000 ideographs in my mind, it is not hard to keep in mind 52 cards."

SINGAPORE AND HONG KONG: Britain's great 19th-Century warrior and native-queller, Field Marshal Sir Frederick Roberts, once said that the history of the world would be decided at Singapore. By this week the Japanese had come within 300 miles of that decision.

The Japanese fought their way down Malaya on a miniature scale. The little men, in light shorts and rubber sneakers, were apparently insufficient targets for the British. As they had used tiny, steel-saving two-man subs at Pearl Harbor, they used in Malaya tiny one-man tanks and two-man gun carriers. The British even said that their doctors cut miniature Japanese bullets out of miniature British wounds.

But there could be no belittling the results. In 14 days the Japanese had driven more than 100 miles through jungles which the British had complacently considered impenetrable. They also landed on the wild and oily island of Borneo. In the Philippines they made a new landing on the southern island of Mindanao, appeared ready to make their big push on the main island of Luzon. And Hong Kong tottered. In its second week of siege, the Fragrant Port was hard-pressed on every side. Japan confessed that the city's defenders were fighting "in a manner even to win the respect of the tough Japanese." But London weighed the odds, wrote off Hong Kong as an inevitable loss. [Critical Singapore, which proved to be strangely undefended against land attack, fell on February 15, 1942.]

MESSAGE FROM WAKE: From the little band of professionals on Wake Island came an impudently defiant message phrased for history. Wake's Marines were asked by radio what they needed. The answer made old Marines' chests grow under their campaign bars: "Send us more Japs." [The island fell December 23, too late for the story to appear in TIME's last issue of 1941.]

FOREIGN NEWS

Japan

The news coming out of Japan week after week made it obvious that the nation, already deeply engaged in China, was preparing for war against the U.S. and Britain. The American government was aware of this danger. The one thing it did not know was that, even as Japanese diplomats continued their talks in Washington, Japanese aircraft carriers were sailing boldly across the Pacific toward Pearl Harbor.

JAN. 6 **SUPERPATRIOTS IN THE SADDLE:** Mitsuru Toyama, a very old man with eyes like flashlight sockets, a ragged white beard which fails to make him look saintly, is the dictator of Japan's network of secret societies. The societies are dedicated to superpatriotism, and in the name of the Emperor they keep the national fervor burning. It has been said that Mitsuru Toyama could call upon any one of 10,000 youths to murder anyone but the Emperor, and the deed would be done.

JAN. 13 **ALMIGHTY MATSUOKA:** Last week smooth, pudgy, pipe-smoking Foreign Minister Yosuke Matsuoka issued a gloomy New Year's message which set a new record for God-claiming: "It may sound unlucky, but in my innermost heart I fear the coming year will prove a most tragic and unfortunate one for all mankind."

FEB. 3 **SPARE EYES:** Japan's new Ambassador to the U.S., one-eyed Admiral Kichisaburo Nomura, sailed for San Francisco with five spare glass eyes and a three-point policy: 1) Japan will stick to the alliance with Germany and Italy; 2) Japan will be boss of the Far East; 3) if the U.S. will accept Points 1 and 2, Japan will try to be friends.

MARCH 3 **SNAKE'S EGG:** The metaphor of the week was produced by the Japanese Army's spokesman, Major Kunio Akiyama.

Said he: "Japan has the heart of a dove of peace, but a snake —the United States and Great Britain—has placed its egg in the dove's nest." The egg, Major Akiyama went on to explain, was "the fortification of Singapore, the arrival of Australian troops in Malaya and the impending fortification of Guam and Samoa." A correspondent asked the Major what he thought would hatch from this egg.

"God knows," he said, "but the dove will protest vigorously."

THE PACT BEGINS TO WORK: Down from a Trans-Siberian APRIL 28 Railway carriage stepped Foreign Minister Yosuke Matsuoka one day last week, home from a visit to Germany and Russia. His hair was full of cinders and his head was full of plans. It was good to set foot once again on the soil of Manchukuo. "I had not expected a neutrality pact with Russia at all," grinned Matsuoka. "It was negotiated in ten minutes."

On to Tokyo sped the pleased little diplomat, through border country from which Japanese troops were already being moved south to new spheres of action. In his briefcase was the precious pact, signed by himself and Russia's Premier Molotov in the presence of Joseph Stalin just a week before. Tokyo newspapers were already hailing it as a "new sword" in Japan's hand, with which Japan would try to settle its differences with Britain, the U.S., The Netherlands Indies and China. If diplomacy did not succeed, Japan now no longer feared attack from the rear. In Chungking last week there was cold fear. By freeing Japanese troops from Manchukuo, Russia had enabled Japan to intensify her attack against South China.

MATSUOKA HOME WITH A HEAD: Busy little Foreign Minister Yosuke Matsuoka last week reported to an anxious Japan the things he had done and the friends he had made on his travels to the capitals of Totalitaria. A member of his suite told of Matsuoka's meeting with Hitler.

"Herr Hitler," said the spokesman, "gradually became so heated in his conversation, and finally was so carried away, that it seemed he didn't know to whom he was talking. He pounded the table with his fist and exclaimed that England must be defeated."

Joseph Stalin and Japanese Foreign Minister Matsuoka drink a toast to the health of Asians, and to saving their own two heads.

With Russia's Stalin the Foreign Minister had a different kind of time. After the Neutrality Pact was signed, Stalin brought out a reddish liquor and proposed a toast to the Emperor of Japan. Matsuoka took a look at the glass, drew himself up to his full five feet two, and grasped the goblet like a man. "I will drink anything if it is for His Majesty the Emperor," said he, and emptied the goblet in a gulp. Much liquor flowed and soon both statesmen grew mellow.

"Mr. Stalin," said Mr. Matsuoka, "the treaty has been made. I do not lie. If I lie, my head will be yours. If you lie, be sure I will come for your head."

"Mr. Matsuoka," said Mr. Stalin, "my head is important to my country. So is yours to your country. Let us use care to keep our heads on our shoulders."

"Let us drink to that," said Mr. Matsuoka.

"You are an Asiatic," said Mr. Stalin. "So am I."

"We are all Asiatics," said Mr. Matsuoka. "Let us drink to the health of the Asiatics."

JUNE 23 **CANDOR:** Now & then, under special pressure, a Japanese diplomat startles the world with a statement of plain, simple candor, and such a statement came last week from bony little Kenkichi Yoshizawa, head of Japan's economic mission to The Netherlands East Indies. He had been politely informed that The Netherlands East Indies had not the least idea of allowing Japan increased shipments of rubber, oil and tin. Speaking to the Tokyo press, Commissioner Yoshizawa said: "The choice before us would seem to be either statesmanship or physical force."

THREE TO MAKE READY: The Japanese Fleet suddenly steamed JULY 21 into the Yokohama harbor last week and dropped anchor with a rattle and splash. The publicity attending this move looked like a sign that Japan was ready for adventure and did not care who knew it. There were other signs. Three in particular pointed to something drastic—and soon.

¶ An unexpected shake-up of the Army High Command.

¶ A Cabinet decree bringing all finance, industry, production and distribution under Government control.

¶ The appointment of two special investigators from the Police Bureau to extend Thought Control (Japanese for suppression of free speech) to all matters of foreign policy.

On the day the Army shake-up was announced, Emperor Hirohito conferred for two hours with War Minister General Tojo. Next the Son of Heaven questioned Navy Minister Oikawa for nearly an hour. Then for two hours more the Emperor listened to Prince Konoye. Apparently Japan was almost ready to strike. But where?

NEW CABINET: One day last week, in the midst of feverish JULY 28 preparations for war, the Cabinet of Premier Prince Fumimaro Konoye suddenly resigned. Prince Konoye backed out of the presence of Emperor Hirohito, threw together a new Cabinet. When noses were counted it was observed that conspicuously missing was the slightly bulbous nose of Yosuke Matsuoka, who as Foreign Minister had promoted the Triple Alliance with Italy and Germany and the Neutrality Pact with Russia. It was evident that one object of the change was to squeeze out Mr. Matsuoka. His elimination enabled Japan to pursue a foreign policy more free of the influence of Germany and Russia.

EMPIRE GAME: All the pieces were on the board for a new AUG. 4 game of Empire. So far the game had followed the rules. But then, so fast that it made Tokyo's head swim, President

Roosevelt issued an order freezing Japanese assets in the U.S. A similar British order followed at once. Axis capitals loosed a stereotyped yell about U.S. aggression in the Far East. But Finance Minister Masatsune Ogura explained that Japan is blessed with an abundance of raw materials.

Japanese-held East Asia, however, is virtually unblessed with petroleum. Almost every drum of gas and gallon of oil that Japan burns in her tanks, planes and other empire-building machinery must be imported. Biggest source of supply, outside of the U.S., is The Netherlands Indies, with whom Japan last year contracted for an annual supply of 1,800,000 tons. Before Japan had a chance to take another step, she received a rude shock. The Netherlands Indies not only froze Japanese assets but slapped a bung in the oil barrel, suspended the contract.

From Japan's point of view, her orderly chess match had turned into a rough-'em-up game of sandlot football. She had counted on facing the U.S., the British Empire, The Netherlands Indies, but she had not expected such swift teamwork. It was disconcerting. Japan was at last playing in the big leagues. The game was war.

AUG. 11 **JUMPING-OFF PLACE:** Into the Indo-Chinese port of Saigon poured fresh, fighting-fit Japanese troops. Day after day the troops debarked and marched: 20,000, 30,000, 40,000 soldiers. They were not occupation troops. They were picked troops for fighting. Behind them trucks shuttled back & forth between the docks and the encampments with crated bombs, munitions boxes, drums of gasoline, guns.

Nobody supposed that the Japanese had moved into French Indo-China to make themselves comfortable. After the U.S. and Britain froze Japanese assets, Premier Konoye spoke grimly of the need for "swift and determined execution" of Japan's national policy. Japan's aims: 1) "to secure the safety of the country"; 2) "to obtain self-sufficiency in various resources"; 3) "to establish a Greater East Asia co-prosperity sphere." French Indo-China was only a jumping-off place for the achievement of those aims.

AUG. 25 **BIG SHOT-AT:** When things grow tense in Japan, somebody often takes a shot at a political big shot. Five of the 18 Premiers Japan has had since World War I were assassinated. Last week the big shot-at was Baron Kiichiro Hiranuma, 75, onetime Premier and currently Vice Premier in the Cabinet of Prince Konoye.

When Baron Hiranuma was Premier in 1939, he lived in an "assassination-proof" house. Now he lives in a modest villa in the Tokyo suburbs. Early one morning last week there came to the door a 33-year-old autograph hunter named Naohiko Nishiyama. While the kimonoed Baron obligingly painted his calligraph, Nishiyama whipped a revolver from a parchment scroll, fired thrice, missed once. Though wounded, the Baron gave chase, caught the visitor by the shirt, held him with the aid of a guard.

Emperor Hirohito sent a basket of fruit to the Baron's bedside. In Japanese court etiquette this meant that the Son of Heaven held hope for his recovery. Had the gift been imperial wine, it would have implied that the Baron's sukiyaki was cooked. The Baron took the hint: at week's end he was reported to be rallying strongly.

HONORABLE FIRE EXTINGUISHER: "All over Tokyo are no SEPT. 22 taxicab." When cheerful Ambassador Kichisaburo Nomura says this the sparkle goes out of his one good eye. To him it is a sentence full of unhappy foreign policy. It means that Japan is desperately hard up for oil and gasoline; that therefore Japan must for the time being say uncle to Uncle Sam—or else fight for oil.

Admiral Nomura would be most reluctant to have Japan fight for oil. He personally likes peace. "I am old man, I am most earnest," he says in his much-better-than-pidgin English. "We maintained ever since opening Japan 87 year ago good relations you and us. Most of time we're happy hours. Now Japanese and United States policy, they are many divergencies. But human being must be able to make some formulas."

Last week, as he had been ever since his appointment as Ambassador, Admiral Nomura was a man in search of a formula. But it did not look last week as if Admiral Nomura or anyone else could make either side withdraw cleanly and permanently from the brink.

In the face of this apparent futility, Admiral Nomura is

cheerful, hopeful and seemingly quite sincere in his desire for peace. "This is time of war crisis," he says. "Almost three-fourths of world burned, and there must be statesmen who play to be the fire extinguisher." Kichisaburo Nomura's difficulty is that he stands between two fires: between a tough Army at home and a tough President in Washington.

OCT. 13 **TIME IN FLIGHT:** Last week a great debate raged in Tokyo. The Navy-and-civilian-dominated government of Premier Prince Konoye wanted to persuade the U.S. to relent. The Japanese Army, struggling for power, felt that U.S. policy was inexorably fixed, that Japan must move before the time limits expired. For ten years a struggle has gone on between Army and Government for control of the nation. Three Cabinets in four years have fallen because of foreign policy. Last week the fourth tottered. The strain of more than a month of fruitless conversations was telling. In Japan the conviction grew that the U.S. was outsmarting Prince Konoye, that the U.S. was spinning out the talks endlessly. Squeezed now by the Allied embargo on scrap iron and iron ore (she imports two-thirds of her steel industry's raw materials) and on oil (she imports 93%) Japan also faced an extraordinarily poor rice harvest, a subnormal fish catch.

The Japanese Army wants to fight now and is backed by a powerful German fifth column, three thousand strong, giving friendly 24-hour service. German technicians swarm through Japan's war industries. Germany wants Japan to throw its weight into the world struggle: against the Allies at Singapore, against the Russians in Siberia, or both.

OCT. 27 **END OF COMPROMISE:** One evening last week newsboys whipped through Tokyo's streets, warm papers under their arms. *"Gogai! Gogai!" (Extra! Extra!)* they shrilled. The Cabinet had fallen.

Behind the darkened windows of his official residence, Premier Prince Konoye told his Cabinet that the Emperor had accepted their resignation. This, they knew, was the end of Japan's effort to compromise with destiny.

The next day Japan's former Premiers conferred on the selection of a new leader. In less than four hours the choice was made: a general, the son of a general, War Minister Hideki

Tojo, was to head the nation. The sloppy uniform, horn-rimmed glasses and sad mustache of Japan's new Premier make him look like a professor at a masquerade, but his bluntly expressed, razor-sharp opinions are anything but mild. General Tojo's hates—Russia, the U.S., Great Britain —were important. More important was the fact that his hates were the Army's hates, his will the Army's will. He is one of the Army's Big Three. This week, at last, the Army moved to front center on the stage, took full responsibility for Japan's future. Japan had turned her corner in history.

Premier Prince Konoye. His cabinet resigns, once and for all. Page 114.   *Premier Tojo. A general who hates the U.S. takes over Japan.*

PINCH HITTER: Japan's new and super-special envoy to the U.S., Saburo Kurusu, was speeding by Clipper to Washington. That jittery, encircled, embargoed Japan proposed to follow months of Washington conversations with still more conversations was a clear sign that Japan still did not dare follow its sword-brandishing with swordplay. A Tokyo editor who shares the Japanese lust for baseball had called Kurusu "a pinch hitter on the diplomatic diamond." Pinch Hitter Kurusu was well aware of the pinch. He left Tokyo on two hours' notice. Just before leaving he told his son, Sub-lieutenant Ryo Kurusu: "Maybe I will not be able to come back. Look after the family." [Immediately after the attack on Pearl Harbor, Kurusu was interned in the U.S. along with NOV. 17

Ambassador Nomura. They were returned to Japan in 1942 in an exchange of prisoners.]

DEC. 8 **MORE TALK, MORE TROOPS:** Just before they let it be known that they wanted to negotiate with the U.S. for two more weeks, the Japanese had been acting particularly tough. Said Premier General Hideki Tojo: "Britain and the United States desire to fish in troubled waters of East Asia. . . . For the honor and pride of mankind, we must purge this sort of practice . . . with a vengeance."

Five formations of Japanese planes roared from Northern Indo-China to bomb supply depots and machine-gun truck convoys on the Burma Road, the first attack on the Road since last spring. Japanese troops continued to pour into Indo-China. It was said that a force of at least 100,000 was ready to strike at the Burma Road.

Perhaps Japan's desire for two weeks more of Washington talk was merely to allow herself a fortnight's more preparation in Indo-China.

In Tokyo, with the weariness of a tired man about to be summoned to a task greater than his strength, the Japanese people waited. Floodlights cut white arcs through the dark as work on inadequate air-raid shelters went on around the clock. Men were at work in one corner of the Palace grounds. No one could see what they were doing, but a good guess was that they were building an air-raid shelter for the Emperor.

Great Britain

In a Britain struggling for existence (see Battle of Britain, page 71), the home front and the front lines were often identical. Nevertheless, the nation at home maintained its special character: behind the war effort was a mighty civil force— under a great political leader.

JAN. 6 **MAN OF THE YEAR:** Those who write history with words sometimes forget that history is made with words. In the autumn of 1917, Nikolai Lenin quietly said: *"We shall now proceed to construct the Socialist State."* In the autumn of

1924, Adolf Hitler wrote in *Mein Kampf*: *"I . . . resolved now to become a politician."* On May 13, 1940, in his first statement as Prime Minister, Winston Leonard Spencer Churchill declared: *"I have nothing to offer but blood, toil, tears and sweat."* Those eleven words summed up the nature of Britain's war, turned Britain's back on the weaknesses of the past, set her face toward the unknown future.

December 31, 1940, was not only the end of a year; it was the end of a decade—the most terrifying of the 20th Century. It saw the unleashing of ruthless war. It saw the U.S. turn to a feverish effort to protect itself and its neighbors. It saw, in the Battle of Britain, the life-&-death struggle of the greatest empire the world has ever known.

The great accomplishments of 1940 belonged across the waters as they did in 1938 when Man of the Year Hitler conquered without fighting in Austria and at Munich, as they did in 1939 when Man of the Year Stalin got half of Poland by a shrewd deal and a free hand to work his will on Finland. But 1940 did not fall like a plum into the lap of dictators. Hitler during the year conquered five nations by arms. But he did not master Britain, as scheduled, before the summer was out.

In most men's minds everywhere—even in Germany, to judge by Nazi denunciations—Winston Churchill out-

Prime Minister Churchill: "blood, toil, tears, sweat" and courage.   *Minister of Labor Bevin: mothers must have babies "on the side." Page 122.*

ranked all others as Man of 1940. He came to power as Prime Minister just as the Blitzkrieg descended upon Britain's outposts. In his first few weeks in office they toppled about him like ninepins. Norway had already been lost. Then fell The Netherlands, Belgium, France.

Against this roll call of defeats, all the victories which Churchill gave his countrymen, aside from isolated success at sea, were such that any Cockney could count them on his thumbs: 1) the gallant evacuation at Dunkirk, really a disaster in which, although upward of 335,000 men were saved, the equipment of virtually the entire British Expeditionary Force was lost; 2) the Battle of the Marmarica which smashed the Italian Army in Egypt.

But Churchill was not without accomplishment. He gave his countrymen exactly what he promised them—blood, toil, tears, sweat—and one thing more: untold courage. It was the last that counted, not only in Britain but in democracies throughout the world.

Man-of-the-Year Churchill does not stand alone. Beside and behind Churchill stands a very small man multiplied a millionfold. He is just an Englishman. When the war came he did not like it. For a moment he knew fear, then he lit his pipe and poured himself a whiskey. When the blackout came, he groused. Churchill took over: the right man for the job. Then came Dunkirk: a bloody shame. Then the stuff fell: St. Paul's, the club, women and children, London afire. He got mad but he did not show it. There was too much to do: business to carry on, children to be sent to the country, people to be dug out of shelters, sleep to be got somehow. A bloody nuisance. On his behavior hung the shape of the future. His civilized toughness, his balanced courage and simple pride altered the course of history in 1940. Without him there could have been no Churchill.

JAN. 27 **THE PHONETIC MURDER:** Professor Arthur Lloyd James of London University is one of the greatest living authorities on the English language and its pronunciation. He taught British Broadcasting Corp. announcers to pronounce Cholmondeley in two syllables (chumly) and Llanfairpwllgyngyllgogerychwryndrobwllllantsiliogogogoch in liquid labials (pronounced   Hlan-fair-poohl-gooin-gill-gogery-coorin-droboohl-hlant-seeleo-gogo-goch). Declaring that BBC announcers were "too haw haw" in their diction, he is responsible for the nickname "Lord Haw Haw" given to Nazi Propagandist William Joyce.

Before Christmas the professor and his wife visited London (from Oxford) and ran smack into one of its most violent air raids. Severely shaken, they were taken to a nursing home, later went back to their London house, where they slept in the basement. Answering an anonymous phone call last week, London police found the professor, wandering dazedly. On his cuffs and under his fingernails were bloodstains. In the bedroom lay the body of his wife, her head bashed in and innumerable stab wounds in her body. From the professor's unphonetic mumblings police gleaned this explanation: "I thought my powers were failing, and I could not cope with my work. Rather than expect my wife to face a bleak future I decided she should die. . . . I thought I would also kill myself." Britons knew the answer: cracked war nerves.

LABOR DRAFT: Last week the No. 1 British trade unionist, MARCH 31 Minister of Labor Ernest ("Big Ernie") Bevin, ordered all British males aged 41 or 42 not already actively defending their country to register for labor service. On April 19 British females aged 20 must do the same. To speed up the process of getting more people to work in munitions factories, shipyards, mines and upon repair of bombed areas, Bevin urged that 100,000 young women volunteer at once. To queries whether newly married women might not be exempted for six months "for population reasons," a spokesman answered: "Oh, they will have time for that on the side."

VITAL STATISTICS: Since the war began [September 3, 1939] APRIL 7 28,859 people have been killed and 40,165 seriously wounded in Britain as a result of bombings.

HOW IT FEELS: In a brick cottage in Liverpool's Merseyside APRIL 14 last fortnight, 19-year-old Ruth Owen wrote a letter to her sweetheart to tell him how it feels to be bombed. Her letter: "The time is now 8:45 p.m. The warning has just gone and the guns are going. It sounds as though the whole German Air Force is over our house. Oh, I do hope they don't drop any bombs. . . . My two aunties are knitting. Mums is just sitting still. Dad is smoking and I am writing to you. Oh, you would laugh if you could see us all sitting by the inside wall, ready to make a dive under the table if things get too hot. . . . My Lord, what a row! Machine guns and bombs and planes, ours and Hitler's. It's our night tonight, all right. I am lying under the table. We have just had an incendiary bomb in the yard. My hand is shaking. . . ." Last week a demolition squad found Ruth's letter beside her body under the table.

MAY 5 **"WHIPPED JACKAL":** On Sunday Winston Churchill stepped up to a microphone to report to the people of Britain and the U.S. Commenting on the difficult campaign against Axis troops in Greece, he turned the full force of his scorn on Germany's partner: "This whipped jackal, Mussolini, who to save his own skin made all Italy a vassal State of Hitler's empire, comes frisking up at the side of the German tiger with yelpings not only of appetite . . . but even of triumph." A realist as always when he meets reversals, Churchill minced no words in describing Britain's peril. "You know I never try to make out that defeats are victories. . . . It is certain that fresh dangers . . . may come upon us in the Mediterranean."

He reiterated his faith in the war's outcome: "No prudent and far-seeing man can doubt that the eventual and total defeat of Hitler and Mussolini is certain. . . . There are less than 70,000,000 malignant Huns, some of them curable and others killable."

One sensation of the year was the sudden and dramatic flight from Germany to Great Britain of Rudolf Hess, a solemn, humorless Nazi who had been a faithful follower of Hitler since the '20s. Second in line to succeed Hitler (after Hermann Goering), Hess apparently grew frustrated as the war thrust him into the background. His trip to England may have been motivated by a fanatical desire to serve Hitler by negotiating a peace agreement.

HESSTERIA: *Hamlet: Ay, marry, why was he sent into*   MAY 26
England?
Clown: Why, because 'a was mad . . . 'tis
no great matter there.
Hamlet: Why?
Clown: 'Twill not be seen in him there.
There the men are as mad as he.

Britons last week merrily quoted *Hamlet* to each other, felt
an obscure contentment that the most fantastic episode in
Britain's greatest war could be cosily tied up with Shakespeare. Rudolf Hess, only two places removed from the leadership of Germany, had quit Germany under his own steam
and gone to the enemy country, where he was imprisoned.

Hess had taken off from the Messerschmitt plant at Augsburg in a new type of reconnaissance plane on a Saturday
evening. He wore a gold wrist watch, a gold wrist compass.
In the pockets of his superbly tailored uniform he had a
photograph of his four-year-old son, two phials of medicine,
one for his weak heart, the other for a gall-bladder ailment.
He also had a selection of photographs of himself; a map on
which was charted a course from Augsburg to the grounds
of Dungavel Castle near Glasgow, the seat of 38-year-old
Wing Commander Douglas-Hamilton, 14th Duke of Hamilton, 11th Duke of Brandon.

It was 11 o'clock, the very end of the long northern twi-
light when he circled the grounds of Dungavel. He zoomed
his plane a few thousand feet, then bailed out.

David McLean, a tenant of the Duke's, saw the Messerschmitt crash and puff into flame, saw also the white bloom
of the parachute drifting down through the dusk. Armed
with a pitchfork, he found Hess lying on the ground with a
broken ankle. In perfect English Hess said to McLean: "Will
you take me to Dungavel to see the Duke of Hamilton?"

Instead, McLean called the Home Guard. At Home Guard
headquarters Hess was turned over to the Army. With Hess
incommunicado "somewhere in Britain," eating better than
many a Briton, the press turned much attention on the Duke
of Hamilton. If the Nazi leader had been looking for an influential Briton to get the Government's ear for him, Dungavel was hardly the right address. The Duke was away on

active service. The world waited anxiously for word on the mystery from Winston Churchill, who had promised to explain all to Parliament. Already it was evident that Hess's flight had disconcerted Germany too much for it to be an elaborate ruse, and that Hess's peace plan, if he had one, had not a slender chance of winning acceptance.

Said Home Security Minister Herbert Morrison: "It does not matter what kind of animal he is, the main thing is that he is caged." [After the war, Hess was tried for war crimes at Nuremberg and sentenced to life imprisonment.]

JUNE 2 **EMPTY CUPBOARDS:** If you had two chops for lunch yesterday, you ate what was for most British civilians a week's ration of meat. Britain's larder is lower than it has been since the lean days of 1917, when food stocks fell within six weeks of exhaustion. For the first time since World War II began, Germans are eating better than are Britons. Citrus fruits have virtually disappeared. No onions can be found in public markets. The weekly egg ration is two eggs per person. The poor man's national supper of fish and chips (French fried potatoes) at a stall is fast becoming fish and mashed potatoes. Reason: no lard for frying.

JUNE 16 **CHURCHILL UNDER FIRE:** Largely by means of sheer eloquence, Winston Churchill had been able to keep most Britons' devotion. But last week, with Crete added to the somber list of defeats, a tide of opinion arose in Britain to the effect that one more major defeat would call for a radical change, if not the exit of the Churchill government. Parliamentary circles were angrily agog with suspicion that the obsolete and stubborn 1914 military mentality was still in charge. The rising criticism was even harder on Churchill for neglecting the war economy. Said the London *Daily Mail*: "When are we going to run machines, factories and shipyards to full capacity? When are we going to see an end of masterly retreats?"

JUNE 23 **CHURCHILL SPEAKS LAST:** In Parliament last week, Winston Churchill finessed rather than faced the hottest critical barrage of his Prime Ministership. Tart and testy, he suggested that any critic whose mind was focused on the small island of Crete was being very small-minded indeed. Said Churchill:

"We provided in Crete a deterrent to enemy attack sufficient to require a major effort on his part, but to attempt to be safe everywhere is to make sure of being strong nowhere." In general, Churchill drew a picture of Britain fighting what the New York *Herald Tribune* called a "guerrilla war of evasion, attrition, maneuver and retreat"—until such time as Britain's armament catches up with the Nazi striking power.

Rudolf Hess. The No. 3 Nazi arrives in England to see the Duke. Page 124.   *King George cuts down on cigarets to share the hardships of his people.*

"NO PEACE, NO REST, NO PARLEY": If Winston Churchill was still far from disarming British critics of his conduct of the war, no one found fault with his spirit last week. Behind the grim, bomb-scarred brownstone walls of St. James's Palace the Prime Minister made one of the most eloquent addresses of his career. Said he:

"Here we meet while from across the Atlantic Ocean the hammers and lathes of the United States signal in a rising hum their message of encouragement and their promise of swift and ever-growing aid. . . . Hitler, with his tattered lackey, Mussolini, at his tail . . . pretends to build out of hatred . . . a new order for Europe. . . . We cannot yet see how deliverance will come . . . but nothing is more certain than that every trace of Hitler's footsteps, every stain of his infected, corroding fingers will be sponged and . . . if need be, blasted from the surface of the earth. . . . We shall be on his track wherever he goes. . . . He will find no peace, no rest, no halting place, no parley."

JUNE 30 **"DISEASE OF OVERCROWDING":** In spite of dire predictions, Britain is extremely healthy after a year of total war. Deaths from many diseases have dropped sharply (partly, doctors think, because of healthier diets enforced by rationing) and only cerebrospinal fever [a form of meningitis], the "disease of overcrowding," has shown a heavy increase.

JULY 21 **LESS SMOKE:** George VI last week put himself on short rations of cigarets—cutting down from 20-25 a day to 15 —in order to share the hardships of his people who now can get only a limited amount. The average British smoker considers himself lucky to get ten a day after protracted queueing.

SEPT. 15 **THE LIFE OF A FIREMAN:** To Verger Stanley Thompson, 60, of London's Church of St. Dunstan-in-the-West was awarded the British Empire Medal last week. Verger Thompson did not know much about putting out incendiary bombs [they were supposed to be covered with sand], but he did the best he could.

During a recent raid a bomb shower fired the wooden desks and floor of St. Dunstan's schoolroom. Verger Thompson doused desks and floor with water, causing the bomb fragments to explode. Undaunted, he stamped out the fragments. The church's dome started burning. Fireman Thompson scrambled nimbly up an iron ladder, picked up a hot bomb, hurled it to the ground. Losing his balance, he tumbled down the dome, got wedged against a parapet. Freeing himself, he spotted another incendiary on the vestry roof, walked atop a twelve-foot wall carrying a water bucket. The bomb responded to the water by exploding and hurling Fireman Thompson to the concrete pavement below.

Fireman Thompson could not seem to learn. Late that night he was discovered astride a 30-foot wall, hauling up a fire hose to drench another fire. Last week he was recuperating, expected soon to take a new job of fire-watching, at which he will try very hard to remember not to throw water on incendiaries.

THE LASSIES STICK TOGETHER: In Buckingham Palace the OCT. 6 Queen opened a letter addressed to "Her Majesty the Queen Personally." She read: "Your Majesty, I appeal to you as one Scottish lassie to another. I am in love with a Polish soldier and he doesn't want to marry me. But, Your Majesty, it is most imperative that he should marry me as soon as possible, and I beg of you to help me." The Queen sent the letter to the wife of the Polish Ambassador, who passed it on to her husband, who passed it on with a very strong note to the commanding officer at a Polish camp in Scotland. The Polish colonel summoned a Polish private, gave him unprintable Polish hell.

Last week, the Queen let it be known that she had got another letter from her Scottish lassie: "Your Majesty, I am now the happiest woman in the world. My Polish soldier married me and I owe it all to you."

Germany

In August 1939, Hitler had signed a Non-Aggression Pact with Stalin that divided Eastern Europe into zones of influence and left Germany free to take over the rest of Europe without Russian interference. Then, in the summer of 1941, Hitler launched a massive invasion of Russia itself (see page 91). That winter, the strain of the war began to tell on Germany. But the nation still appeared all-powerful. Hitler's propaganda machine was in high gear, and on the home front the thought that Germany might lose the war had not yet begun to penetrate.

PROBLEM IN SUBTRACTION: The arithmetic that Hitler has MARCH 3 taught the Jews in the Third Reich has been the misery of subtraction. From all of them he has taken something: privileges, property, homes, life. Within the last fortnight two sardine-packed trains left Vienna. Aboard each were more than 1,000 Jews bound for limbo—the new barbed-wire ghetto near Lublin in Poland. Elsewhere sealed trains crossed the border with more Jews (mostly very old and very young) for the concentration camps of unoccupied France. Hitler's final solution to his problem in subtraction is zero—to be reached, according to the most sanguine reports from Germany, in just six more weeks.

APRIL 14 **A DICTATOR'S HOUR:** The crucial spring of his career came last week to Adolf Hitler. He could see it in sheltered, sunstruck places around the Berghof where lilies of the valley, violets, Alpine roses, blue gentians, and wild azaleas bloomed, and in the green showing through the white on the Untersberg's slopes across the way. But he could feel it even more strongly in his bones: spring, when armies march.

If the campaigns Hitler launches this spring are as successful as those he launched a year ago, he will almost indisputably soon be master of at least half the world. If they fail, the least that can be expected is that the tide of world power will begin to run against him as the weight of U.S. economic power begins to pour to the aid of Britain. For Hitler this spring is destiny.

Though not a noisily sturdy man like Mussolini, Hitler is a healthy man, who in ten years has changed physically less than most men between 42 and 52, and who has suffered no greater hurts than a finger broken in an automobile accident and a polyp removed from his larynx. The wiglike wad of hair which hangs across his forehead has no grey in it; nor has his curt mustache.

For Adolf Hitler is an ascetic. He never smokes, and says: "I like to have my enemies smoke as much as possible, but I do not like to have my friends smoke." He never drinks anything stronger than his private near-beer, 1.5% alcohol. He eats no meat. Sex has no place in his life. In springtime, with Germany at war, he gives up even his little pleasures. There are no more evenings now of dressing to the ears and listening for hours on end to the stupendous heroics of Richard Wagner. No more lavish entertainments now, no more evenings amusing everyone by mimicking the fat Goering and the thin Goebbels, no more long, lazy conversations about art. And no friendly picnics in Bavaria. His society must now be his soldiers, who he says are "quick as greyhounds, tough as leather, and hard as Krupp steel."

SOMETHING BREWING: From Moscow last week came a strong   MAY 12
smell of diplomatic fermentation. The Russian press announced that 12,000 German troops had landed in Finland,
within 50 miles of the Russian base at Hanko. As always hap-
pens when Russia or Germany makes a move which by the
use of a little imagination can be interpreted as hostile to the
other, wistful thinkers saw in the announcement that Germany and Russia would soon be at each other's throats.

THE MAN WHO FAILED: "Yes, the big things in the world are   JUNE 16
always done by just a man—one man—one strong person-
ality. History in its times of crisis cried out for a man. . . .
You may gather all the wisdom in the world in a Parliament chamber, but you will never get action out of a Parliament chamber. One man has got to lead." Last week, the
man who spoke these lines was dead, having given up the job
of leading almost 23 years ago. For the speaker was Kaiser
Wilhelm II of Germany.

SOMETHING WRONG?: The silent war of nerves being waged   JUNE 23
between two masters of the nerve technique, Adolf Hitler
and Joseph Stalin, last week reached a new climax.
¶ Germany was moving heavy troop concentrations to the
Russian frontier.
¶ Russia also had troops concentrated close to the frontier.
¶ More German troops moved into Finland.
¶ German diplomats showed the latest Blitzkrieg films to
the Red Army's general staff in Moscow.
   If all these facts did not add up to an impending Russo-
German war, at least they summed up a crisis.

WAR AT HOME: From a TIME correspondent until recently   JUNE 30
in Germany came these facts:
¶ Germany was rumbling with spontaneous discontent.
¶ Adolf Hitler has lost contact with his people. No one but
the generals makes suggestions to the great dictator any
more; he has made it known that he does not like advice.
¶ Rudolf Hess knew of Germany's discontent better than
anyone else, for to him were delivered the official reports on
civilian morale. Hess's flight to England was his own individual project. Hess wanted to urge the British to sue for peace

with Germany immediately. He wanted to warn the British that if Russia accepted the German demands, the German military machine was prepared to wage an all-out war on Britain and its Empire, with the probable invasion of the British Isles this summer.

JULY 21 **POWDER ROOM:** When plans were drawn for converting the Blücher Palace in Berlin into the U.S. Embassy, architects included a "powder room" for visiting ladies. Last week, Gestapo agents marched into the Embassy with a copy of the architect's plan in which "powder room" was literally translated *Pulverkammer*. They demanded to see it, accusing the Embassy of the storing of munitions. They were shown to the ladies W.C.

JULY 28 **BEGINNING TO PINCH:** The grimness of the war was coming home to the German people. The Russian campaign had been neither swift nor bloodless. The R.A.F. was pounding harder by day as well as by night. And though midsummer had come as a late blessing to homes heatless by decree since May 1, warmth was the only mitigation of Germany's joyless and complicated living. Other signs that the war is beginning to pinch:

¶ Beer is scarce in Germany and the *Kneipen* (corner beer saloons) sell beer only between 11:30 a.m. and 3 p.m. and between 7 and 10 p.m. (one glass to a customer).

¶ There are few bicycles remaining to civilians and no new ones available. (The German people have long gone without autos.)

¶ Clothing is tightly rationed and of bad quality.

¶ The monthly soap allowance, used daily for the hands and weekly for the bodies, withers away by the third week of the month.

¶ For fun when work is finished, workaday Germans go to parks and sit.

NOV. 17 **LAST CHANCE:** For months it has been reported that many Hitler-weary Germans continue to support Hitler only because of their fear of what might happen to them at the hands of a vengeful Europe if Hitler lost. Last week Adolf Hitler and his mouthpiece tacitly confirmed these reports by using that fear for propaganda purposes. Propaganda Minister Paul Joseph Goebbels called on the German people to keep fighting for the most negative—and perhaps strongest—of reasons: fear of defeat and revenge. Said he:

"If we win, all is won: raw materials, freedom, nourishment, *Lebensraum*, the basis for social reform of our state and the opportunity of full development for the Axis powers. If we lose, all this, this and still more, will be lost—namely our whole national existence. . . . Germany will be destroyed, exterminated and extinguished. . . ."

Nazi Propaganda Minister Goebbels, meeting a Russian prisoner of war, has a wish for Christmas: blankets for the German troops.

OLD SCHOOL EYE: German officers of the old school blinked NOV. 24 with dismay over a Government economy edict forbidding further production of monocles.

CHARTER OF ANTI-SEMITISM: Jew-baiting Propaganda Minister Goebbels, alarmed by the German people's growing sympathy for the persecuted Jews, last week saw fit to publish a charter of anti-Semitism. Excerpts:

¶ "The Jews are our ruination. They contrived and brought on this war. With it they want to destroy the German Reich and our people."

¶ "There is no difference among Jews. Every Jew is the sworn enemy of the German people."

¶ "Anyone who . . . still cultivates private relations with him . . . must be appraised and treated the same as the Jew. Jews are the enemy's emissaries among us. Whoever stands at their side deserts to the enemy in war."

DEC. 29 **CHRISTMAS IN GERMANY:** Over every radio station in the Third Reich, nervous Dr. Paul Joseph Goebbels last week broadcast a Christmas message to the German people. It was no message of cheer. After a perfunctory mention of "the accomplishments of our Army" (now retreating in Russia), the little Minister got down to business. What he wanted was Christmas presents for the soldiers on the Eastern Front: overshoes, stockings, woolen underwear, furs, blankets, gloves, earmuffs—anything, in fact, that would turn the keen winds of the Russian winter.

Russia

From the Russian point of view, the Non-Aggression Pact which Stalin concluded with Germany in 1939 had been successful at first. Russia was awarded part of Poland, and, in the summer of 1940, under terms of the agreement, Stalin moved to annex the Baltic states of Estonia, Latvia and Lithuania. But by 1941 tension was beginning to rise between Germany and Russia. When Hitler moved troops into the Balkans, Stalin accused him of violating the 1939 pact. At last, in midsummer, the agreement was shattered once and for all as Nazi troops advanced into Russia.

FEB. 24 **DIRTY CAPITALISTS:** The National Conference of the Soviet Communist Party met last week for the first time in four years, and all was not brotherhood at the meeting. The brotherhood heard a bitter speech by a member of the Central Committee's Secretariat, Georgi Malenkov, admitting that Soviet industry had been slowed down by a top-heavy bureaucracy, buck-passing, lazy administration. Shops, depots, harbor and railroad works, he said, were suffering a "reign of dirt." Dirt, he said, is "the bulwark of capitalist traditions."

COMRADE STALIN EXPLAINS: Last week Comrade Stalin gave JULY 14
his countrymen the explanation he had owed them since that
Sunday morning when Russians woke up to learn that Germany
had invaded their country. It was his job to explain why he had
promoted the 1939 Non-Aggression Pact with Germany, which
enabled Adolf Hitler to pick off his enemies by ones and twos
until he was free to tackle Russia.

Taking to the microphone with a big pitcher of tea at his el-
bow, Comrade Stalin saluted his fellow comrades in patriarchal
tones: "Comrades, Citizens, Brothers and Sisters, Men of our
Army and Navy! I am addressing you as my friends. . . . A
grave danger hangs over our country. . . . [Germany] suddenly and treacherously violated the Non-Aggression Pact. . . .
It may be asked: How could the Soviet Government have con-
sented to conclude a non-aggression pact with such treacherous
fiends as Hitler and Ribbentrop? Was this not an error on the
part of the Soviet government?"

Pouring himself a glass of tea to cool his throat, Comrade
Stalin answered his own question: "Of course not! . . . Could
the Soviet Government have declined such a proposal? I think
that not a single peace loving State could decline a peace treaty
with a neighboring State, even though the latter was headed by
such fiends and cannibals as Hitler and Ribbentrop."

The next day being July 4, the Russian radio had a good opportunity to plug in Comrade Stalin's newest party line. It devoted an hour to an English-language program, the theme of
which was: "The people of the Soviet Union, now fighting a
great patriotic war in defense of their country . . . extend their
ardent greetings to the American people on the occasion of
their glorious national holiday. . . . It is altogether fitting on
this occasion for the American and Russian people to clasp
hands more firmly."

MORALE IN MOSCOW: Confounding outside observers, who a JULY 28
month ago predicted that the whole Soviet system would shiver
and collapse like a card-house at the breath of modern war,
U.S. newsmen in Moscow painted a far different picture. The
people of Moscow, they said, were going about their business as
calmly as Londoners, organizing an effective blackout for their
as-yet-unbombed city. The queues that used to form in front
of banks, food and kerosene stores were gone, and though ra-

tion cards were issued for food, clothing and manufactured goods, Moscow's stores were generally better stocked than they had been before the war began.

It seemed obvious that the Soviet Government had released some of its reputedly enormous food reserve. Civilian morale in Russia had two great advantages. Russia's very vastness and lack of communications kept bad news at the front from spreading easily to the rest of the nation; and Russian communiqués kept the results of the fighting in a convenient haze. Hub of the Communist universe, Moscow might be expected to have the highest morale. From the smaller cities there was little word, from the farming villages (where anti-Stalin feeling is strongest) none. But along the Trans-Siberian Railway travelers saw much the same sights they had seen in Moscow: swift, purposeful mobilization, ample food. They also saw an average of three trains an hour clanking westward with materials for the front.

DEC. 1 **NICE OLD GENTLEMAN:** Dictator Joseph Stalin, who disposed of his Russian opposition simply by shooting it, was once widely regarded in the democracies as a sort of unwashed Genghis Khan with blood dripping from his fingertips. But as his armies have provided the principal opposition to Adolf Hitler, Dictator Stalin has come to seem increasingly benign to his new democratic friends. Last week United Press Correspondent Wallace Carroll, just out of Russia, reported that one U.S. official, after being a guest at a Kremlin dinner celebrating the completion of aid-to-Russia arrangements, described the Dictator as "a nice old gentleman."

At the dinner, grey-clad and booted, Dictator Stalin regaled his guests with a seven-hour, ten-course meal including flagons of cognac and vodka. Thirty-one bottoms-up toasts were drunk (some guests hazily estimated 37); Dictator Stalin preferred cognac. At length the Dictator himself proposed a toast to President Roosevelt, and added: "May God help him in his task." Several Americans, unable to believe their ears, checked the translation of these words with their Russian table companions. They discovered that it was correct.

The dinner over, Dictator Stalin led his bulging, elated guests from the banquet hall. Turning to them, he courteously observed: "The lavatory is on the left." Again, he was translated correctly.

France

France had fallen to German troops in June 1940. Under the armistice terms, the Germans occupied three fifths of France, leaving an unoccupied zone in the south and southeast under the presidency of Marshal Henri Pétain, whose capital was at Vichy. Under the original terms, Vichy France was supposedly free to govern itself; but the Germans kept adding new conditions and continuing the pressure for Vichy to collaborate with Germany. But France refused to do the one thing that Hitler wanted most—turn its fleet over to Germany. The Germans finally occupied all of France in 1942, but they still did not get their hands on the fleet. The French scuttled it.

END OF A LINE: The 20th Century's greatest defensive position, the 125-mile Maginot Line, last year proved worthless in spite of its 1,600,000 cubic yards of concrete, 50,000 tons of steel plate, its cost of $500,000,000. Last week Berlin announced the dismantling of the Maginot Line. Some of its heavy guns have already been set up along the English Channel. Eight thousand of its coal stoves are now heating Berlin air-raid shelters, which are also equipped with its bunks and mattresses. JAN. 27

Once the tank traps, entanglements and other defensive devices have been removed, the terrain in front of the line will be turned into fruit and vegetable farms. Like the Great Wall of China, which was crossed time and again by Mongol and Manchu armies, its labyrinthine corridors and concrete chambers will remain, anachronisms to awe tourists and recall outdated military conceptions.

THE MARSHAL WAITS FOR NEWS: In Vichy, the cold, cheerless onetime health resort which is now the capital of unoccupied France, Marshal Pétain last week proceeded with the construction of a state designed to suit both him and Adolf Hitler. Hitler's terms of "collaboration" were reported to include a demand that German troops be allowed to cross Tunisia for an attack on the British in Libya. When this proposition was made to the Marshal a fortnight ago by his FEB. 3

ousted Vice Premier Pierre Laval, Marshal Pétain was adamant on adhering to the original Armistice terms. But since then there have been signs that the Marshal might waver. [Pierre Laval, a longtime French politician and onetime premier, was named foreign minister in the Vichy government and successor designate to Pétain in June 1940. He was dismissed in December, when, because of Laval's close ties to the Germans, the suspicion arose that he was plotting to overthrow Pétain. In 1942 he was reinstated. After the Nazi defeat in 1945, Laval fled to Spain, was deported to Austria where he was captured by American troops and extradited to France. He was tried for treason, sentenced to death, and executed in October 1945 after a futile attempt at suicide.]

Last week U.S. Ambassador to Vichy, Admiral William Leahy, had a talk with Marshal Pétain about the French Fleet. Admiral Leahy has let it be known that if German demands should force France to re-enter the war on the British side, the U.S. would support her as fully as the U.S. now supports Great Britain. But the U.S. and U.S. aid are far away, and Germany just around the corner.

FEB. 10 **THE MARSHAL GETS THE NEWS:** The terms of Adolf Hitler's new demands had come at last. Marshal Pétain learned of them by telephone from his Ambassador to Paris. They were

Marshal Pétain and Admiral Darlan, leaders of Vichy France. Their problem: how to fend off new German demands for collaboration.

harsher than the old Marshal had expected. Not only did Hitler want the restitution of Pierre Laval to power and passage for German troops across Tunisia for an attack on the British in Libya, but he also now wanted to occupy Mediterranean ports in France as well as North Africa.

People who saw the 84-year-old Marshal after he had heard this news reported that he was calm and serene. But France's Chief of State was going through the same mental and emotional experience that had broken such men as Austria's Chancellor Kurt von Schuschnigg [whom the Nazis imprisoned at Dachau] and Czechoslovakia's Eduard Beneš [who fled to England to lead a government in exile]. Like them Pétain tried to make little concessions, apparently unwilling to believe that the only concession that ever satisfied Adolf Hitler is capitulation.

BIRTHS AND PETS: Last week Marshal Pétain, France's ear- APRIL 21 nest Catholic Chief of State, drafted a decree which he hopes will keep French home fires banked if not burning. There will be no more quick divorce in the France that Vichy rules. Instead of allowing couples 20 days to think things over, the new law will require two years for an attempted reconciliation. A spokesman denied that Pétain's decree was dictated by religious considerations, insisted it was one more effort to halt the downward spiral of France's birth rate.

While Vichy was encouraging human procreation in Unoccupied France, German-occupied Paris cracked down on animal increase. The Society for the Protection of Animals asked owners to prevent their cats and dogs from mating. Reason: food is so scarce that Paris pets are already starving.

JEWS ARE EQUAL: "Racial" collaboration was already in MAY 26 frightening motion. Three weeks ago Adolf Hitler made the Jews of Occupied France equal to the Jews of Germany—forbade them practically all business or professional activity, and the Vichy Propaganda and Information Secretariat declared: "The intention is simply to put Jews in a position where they can no longer harm the country."

BOONS TO FASCISM: Stubbornly patriotic as Marshal Pétain may be, his patriotism has never reflected the French egalitarian spirit. Even as an officer in World War I he was a professed Royalist. During the Spanish Civil War the Hero of Verdun strongly favored the cause of his old friend, Francisco Franco. Since the fall of France, when Pétain was drafted by a reactionary bloc of deputies to reconstruct the country, he has developed an aptitude for sonorous political pronouncements whose vague and lofty words do little to conceal their totalitarian direction.

But perhaps the best proof of the Marshal's sympathies lies in his choice of a No. 2 man to carry out the hard, detailed work of statesmanship that an 85-year-old can hardly be expected to do. Fifty-nine-year-old Admiral Jean François Darlan is a spruce, magnetic little figure from his flattish bald head to his impeccably polished shoes. He has the eyes of an amused gambler and his career exhibits him as having the principles of a cat. He has constantly and glibly shifted his politics to suit his career.

The Admiral of the French Fleet loathes the British. Of the British blockade he has said: "Germans are more generous and more understanding of the needs of humanity than the English." He is a great eater and drinker, and on the night France collapsed he luxuriated so heartily and publicly at a Bordeaux restaurant that the next day a number of his officers resigned out of shame.

But he still has a Navy under him—one battleship, 13 cruisers, some 20 destroyers and some 50 submarines. He is Commander of France's only surviving, if heavily battered, military arm. As Vice Premier, he is second in command of France. He is a neat French edition of the able, scheming, ruthless personality-type which has been a boon to Fascism wherever it has risen.

JUNE 2 **"SOVEREIGNTY":** Making his first radio address to the nation, Admiral Darlan declared that Hitler "did not ask me to hand over our fleet to him. Everyone knows . . . that I will never hand it over. The Chancellor did not ask me for any colonial territory. He did not ask me to declare war on England. . . . At no moment was there any question of France abandoning her sovereignty."

It seemed apparent that Admiral Darlan had put more weight on the word "sovereignty" than it could possibly bear.

It remained clear last week that Germany was enjoying a good part of France's agriculture and industrial output. If the Nazis had not got the French Navy, they apparently controlled the perhaps even more helpful French merchant marine. London sources said that heavy French shipments of oil, rubber, lead, wool and foodstuffs have been moving from U.S. Gulf ports into Nazi hands.

ALCOHOL: *Le Temps* reported that since the fall of France the nation has suffered a wave of alcoholism, adding that "unless the fight against excessive drinking is pursued with energy, it is certain that efforts for national reconstruction are due for a definite check."

"DE GAULLE SOUP": General Charles de Gaulle's Free France AUG. 4 is an army of 40,000 men, an air force of 1,000 and a navy of 17 fighting ships. It does not pretend to be a government. To General de Gaulle and his brave, fanatical followers, Free France is the trustee of the French Republic, and one day, he hopes and believes, it will return France to its people. Meanwhile his task is to fight to free Frenchmen and French subjects from Nazi and Vichy Fascism.

He is doing his part to hold Hitler in check. In Syria Free French and British forces stand guard over the northern approaches to the Suez. French Equatorial Africa, where de Gaulle now has his capital, is a possible base for Anglo-U.S. operations along Africa's west coast, a dagger pointed at Axis Libya.

Charles André Joseph Marie de Gaulle has a too-tall (6 ft. 4 in.) body, big hips, a small head and the undynamic appearance frequently found in big men. He is an inexperienced politician, a bad salesman. But he has the unique advantage of being the one Frenchman who knew what was wrong with the French Army. The army of the future will move on caterpillar treads, he wrote in 1934. The Maginot Line can be crossed, he warned. Nobody paid any attention.

On the day after the Germans broke through at Sedan, de Gaulle was made a general in command of a hastily assembled armored division. He held up the Germans for four days. Premier Paul Reynaud made him Under Secretary of State for Defense, and General de Gaulle helped to persuade Reynaud to continue the war; and he flew to London to tell Winston Churchill that France would see it through. When Reynaud lost heart and resigned in favor of Pétain, de Gaulle flew to London for keeps.

Now he leads the movement to restore France's freedom. His followers have all braved dangers to join him. Gaullists slip into France at every opportunity and can rely so much on popular support that they knock on doors at random, announce simply: "I am here." Sometimes they are caught. But few Frenchmen want or would dare to turn a Gaullist in. They get a night's lodging, a meal or whatever help they need and go on about the business of organizing sympathizers for an eventual uprising. If Vichy and Hitler begin to crumble, the Free French in France will have not merely a fifth column. They may have the nation. Already, restaurants are unofficially calling *Vichyssoise* "De Gaulle soup."

SEPT. 15 **TERROR FOR TERROR:** In Paris a night-walking German civilian was savagely beaten. Pistols suddenly cracked in the streets—at a Nazi sergeant, a German official, a second Nazi noncom. Despite death sentences threatened for railway sabotage, round-house turntables on the Paris-Brittany main line were blown up. In retaliation, the enraged Nazis seized hostages, backed three of them against a wall near Paris and executed them. It had obviously become a question of terror for terror.

NOV. 3 **100 FOR 2:** When two Frenchmen slipped up to the Nazi military commander of Nantes early last week and riddled him with bullets, the Germans knew exactly what to do. From Paris General Otto von Stülpnagel, commanding the German Army of Occupation, issued a terse communiqué. He offered a reward of 15,000,000 francs [$300,000], to be paid by France, for the killers, promised he would execute 50 French hostages if the killers were not arrested in two days.

The general was as good as his word. Forty-eight hours later 50 French prisoners stumbled out of their cells and were shot by firing squads. But still the men who had killed Lieut. Colonel Karl Friedrich Holtz were free. Not even the promise of a sizeable fortune had persuaded their friends to betray them. General von Stülpnagel announced that he would shoot 50 more hostages.

That same day the Nazis had another dead officer on their hands. Early in the evening four men waylaid a Nazi major in Bordeaux, shot him. Again the Germans clamped down. They fined the city 10,000,000 francs, picked 50 more hostages to die for the new killing.

From Vichy old Marshal Pétain broadcast an appeal to the people of France. In his tired, halting voice he begged: "Frenchmen . . . put an end to this butchery. Do not let more evil be done in France." The Bordeaux hostages were shot.

A FUNNY RACE: The German conquerors of France had anticipated an upsurge of national feeling on Armistice Day and had destroyed all monuments commemorating French victories on the old World War I battlefields. Unable to display their feelings openly, Frenchmen prepared in gardens and cellars. On the morning of Armistice Day, Colmar, in Alsace, beheld a strange parade. Hundreds of snails crept through the streets. They were smeared under the wheels of traffic, squished under the boots of Nazi troops. Across the shell of every snail was painted the red, white and blue of the Tricolor. NOV. 24

COLD v. ART: Governor Charles Magny of Paris does not believe in letting a coal shortage interfere with the output of art. He allotted an extra ration of coal to artists who employ nude models. DEC. 15

Italy

BENITO MEETS FRANCO: On the Italian Riviera, Spain's Generalissimo Francisco Franco paid a visit to Benito Mussolini, which caused a bright Englishman to observe that he had never before heard of rats boarding a sinking ship. FEB. 24

Things had not been so well with Il Duce since he chiseled into the war last summer. His Army in the Balkans needed rescuing from the Greeks. Another Army, or what was left of it, was making dust across Libya and needing rescue from the British. And so last week, for the first time, Benito Mussolini took the trouble to meet the man he helped to power in Spain—in the hope that Generalissimo Franco would help to close the Strait of Gibraltar.

While an Italian armored train, its guns turned on the Mediterranean, chuffed nervously up & down the Riviera between San Remo and Grimaldi, Il Duce and El Caudillo sat down to talk. Whatever he may be as a soldier, Il Duce is a very good diplomat. He told El Caudillo some of his friend Adolf Hitler's plans for the conquest of Britain and for the New Order in Europe after the war. El Caudillo had nothing but the warmest wishes for the success of the Axis plans. He would like to participate, but there was a little matter of bread. Bread is Spain's great problem, and bread to keep the people from starving is going through the British blockade, both from the U.S. and from Argentina.

What Mussolini and Franco cooked up in their conference was anybody's guess, but a good one was that Spain would continue to trade neutrality to Britain for bread until Britain looks nearly beaten. Then, if that time ever comes, Spain will step in and—with France—will be glad to share *Mare Nostrum* with Italy. Otherwise, she would rather eat.

MARCH 10 **FOR SERVICES RENDERED:** In the Spanish Civil War, Italy last week sent this bill to Debtor Francisco Franco:

763 planes
1,414 motors
1,672 tons bombs
1,930 cannons
7,668 motor vehicles
10,135 automatic guns
240,747 small arms
9,250,000 rounds aircraft ammunition
7,514,534 rounds artillery ammunition
324,900,000 rounds small-arms ammunition

TOTAL 7,500,000,000 lira
Less discount (for good will) 2,000,000,000

NET 5,500,000,000 lira
($277,750,000)
TERMS: 24 annual payments

IMPERIAL BULLFROG: This week Benito Mussolini, the loud, JUNE 9
guttural Bullfrog of the Mediterranean, went to Brennero to
confer with Adolf Hitler. It was the sixth time the two dictators had met since World War II began. Much had happened
since they last conferred, January 20. Were Mussolini a man
to be amused by his own misfortune, he might laugh guttur-
ally at the paradox of his position:

If his ally wins the war, Italy may rule an empire of sorts,
but Germany will rule Italy. Mussolini is now a puppet of
Hitler's.

After more than 18 years of dictatorship, Mussolini is no
lusty athlete, but a sick, neurotic old man of 57. He has had
stomach ulcers for years, has used no meat, tea, coffee, hard
liquor or tobacco. There is a suspicion abroad that both his
heart and brain have been affected by syphilis. Last April
Chicago *Daily News* Correspondent John T. Whitaker reported that in the spring of 1939 Mussolini suffered a
stroke. He was confined to his bed for five weeks, his face
partially paralyzed and his left eye affected. Since then, said
Whitaker's trustworthy sources, the Duce has suffered from
paranoia. Paranoia is often characterized by delusions of
grandeur.

OFFENSIVE: "When one wants to remember a dictator in the JUNE 23
pure classical meaning of the term," spouted Dictator Mussolini over Italian radio, "one cites Sulla. Well, Sulla seems
to us a modest amateur compared to Delano Roosevelt."
Accented as it was, "del ano" in Italian means "of the anus."
Benito Mussolini has always found that the best defense is to
be offensive.

BRUNO'S LAST FLIGHT: Benito Mussolini hates death. He AUG. 18
wants perpetual strength for his own body, for his loved
ones, for his Italy. One morning last week he was at his desk
in Rome. A few minutes after 10 o'clock the telephone rang.
San Giusto Airport, Pisa. An accident. Three killed, five injured. And one of the dead was Benito Mussolini's second
boy Bruno, the brown one, the good flyer.

Mussolini flew at once to Pisa. There he went to Santa
Chiara Hospital, and stood a long time beside the boy's body.
He remembered the day when he pinned gold wings on Bru-

no's chest to make him, at 17, the youngest pilot in Italy. He remembered what the generals said about how the lad acquitted himself on bombing missions in Ethiopia.

Now, only 23, he had broken himself test-piloting a big new four-motored bomber. Benito Mussolini stared for a time at the scene of the crash. Then he returned to the bedside and sat there all night. In the morning came the Pope's blessing on this agnostic father and a brief service for the son. Then the coffin was taken off to be buried on one of the little Romagna hillsides where the Mussolinis, the makers of muslin, had always lived.

But before he left Pisa, Benito Mussolini went to talk with the five injured survivors. One unwittingly asked how Bruno was. "Bruno," said Benito Mussolini, who hates death, "is quite well. He is no longer in danger."

PANTS UP, PANTS DOWN: Last fall, in order to save cloth, Italy's Supreme Council of Autarchy, headed by Benito Mussolini, urged Italian manhood to get out of long pants, get into shorts. Newspapers insisted shorts were "not only hygienic but masculine and patriotic."

Last week came an abrupt style switch, a harsh pull-'em-down order. Snarled *Telegrafo*, newspaper of Mussolini's son-in-law, Count Galeazzo Ciano: "Men wearing short pants look absurd. . . . Grown men with hairy legs . . . and short panties resemble ridiculous absent-minded professors. . . . This mediocre idea proved a failure."

DEC. 1 **WORKING, BREEDING, ENDURING:** Italy had amassed all the necessary ingredients for a first-class revolution. Favored Fascist bigwigs prospered from wartime grafts. The tightened food-rationing system reeled along under the weight of flagrant violations. Military morale ebbed to a new low as the British Army pushed into Libya.

The ingredients were there, but the will to combine and ignite them was pathetically lacking last week. The people watched the country's slow disintegration, its gradual absorption by its Axis ally and did not move. After 16 months in Rome for the New York *Herald Tribune*, Correspondent Allen Raymond thought he knew why:

"The Italian people have lost faith in Mussolini, faith in

their King, and sometimes it seems . . . faith in themselves, except in their capacity to work hard, to breed, to endure hard standards of living and to survive. . . . Apathy and pessimism grip the people. . . . They pray for some miracle that may bring them peace."

Belgium

The Nazi blitzkrieg had struck Belgium on May 10, 1940. When Belgian defenses crumbled under the attack, British and French troops were sent in to reinforce the line. But then the Germans broke into France, and the Allied positions in Belgium were outflanked. At this point King Leopold III of Belgium surrendered unconditionally to the Germans. In Britain and France he was bitterly accused of letting down his allies and he was also criticized for not trying to flee and set up a government in exile as other European monarchs had done. Interned as a prisoner in one of his own castles, Leopold was later moved to Germany, where he was freed in 1945 by Allied troops.

THE FACTS IN THE CASE: Since Leopold, King of the Belgians, JUNE 23 surrendered to the German Army on May 27, 1940, thousands of words have been written to prove that he was: 1) a traitor, 2) a defeatist, 3) a humanitarian, 4) a patriot. The man who knew most of the facts in the case was Admiral of the Fleet Sir Roger Keyes, who, as a special British liaison officer to Belgium, was with King Leopold the day he surrendered. Last week he made the facts public at last. His story:

Fighting on the Belgian front had been continuous for ten days. On May 20 the Belgian King sent word to the Allies that should his troops lose contact with the French and British, "capitulation would be inevitable." By May 27 the Belgians were running short of food and ammunition, and they were being attacked by at least eight German divisions and wave after wave of dive-bombers.

That morning King Leopold asked Admiral Keyes to inform the British authorities that he would be obliged to surrender before a debacle took place. A similar message was given the French. By afternoon of that day the Germans had driven a wedge between the Belgians and the British. Hundreds of thousands of refugees, men, women and children, were being mercilessly machine-gunned and bombed by low-flying aircraft.

In these circumstances King Leopold at 5 p.m., May 27, informed the British and French that he intended at midnight to ask an armistice to avoid further slaughter of his people. Reports that he quit the Allies without warning were groundless. The King's 5 p.m. message reached London and Paris quickly, but after that the lines were cut. King Leopold carried out his decision. [In 1950, after years of exile in Switzerland, Leopold returned to Belgium, but popular opinion soon forced him to abdicate in favor of his son, Baudouin.]

Bulgaria

FEB. 3 **BALKAN TOUCH:** Travelers who visit the Balkans without losing a watch or wallet are regarded by Western Europeans as exceptions, by the Balkan people as geniuses. Balkan gentlemen even joke about the dexterity of their own restless fingers. One of their stories recounts that during a diplomatic dinner the British Ambassador missed his watch. Unembarrassed, the host announced: "I shall place a silver platter on the table, the lights will be out for a minute, and I expect the watch to be placed on the platter." When the lights came on, the platter contained six watches. According to another version, the platter was missing.

Colonel William Joseph ("Wild Bill") Donovan, U.S. observer inspecting countries at war or expecting war [and later founder of the wartime U.S. espionage agency, the OSS], arrived last fortnight in Sofia, Bulgaria, where he straightened his tie and went to call on the King. Leaving the Royal Palace, he discovered that his wallet containing passport, money and letters of introduction was missing. A search began and an appeal was made for its return. As "Wild Bill's" hour of departure arrived, the Orient Express was kept waiting 20 minutes while the Royal Palace was ransacked. Finally, he departed for Yugoslavia, Greece, Albania, Turkey minus wallet and passport. He still had his watch.

BOTTLE BATTLE: The U.S. Minister to Bulgaria is husky, MARCH 3 200-lb. George Howard Earle, a deceptively sleepy-looking native of Philadelphia's archconservative "Main Line" who in 1935 shocked his background by becoming the New Deal's liberal Governor of Pennsylvania. The conditions of World War II have often reminded the Minister of World War I, when he got the Navy Cross for risking his life to save the crew of his burning submarine chaser.

"Wild Bill" Donovan. His wallet is stolen at the palace. Page 147.   *U.S. Minister George Earle. He slugs a German in a nightclub brawl.*

In a Sofia café last week the Minister felt reminiscent and asked the band to play *Tipperary*. A sabre-scarred German in civilian clothes protested that the song was anti-German. The Minister replied that Bulgaria was neutral and that he would comport himself as he pleased. Thereupon the German threw a champagne bottle at the Minister, who got a six-inch bruise in his forearm. The Minister promptly socked the German in the face, knocking him down.

It was the Minister's third personal café tangle with the Axis since taking this job. "The incident was regrettable," he stated later, "but I saw no other course."

BOTTLE BATTLE (CONT'D): The diplomatic incident was re- MARCH 10 interpreted last week by the German in question. He proved to be a middle-sized battler with an adhesive patch on his

forehead. He introduced himself as Dr. Karl Becker, 42, a
metal type salesman. He admitted protesting to the management that it was unpleasant to hear an English tune repeated.
He said he had asked for a German waltz and that Mr. Earle,
unknown to him as the U.S. Minister, had then called him
a "dirty Nazi" several times and finally struck him with a
bottle. Dr. Becker said he had retaliated—but didn't say how
—and that Minister Earle had thereupon retired to an al-
cove and thumbed his nose.

Dr. Becker claimed that his forehead injury had been certified by a doctor as having been caused by a harder object
than a fist, said he had filed insult-and-injury charges against
Minister Earle.

Denmark

AUG. 11 **LANGUAGE LESSON:** In German-occupied Copenhagen a
newsdealer displayed a textbook, *English in 50 Hours*, under
a poster saying: LEARN ENGLISH BEFORE THE TOMMIES ARRIVE.
Nazi occupation authorities made him take down book and
poster. Next day the newsdealer displayed a new book, *German
in 50 Hours*, under a new sign: LEARN GERMAN BEFORE OUR
FRIENDS THE GERMANS DEPART.

Greece

APRIL 28 **80-DAY PREMIER:** For the second time this month a Balkan
Premier looked into the future and could see in it no solution
but his own destruction. Alexander Korizis read the hourly
tale of Greek and British retreats in the northern mountains,
heard the air-raid alarms as Nazi planes swooped over Athens,
chose to die by his own hand.

For 80 days Korizis had done his best to defend Greece,
killed himself when he felt he could do no more. Athens gave
the unsoldierly man who had filled a soldier's job the honor
of a hurried military funeral. As the procession neared the
cathedral an air raid started and the funeral service was read
to a crackling background of anti-aircraft fire. At week's end
amiable, Gable-eared King George II announced that he had

taken over the Government. That it could stop the flood of the Nazi invasion few could hope, but Britain's George VI's cousin George II evidently intended to stick to the end. [Greece fell to the Nazis on April 23 and King George fled to the island of Crete.]

HUNGER IN ATHENS: As early as mid-September men and NOV. 24 women fainting from hunger were a common sight in the streets of Athens, Salonika, Piraeus. Bread, wheat and flour were the first commodities the Germans confiscated. Later they took tomatoes, sent them to Libya where German troops were suffering from scurvy. Dried figs and raisins, now the staples of Greek diet, are also being commandeered, shipped to Germany. To a young woman who pleaded to be left one sack of potatoes after all the food in her house had been requisitioned, a German officer said politely: "I am sorry, but you must realize there are at present twice as many Greeks as we need here. Half must die. . . . I am unable to make an exception in your case."

Hungary

Hungary was an early ally of Hitler and Mussolini and was rewarded with a slice of Czechoslovakia in 1938. In the spring of 1941, Hungary joined the Axis as a full partner and took part in the German invasion of Russia in June. But before that happened her premier died under mysterious circumstances that indicated the alliance with Hitler was not altogether smooth.

END OF A TIGHTROPE WALK: From its perch on the towering APRIL 14 crags of Buda one dawn last week the Hungarian Foreign Office abruptly announced that Premier Count Paul Teleki had just died of a heart attack. Intimates of the Teleki family whispered that Count Teleki had taken poison. Finally doctors who examined the body signed a one-sentence communiqué: "Premier Teleki committed suicide at dawn."

Whether Count Teleki had committed suicide in despair—perhaps even to arouse his people—because he believed Hun-

The late Count Teleki (with Hitler). When the Germans ask him for too much, the premier takes poison at dawn.

gary was about to be completely engulfed by Hitler, or whether he had been killed by the Gestapo lest he initiate an Anti-Axis *coup d'état*, he died because his policy was fatal.

In the last two years Count Teleki had succeeded in getting back for Hungary large pieces of territory she once owned. But Count Teleki had to pay for these gains. Last year Hungary issued over 6,000 visas to Nazi fifth columnists entering the Balkans disguised as tourists. Premier Teleki also obliged by letting German fighting forces and supplies pass across Hungary on their way to browbeat Rumania and Bulgaria.

But when he was asked to help invade Yugoslavia, Teleki's unrelenting conscience toppled him off his tightrope. Last year U.S. Columnist Dorothy Thompson asked him: "What will you do if the Germans insist on using Hungary as a base of operations against another State?" He replied: "It will be Hungary's historic catastrophe. . . . I do not know. I shall have to make up my mind when the moment comes." The moment came last week.

International

JULY 28 **V FOR VICTORY:** A Belgian refugee named Victor de Laveleye first had the idea. In a shortwave broadcast from London to his countrymen he asked them to chalk the letter V (for *victoire*) in public places as a sign of confidence in their deliverance. That was six months ago. Last week the world awoke to the fact that something almost as frivolous as a parlor game might play an important part in international politics.

On a BBC shortwave program one night last month, a mystery voice named Colonel Britton plugged the V campaign in English, French, German, Dutch, Polish, Czech, Norwegian. He told people how to tap it out in Morse Code, three dots and a dash, recommended it as a signal for calling waiters, blowing auto horns and train whistles, knocking on doors. Soon that tat-tat-tat-too was heard all over Europe.

The Colonel told Europeans how to sit in cafés with their legs stretched out V-wise. He told them to wave to one another with the first two fingers of the hand spread V-wise. He told them to make the letter V with their knives and forks in restaurants, to set stopped clocks at five after eleven.

Like a fresh wind blowing in from the sea, the campaign spread over .Europe. V became *vrÿheid* (freedom) in Dutch, *vitezstvi* (victory) in Czech, *vitestvo* (heroism) in Serbian, and in Norwegian *ve vil vinne*, which means just what it sounds like in pidgin English.

First the Nazis tried to suppress or ignore the eternal tat-tat-tat-tooing. Growled Norway's Quisling Propaganda Minister Gubrand Lunde: "Don't think you will win the war by making silly noises in restaurants." Then Germany's Propaganda Chief Paul Joseph Goebbels had what he thought was a bright idea. On the principle of if-you-can't-lick-'em-join-'em, his ministry announced that V stood for *Viktoria*— Nazi victory.

The Netherlands

Germany seized the Netherlands on May 14, 1940, and the country was ruled thereafter by Nazi High Commissioner Arthur Seyss-Inquart. After the war he was tried at Nuremberg for war crimes, was found guilty and was executed on October 16, 1946.

JAN. 6 **IT BEATS THE DUTCH:** The placid Dutch find something to laugh at in everything, and Germany's failure to cross the English Channel is the subject of many jokes. After Commissioner Seyss-Inquart ordered a bookseller in the Hague to remove a picture of Queen Wilhelmina from his window, the bookseller complied, replaced it with a full-length photograph of Hitler. Around the Fuehrer's photograph he arranged a display of copies of a book by the famed Dutch swimming coach, Frau Braun. Title: *How Do I Learn to Swim?*

MARCH 17 **BEGGARS UNDERGROUND:** In none of her unwilling provinces does the Third Reich find stiffer, more stubborn resistance than in the Netherlands. Focus of stolid Dutch hatred of the Nazis is a secret society called "Les Gueux" (The Beggars), blamed by the Germans for recent widespread riots. Fortnight ago, breathing brimstone, a German military court sent 18 of the Beggars to face a firing squad, imprisoned 19 more, hoped without conviction it had broken the Beggars' back.

Formed in the 16th Century to harass Spanish conquerors, Les Gueux was revived last year by students of the Nazi-shuttered Universities of Delft and Leiden. It has become a truly underground organization, with many of its members hiding out in cellars of bomb-wrecked buildings.

With as many countersigns as a dime novel, the Beggars have methods as effective as they are penny-dreadful. Routine and deadly are sniping isolated German soldiers, drowning them in convenient canals. Cocktails spiked with sulfuric acid were served so freely that Germans no longer care to drink in public bars. Other favorites: poisoned pencils to be jabbed into Germans in crowds or the darkness of theatres, strychnine crystals dropped into plates of food from under the fingernails.

Spain

FEB. 24 **ALFONSO'S GESTURE:** Deathly ill with angina pectoris in Rome, dandified, talkative King Alfonso XIII added another egg to the Spanish omelet. He announced that he had abdicated his vacant throne in favor of his son, 27-year-old Don Juan, Prince of the Asturias (Crown Prince of Spain).

Don Juan is the third son of a family famed for its Bourbon nose and its unhappiness. Alfonso's Queen, Victoria Eugenia, carried hemophilia to two of her four sons. Hemophile Don Alfonso bled to death after an auto accident in Florida three years ago. Earlier, the youngest son, Don Gonzalo, also a bleeder, died after a minor car smash.

Second son Don Jaime never took the title of Crown Prince. No hemophile, Don Jaime was born deaf, was for years mute as well, although he now croaks intelligible Spanish, English, French. Always a model son, Don Juan has been a proper princeling. His only independent act to date was to volunteer for Franco's Army and to be firmly escorted over the border by the General's minions.

END OF A KING: For his Catholic Majesty, King Alfonso XIII MARCH 3 of Spain, the God in whom he devoutly believed had reserved the most painful death a man can die. Death came to him slowly last week with the agony that crept from his chest around his diaphragm, up into his neck and down to the tips of his slender, beautiful fingers. His physician had moved him from his bed to a chair to give him an injection, then had been afraid he could not survive the effort of being carried back to bed.

At the week's end, quiet as death in the chair he had not left for three days, Alfonso XIII received extreme unction. Still he lived on, breathing shallowly over the band of pain in his chest, dying with the dignity he had expected of himself as a king. He had never felt or behaved any other way.

Alfonso never questioned his aristocratic right to be a king, never ducked his regal responsibilities as he saw them. He had courage. In Paris once, when a bomb meant for him killed two of his carriage horses, he remarked that bombings were "only the risks of a king's business." In small things, too, he followed the pattern, was a gourmet, a dandy, a lady-killer —all with impeccable taste.

No dictator himself, he put his country in the hands of Dictator Miguel Primo de Rivera, ousted him too late to divert his people's resentment from himself and his office. When the Republicans sent him into exile in 1931 he drove his own car to Cartagena, jauntily boarded a cruiser. His exile changed nothing. He was merely a king on his travels. Almost daily, he studied long dispatches from Spain, awaited confidently his restoration as a constitutional monarch.

A guest of Spain was former King Carol of Rumania, who had ruled his country as a dictator for a decade following his return from exile in 1930. Deposed again by the military in 1940, Carol fled with his longtime mistress, Madame Magda Lupescu, leaving his son Michael on the throne.

MARCH 17 **HOHENZOLLERN HEGIRA:** It took a hurricane to get Carol Hohenzollern and Magda Lupescu out of Spain. Since the ex-King and his plump Pompadour fled from Rumania last year amid a hail of brickbats and the spat of lead against their armored train, the Spanish government has given them asylum but refused to let them push on to Portugal. "I am desperate," said chain-smoking Carol. "If I do not get a favorable reply to my application to leave Spain tomorrow, I will go on a hunger strike!"

Carol and Magda continued to eat heartily in the luxurious Andalusia Palace Hotel. Madame Lupescu continued to stroll in the gardens with her four dogs while Carol showed the same roving eye as ever for beauteous female bar-flies. No longer a great romance but the tie-up of a weak man and a strong woman, the Carol & Lupescu combine was again in a crisis which required all of her notable resources.

Last week she gathered up a purse containing her jewelry, and with Carol at the wheel stepped into his Mercedes "for a drive." They were soon bowling along in the suburbs of Seville, trailed as usual by a police car. Then Carol tramped full down on the accelerator. Over the Andalusian and Estremaduran plains they tore. The police were left far behind and, since most telephone and telegraph lines were still out of business due to a recent hurricane, there was no way to intercept the fugitive pair. They abandoned the automobile near the frontier, proffered fake passports and entered Portugal. [Carol and Mme. Lupescu eventually married in Brazil in 1947. He died in Portugal in 1953.]

Turkey

*By the spring of 1941, German conquests in the Balkans had
isolated Turkey strategically. Despite pressures from both the
Axis and the Allies, Turkey remained neutral through most of
the war, finally declaring war on Germany and Japan in January 1945, four months before the European fighting ended.*

BOMBS IN THE BAGGAGE: On the brink of Europe, facing MARCH 24
Asia across the shimmering Bosporus, the Hill of Pera is
crowned by one of the swankiest old hotels in the world, Istanbul's famed Hotel Pera Palace. Last week a great belch of
flame and smoke pushed out the whole first floor of the hotel
with a crunching, grunting roar. Inside the fiercely burning
hotel screaming chaos reigned.

Cables flashed all over the world that a bomb attack had
been made upon His Britannic Majesty's Envoy Extraordinary and Minister Plenipotentiary to Bulgaria, George William Rendel. The slight, dry and extremely shy British Minister was not killed, because at the moment of the explosion he
was upstairs. He had just entered the Pera Palace with an entourage of 50 persons, whom he had brought from Sofia because Britain had broken off relations with Bulgaria. It was
typical of George William Rendel that he went straight to
his room and began to check over personally his Legation's
more important papers. Other members of the British group
were signing the hotel register or chatting in the lobby when
the blast went off.

Said Vice Consul C. H. Page: "I was standing near the porters' desk, close to the luggage room, when there was a blinding flash. Long tongues of flame shot out from the luggage
room. I was thrown to the ground and got up to find myself
in a crater, out of which I was only able to look. . . . Lying
in the midst of the flames was a woman screaming terribly. I
rushed to carry her away and asked the Reverend Mr. Oakley to take her by the legs and help me. He shouted something at me which I could not at first understand. He repeated it and I was horrified to understand him to say: 'Her
legs are gone.' Somehow we got her out . . . where the ambu-

lance picked her up. Later I found she was Miss Armstrong."

Terese Armstrong, 23-year-old British Legation stenographer, had also lost an arm, but death did not come to her for more than 30 hours. Instantly killed were four Turks. The toll of wounded was 30, including Minister Rendel's private secretary, Miss Gertrude Ellis. His daughter and Legation Hostess, Ann Rendel, 21, lay dazed but uninjured on the floor. Her father sent her upstairs to get his personal documents.

Before it was bombed, the lobby of the Hotel Pera Palace. There was an infernal machine in the British baggage.

Out of the flaming Pera Palace darted Legation Clerk John Embury. He had suddenly remembered an extremely heavy and mysterious suitcase left with part of the Legation luggage in his room at another hotel. This was one of two suitcases noticed on the train to Istanbul, opened and found to contain soiled clothing and what looked like a big radio battery. The clerks could not find any Briton to whom these belonged, but they did not like to throw them away. Now Clerk Embury, with a hunch that the mysterious suitcase in his room contained an infernal machine, heaved it out the window onto an adjoining vacant lot. Turkish detectives cautiously opened it, found the "radio battery" to be a bomb.

The British aired no theory about the explosion. The bombs had been carried onto the train in Sofia under the noses of

Bulgarian detectives and Gestapo operatives. But, when asked if they thought Nazi agents were to blame, the British said that this seemed "too fantastic to be probable."

DOOR TO DREAMLAND: As the late afternoon sun fell gleaming on the domes and minarets of Istanbul one day this week, a bird of ill omen winged in from the west. It hovered above the city for a moment, then settled down at the airport. From the plane stepped dapper old Franz von Papen, German Ambassador to Turkey and the man who Adolf Hitler expects to open for him the door to the rich Middle East, Germany's dreamland for half a century. Turkey was about to learn whether von Papen meant to burst the door, pry it, or slip in the back way and unlock it. MAY 19

British Minister Rendel escapes a bomb by going to his room. Page 156.

German Ambassador von Papen spies his daughter in the arms of an Italian.

Turkey stands in the way of Germany's *Drang nach Osten.* If Germany could get around to the back door via Syria or Iraq, Turkey, encircled, would have to talk turkey. If the decision is to burst, Russia must be reckoned with, and Russia has promised Turkey not to join in any attack on her. In the meantime, in Ankara, Franz von Papen already had a jimmy in the doorjamb. He had laid plans for the "commercial encirclement" of Turkey, persuading such satrap states as Hungary, Rumania and Bulgaria to make economic agreements with her. Cut off from her best markets for tobacco and grains, Turkey had to accept. Such Nazi agreements have a way of corrupting by persuasion and bribery a nation's business element.

NOV. 10 **DIPLOMATIC INCIDENT:** In the crush at a Turkish People's Party ball the brocaded dress of Mrs. George Eric Mexia O'Donnell, wife of the British Naval Attaché, caught on the brocaded gown of Frau Franz von Papen, wife of the German Ambassador. Held tight, in the boomps-a-daisy position, the ladies waited in stony silence until a Turkish protocol officer uncoupled them.

NOV. 17 **AXIS IN A GARDEN:** A Turkish Army searchlight, poking its white eye into the garden of the German Embassy one night last week, disclosed a daughter of German Ambassador von Papen in the arms of a secretary of the Italian Embassy. Next day Ambassador von Papen, who had been watching the searchlight practice for professional reasons, packed his daughter off to Berlin, had her lover sacked.

MILESTONES

DIED: Willis Van Devanter, 81, Associate Justice of the Supreme Court from 1910 to 1937; of a heart attack; in Washington. One of the four conservative justices whose undeviating hostility to New Deal legislation led to the Administration's bill to enlarge the Court's membership, Van Devanter announced his retirement in the thick of the 1937 fight, thus helped defeat the President's bill.

MARRIED (for 50 years): Al Shean, 72, Bowery-voiced comic favorite in the old-time vaudeville team of (Positively) Mr. Gallagher and (Absolutely) Mr. Shean, uncle of the Marx Brothers; and Mrs. Johanna Shean, 70; celebrated in Manhattan a week after Comedian Shean observed his 60th year on the stage.

DIVORCED: Barbara ("Poor Little Rich Girl") Hutton, Countess Haug-witz-Reventlow, 28, five-and-dime store heiress ($20,000,000); from Danish Count Court Haugwitz-Reventlow, 44. Son Lance, 5, will spend most of the year with his mother.

MISCELLANY

JOKER: In Brooklyn, N.Y., Stanley Koprowski asked for a divorce because his wife insisted on telling him jokes in bed.

MEMORY: In Albany, the New York Bureau of Motor Vehicles got a letter from a lady who wanted a low license number because her memory was bad. She forgot to sign her name.

PURR: In Winchester, Va., Robert Wilt complained about the whine in his motor. Mechanics took out a kitten.

PEOPLE

"Names make news." In 1941 the following names made the following news:

Declared white-haired, deep-eyed Philosopher BERTRAND RUSSELL in Chicago: "Although I have preached pacifism all my life, I am convinced now for the first time that freedom cannot be preserved without military struggle. Liberty will die out over the world unless totalitarianism is defeated."

In Los Angeles court, Hedwig Eva Maria Kiesler Mandl Markey got her name legally changed to HEDY LAMARR.

To a thousand-throated freshmen yell of "take them off," SALLY RAND, at a Harvard smoker, thoughtlessly retorted, "I will if you will," danced in a blizzard of cast-off gents' furnishings.

AL CAPONE was served with papers in a $119,367 suit against him for unpaid taxes on illegal beer vintages of the '20s. To the marshal who served him at his walled Palm Island, Fla. estate, paretic Al pouted: "This won't make me feel very good." [Gangster Capone had gone to prison in 1932 for income tax evasion. He was released because of illness in 1939 and died from complications of syphilis in 1947.]

TOMMY MANVILLE, Manhattan's silver souvenir of the trivial '20s, took another wife— his fifth. The bride was Bonita Francine Edwards, 22, a blonde showgirl whom 47-year-old playboy Manville had met four days before. "We're glad we waited till we were sure," said the groom. The bride said frankly: "I'm not in love with Tommy—I'm just infatuated. I hope to fall in love with him after a while." [She left him 17 days later.]

Corporal WINTHROP ROCKEFELLER returned to Manhattan from maneuvers in North Carolina with advice on how to stay rich in the Army. "The best investment I ever made," he confided, "was not learning how to play craps or poker." [In 1966 Rockefeller was elected the first Republican governor of Arkansas since Reconstruction days.]

BRENDA DIANA DUFF FRAZIER, 20, perennial Glamor Girl No. 1, finally decided to wed her longtime escort, socialite Insuranceman John Sims ("Shipwreck") Kelly, 31, one-time pro football player. Brenda, whose allowance has been $1,000 a week, said they would live on Ship's insurance commissions, at least until she comes into her $3,500,000 next year.

Veteran SHIRLEY TEMPLE, 12, neither blonde nor chubby anymore, came out of her 14-month retirement to go to work on the first of four pictures, at a salary of $50,000 a picture.

GEORGE HERMAN ("BABE") RUTH walked into Manhattan's defense-bond headquarters in late December, asked for $100,000 worth. Informed that Treasury restrictions let him buy only $50,000 worth a year he left a $50,000 order for Jan. 2.

Tumbling only at the last two gates on the course, pert, pear-faced Cinemactress CLAUDETTE COLBERT skied off with first-place honors in Sun Valley's first guest slalom race of the season. Her time for the $3/8$-mile track: 1 min., 6 sec.

NAPOLEON BONAPARTE's pickled intestinal tract has been blown to glory, according to Britain's Surgeon Rear Admiral Gordon Gordon-Taylor. It went the way of all flesh when London's Royal College of Surgeons (and its Hunterian Collection) was bombed. Also gone: the tract of "one of the lady friends of RICHARD III."

BRIDGET ELIZABETH HITLER, the Fuehrer's Irish-born sister-in-law, went to work in Manhattan for British War Relief. Said she: "Adolf should be killed by slow torture, a little bit every day."

A furor in Newport over the dilapidation of MRS. JAMES JAY COOGAN'S empty mansion on aristocratic Catherine Street turned the spotlight on one of the world's wealthiest recluses: for 25 years Mrs. Coogan, now well into her eighties, has seldom left her Manhattan hotel suite in the daytime, but each night at 9 o'clock she goes down in the freight elevator heavily veiled, drives to her cubby-hole office in a loft building, puts in five hours administering her real estate fortune (which includes Coogan's Bluff, the Polo Grounds where the New York Giants play). She and her daughter, Jessie, do all the chores about their suite, which neither maid nor bellboy may enter. She never answers letters, for years has hardly glanced at a newspaper. But before her Tammany husband died in 1915 she spent eight years vainly trying to crash Newport society. The book found on her bedroom table in Newport was Burke's *Peerage*—for 1910.

Few days after his New York City bus strike had ended, Transport Union Chieftain MICHAEL J. QUILL was flagged to the curb by an angry policeman for steering his car down the wrong side of Riverside Drive. "Don't you know who I am?" complained Busman Quill. "Who?" said the cop. "I'm Mike Quill." "Never heard of you," grunted the cop, wrote out a ticket.

Ordered to report April 16 (a month earlier than expected) for his year's military service was bespectacled, Sabbath-observing, unmarried WILLIAM McCHESNEY MARTIN JR., 34, $48,000-a-year president of the New York Stock Exchange.

To a gag-minded Chicago couple who sent left-over wedding invitations to assorted bigwigs they didn't know, MR. and MRS. IRÉNÉE du PONT sent formal regrets, a solid silver coffee urn, creamer and sugar bowl.

The fabulously wealthy MAHARAJA OF JAIPUR, 29, joined the British forces in Egypt as a captain. At home he has a private army of his own, rides in a solid gold-and-silver coach.

THE THEATRE

JAN. 6 **"PAL JOEY"**—Since he came of age, John O'Hara has spent more time in nightclubs than many men have in bed. He has stayed till closing, seen all the sights, heard all the jargon. His short novel *Pal Joey* consists of the magnificently illiterate letters of a nightclub crooner and hoofer, an attractive, low and decidedly rubbery heel, describing his greedy world of mice and moola (women and money). Joey has now become the combination hero-and-heel of a bang-up George Abbott musicomedy, a profane hymn to the gaudy goddess of metropolitan night life.

As Joey, lean, dark Gene Kelly has a treacherous Irish charm, a sweet Irish tenor, a catlike dancing grace that makes vice almost as appealing as virtue. This impression is confirmed by Vivienne Segal as the loose Chicagoenne. The amours of these two are accompanied by great Richard Rodgers tunes: *I Could Write a Book, Bewitched, Bothered and Bewildered* (lyrics by Lorenz Hart). For those who can park their morals in the lobby, *Pal Joey* is a wow.

"MY SISTER EILEEN"—Several years ago *The New Yorker* ran some wry, funny sketches by Ruth McKenney describing the screwy plight of herself and her sister Eileen on first moving into Greenwich Village. Last week Eileen McKenney and her husband, Novelist Nathanael West *(Miss Lonelyhearts, The Day of the Locust),* were killed in an auto accident while returning to California from a Mexican hunting trip. And last week sister Ruth's sketches were the basis of a new Broadway comedy hit, directed by George S. Kaufman.

The fictional sisters from Columbus, Ohio move into a characteristic Greenwich Village mare's nest—a furnished, one-room basement apartment suggesting a cross between a Gothic crypt and a rummage sale. There are racking vibrations from a subway excavation just underneath. Drunks leer and bellow in the window.

In the end the girls (Shirley Booth and Jo Ann Sayers) seem well on their way to a saner life, but the comedy has conclusively proved the fact well known to residents that Greenwich Village is still full of loony threats and humors.

"ARSENIC AND OLD LACE" is absolutely top farce. A violent- JAN. 20 ly funny and batty murder play, it might be described, in the words of one of the cast, as what could be expected "if Strindberg had written *Hellzapoppin*."

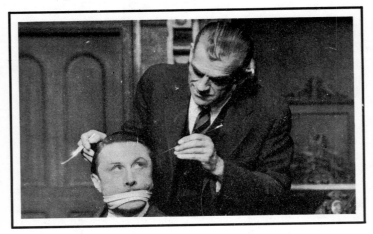

Boris Karloff (with Allyn Joslyn), in "Arsenic and Old Lace," is every bit as sinister as he was in "Frankenstein."

The story concerns a family in which insanity not only runs but "fairly gallops." Two sweet Brooklyn spinsters (Josephine Hull and Jean Adair) have taken to putting lonely old men out of their loneliness with a compound of elderberry wine, arsenic, strychnine and cyanide. In these obsequies they have been assisted by a potty nephew who regards himself as Teddy Roosevelt, the cellar as the Panama Canal, the bodies as yellow-fever victims, and the stairway to the second floor as San Juan Hill.

Another nephew, an international killer, brings home with him a shady plastic surgeon who has disguised him to look just like Boris Karloff of the movies. The part is played by Boris Karloff. Making his Broadway debut, he is every bit as sinister as he was in *Frankenstein*.

Playwright Joseph Kesselring, 39, got the idea for *Arsenic and Old Lace* by considering what would be the most unlikely thing his gentle grandmother might do.

FEB. 3 **GERTIE THE GREAT:** In Moss Hart's play, *Lady in the Dark*, a hard-working editress of a fashion magazine goes to get herself psyched. With that the play dissolves into a psychoanalytical circus with four revolving rings. The play has blandishing music by the German refugee composer Kurt Weill; and droll lyrics by Ira Gershwin. *Lady in the Dark* has swarthy Victor Mature, latest in Hollywood's series of almost outrageously beautiful young men. And Danny Kaye is very funny as a pansy fashion photographer who photographs a suit of armor with a blue chiffon wrapped around its metal neck.

But the secret of the show's success is its heroine. Gertrude Lawrence, known to her intimates as "Gertie" or "G," has long had reviewers dithering about her large wistful eyes, her tiptilted, crinkling nose, her mischievous smile, the huskiness of her voice, her exquisite back, the grace of her slim, long-legged, clothes-horse figure.

Gertie (aged 42), who offstage has never been in a psychoanalist's office, runs an emotional gamut from the romanticism of a school girl to the neurotic distress of a mature young woman. Naturally in *Lady in the Dark* she has no understudy. The show business knows no one who could fill the bill. [In the movie version the bill was filled by Ginger Rogers.]

APRIL 7 **"NATIVE SON"**—Playwright Paul Green has helped Negro Novelist Richard Wright turn his best-selling *Native Son* into by all odds the strongest drama of the season. The story is of Bigger Thomas (Canada Lee), a brooding violent Negro whose father is killed in a Southern race riot, who lives with his mother, sister and kid brother in one room in the Chicago slums. With his pals he indulges in fantasies of machine-gunning white enemies. Bigger gets a job as chauffeur to a wealthy landlord. The landlord's handsome daughter is a neurotic, alcoholic Fellow Traveler who adopts an intimate manner toward Bigger.

One night after Bigger has driven the girl home from a

party, he helps her stagger to her room. The girl's blind mother enters and, in desperately trying to prevent the girl from giving his presence away, Bigger accidentally smothers her to death. He is convicted, sentenced to the electric chair.

"WATCH ON THE RHINE"—Lillian Hellman, No. 1 U.S. APRIL 14 woman playwright (*The Children's Hour, The Little Foxes*) has written an uneven play concerning Nazism, but it is by far the best on the subject to date. There is not a single Nazi in it. It tells of the daughter of a dead American diplomat (Mady Christians), who returns from Europe, bringing with her the German engineer (Paul Lukas) she married 20 years before and their three children. Her husband has been an underground fighter against Hitler and he is about to sneak back into Germany with funds for the movement. His secret is discovered by a decadent Rumanian (George Coulouris), who threatens to inform the Nazi embassy. The German finally kills the blackmailer, says farewell to his wife and children, and leaves on his frightening mission.

"THE BEAUTIFUL PEOPLE"—Playwright Saroyan is still sell- MAY 5 ing his big but ancient idea—that living can be pretty fine if people can relax and savor it. *The Beautiful People* has a boozy, poetical father living with an adolescent son and daughter in a decaying mansion on a San Francisco hill. They are supported by a monthly pension check mistakenly addressed to a dead man. The daughter tends the mice in the house. Brother writes "books"—each consisting of a single pregnant word. One "book" reads "tree."

A shy official arrives bent on canceling the pension check, but is so beglamored by the fey, bemused life of the household that he arranges to have the payments continued. Notwithstanding its whimsical deadweight, the inventive, germinal quality in Saroyan is one of the most fertile forces in the U.S. theatre.

CRITIC'S CHOICE: The New York Drama Critics' Circle, polling its annual vote for the season's best American play, last week got into its usual politico-dramatic wrangle. Six ballots and three hours of electioneering produced no decision between Lillian Hellman's *Watch on the Rhine* and William

Saroyan's dreamy *The Beautiful People*, which had opened the night before. On the seventh ballot Lillian Hellman's *Watch on the Rhine* triumphed.

JUNE 9 **END OF THE ROAD:** Broadway last week reached the end of *Tobacco Road*. After seven and a half years, the 3,180th and last performance of history's longest continuously running drama was signalized by no valedictory speeches or mortuary effects. Last week Playwright Jack Kirkland (who adapted the play from Erskine Caldwell's novel) announced that he would give several of *Tobacco Road*'s props—a wagon wheel, a tree branch, a shack—to the Smithsonian Institution.

NOV. 17 **"BLITHE SPIRIT"**—Last spring Noel Coward, erasing the war from his mind, stole out of bomb-scarred London to a quiet Welsh country house and in five days tossed off an "improbable farce." At the same time, he pulled off a nearly impossible job. One stage ghost was usually a little more than even Shakespeare could handle; Coward has done handsomely with two. One sprightly stage joke usually gives a playwright a good first act; Coward has wispily but brightly spun out his joke through a whole evening. *Blithe Spirit* can be aptly tagged with a single word: it is gay.

MILESTONES

DIVORCED: Gypsy Rose Lee (Rose Louise Hovick), 27, No. 1 U.S. stripper; from Robert Mizzy, 35, Manhattan dental-supply manufacturer; after four years of marriage; in Chicago. Grounds: he knocked her down twice.

BIRTHDAY: Man o' War, glamor race horse of American thoroughbreds, longtime champion sire; in fine fettle; his 24th; at Faraway Farm, near Lexington, Ky.

MISCELLANY

SNOWDROP: In Winter, Wis., Dr. H.A. Smith rushed a semi-conscious woman to the hospital before she could give birth to a baby. On the way, he skidded into a ditch, wrecked his car. He hailed another car and took her to the hospital in it. At the hospital, it was discovered that the baby had already been born. Meanwhile, Farmer Joseph Siefert, on his way to town, saw something in the snow near the doctor's abandoned car. It was the newborn baby. He wrapped it in a blanket and rushed it to town. "We must have dropped him in the snow," announced the incredulous Dr. Smith. "The baby hasn't even developed a sniffle."

SELECTED SERVICE: In Des Moines, a young man asked the draft authorities if he could do his year's training by correspondence. He was, he explained, "allergic to beans and prunes."

$$\boxed{\textbf{SPORT}}$$

NOT-SO-SIMPLE SIMON: When Heavyweight Champion MARCH 31 Joe Louis embarked on his fight-a-month campaign last fall, Broadway wags dubbed his opponents the Bum-of-the-Month Club. Last week, in Detroit's Olympia Stadium, Louis took on his pushover for March: 255-lb., 26-year-old Abe Simon of Richmond Hill, Long Island.

Simon was no more worthy a challenger than Red Burman, knocked out by Louis in five rounds in January, or Gus Dorazio, knocked out in two rounds in February. [Louis knocked out one more, Tony Musto, in nine rounds in April.]

"Simple Simon," sneered the experts, and bet 4-to-1 that Louis would polish him off before the end of the fifth round. But round after round Simon still stood on his feet, and the crowd went wild. How much punishment could this behemoth take? In the 13th round they had their answer. Dazed, dead-armed, after paralyzing rights to the jaw had floored him a third and a fourth time, the challenger suddenly turned his back on the champion, staggered over to the ropes. His fellow townsmen cheered the most exciting fight of the year, agreed Simon should be expelled from the Bum-of-the-Month Club.

UNFIT: A noteworthy series of sports news items was last week APRIL 7 completed:

¶ On Feb. 8, at the Boston Athletic Association track meet, pony-legged Gregory Rice, Notre Dame '39, ran two miles in 9 min., 3.3 sec., for his twelfth consecutive victory in two years of big-time distance racing.

¶ On Feb. 15, at the New York Athletic Club Games, Greg Rice set a new world's record for two miles: 8:53.4.

¶ On Feb. 22, at the National A.A.U. championship meet, Greg Rice set a new world's record for three miles: 13.51.

¶ Last fortnight, at Chicago's *Daily News* Relays, last big invitation track meet of the indoor season, Greg Rice ran two

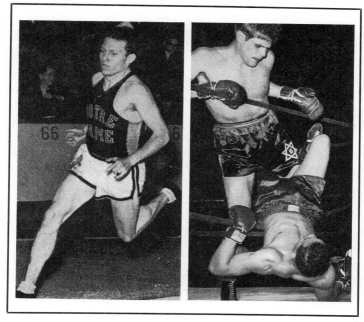

Greg Rice runs the fastest two miles, but is physically unfit for the Army.

Joe Louis hangs over the ropes, but still beats Buddy Baer. Page 170.

miles in 8:51.1—the fastest two miles ever run, indoors or out. [This record was broken in France in 1965 by Michel Jazy, who ran two miles in 8.22.6.]

Last week, four days after his record-smashing race, 25-year-old Greg Rice, recently voted foremost U.S. amateur athlete, was declared physically unfit for the U.S. Army. Reason: triple hernia.

APRIL 21 **FIRST FOURSOME:** Last week golf's bigwigs announced the establishment of a Hall of Fame. Patterned after baseball's Hall of Fame at Cooperstown, N.Y., golf's shrine will stand on a hillock overlooking the Augusta National Golf course at Augusta, Ga. First foursome to be immortalized in bronze: Bobby Jones, Francis Ouimet (pronounced we met), Walter Hagen, Gene Sarazen.

MAY 12 **NAME CHANGE:** First crack out of the box the new owners of the Boston National League Baseball Club last week changed its nickname back from The Bees to the Braves. Its previous nicknames: Doves, 1907-12; Bean Eaters, 1876-1907.

WRIGHT THIS TIME: It took a lot of courage to stick to Whirlaway. Bred at Millionaire Warren Wright's farm in the heart of the Blue Grass, he is a handsome golden chestnut colt with a tail that almost sweeps the ground. But Whirlaway has inherited a tendency to run out (veer away from the inside rail) at the turns. That trait cost him several important races last year. But last week, in the Kentucky Derby, Whirlaway proved that he was a stretch-running fool. He not only finished eight lengths in front, but ran the mile and a quarter in 2 min., 1 $^2/_5$ sec., $^2/_5$ of a second faster than the Kentucky Derby record set by Twenty Grand just ten years ago. Said Jockey Eddie Arcaro, grinning from ear to ear: "He's the runnin'est horse I ever rode."

GREENBERG TRADES UNIFORMS: Last week in his 1,049th MAY 19 game with the Detroit Tigers, 30-year-old Hank Greenberg smashed out two home runs, drove in a third run to lick the New York Yankees 7 to 4, then turned in his uniform. Next morning, in an old corset factory in downtown Detroit, Henry Greenberg, baseball's highest-paid player ($55,000 a year), was inducted into the U.S. Army.

THIS IS FAST: Behind a racing car at Bakersfield, Calif., French- MAY 26 man Alfred Letourner, crack six-day bike racer, last week reached a speed of 108.92, a new world's record for a motor-paced bicycle rider. Even though using an oversize pedal gear, Letourner's feet were going around about 2 $^1/_2$ times a second.

BABY BAER: In Washington's Griffith Stadium one night last JUNE 2 week 25,000 fight fans yelled themselves limp. It was the first round of Washington's first world-championship heavyweight fight, and there, hanging over the ropes head first, was Joe Louis, the champ. The boxer who had dumped him onto the ring apron was 25-year-old Buddy Baer, baby brother of one-time champion Max Baer. [Max Baer, who won the heavyweight title from Primo Carnera in 1934, enlisted in the U.S. Army in 1942. He died of a heart attack in 1959.]
Baby Baer in the fifth round brought the crowd to its feet

again when he opened a gash over Louis' left eye. With blood streaming down his cheek for the first time in his career, the champion went after Baer with the savageness for which he is famed. In the sixth round he weakened the giant with chopping rights & lefts, then felled him as though he were a redwood tree. At the count of seven, Baer staggered to his feet, only to be toppled again with another right to the jaw. Just as the time-keeper counted ten, Baer's gloves slowly left the canvas. Referee Arthur Donovan motioned the fighters to continue. Once more Baer toppled to the floor—out.

JUNE 16 **CLEAN SWEEP:** Warren Wright's Whirlaway, with Eddie Arcaro up, won the Belmont Stakes at New York's Belmont Park. Winner of this year's Kentucky Derby and Preakness Stakes, Whirlaway is the fifth horse in the history of U.S. turf to win America's three major races for three-year-olds. [The others: Sir Barton (1919), Gallant Fox (1930), Omaha (1935), War Admiral (1937).]

Billy Conn unwisely aims a punch at the Champ, before he goes down under a barrage of rights and lefts from Louis. Page 172.

JUNE 30 **HEARTBREAKER:** On the anniversary of the Battle of Water-loo, last week, Emperor Joe Louis met the 17th challenger for his world's heavyweight crown: 23-year-old Billy Conn of Pittsburgh. On the night of the fight 55,000 fans crammed into Manhattan's Polo Grounds.

In the fourth, The Kid began to tattoo the champion with lightning-quick pokes. Four rounds later the rapier began to sting. Young Billy began to maul the Big Boy. By the end of the twelfth round, Conn's sustained attack had the crowd on its feet, yelling.

Aglow with confidence, Conn came out for the 13th round. "I got you, Joe," he had taunted. But the champ was not the champ for nothing. And The Kid was still a kid. Instead of continuing to jig & jab, Conn did just what he was warned not to do: he sailed into shufflin' Joe, began swapping punches. This was what the cool-headed champ had been waiting for. Before the swaggering youngster knew what had struck him, he was staggered under a bombardment of rights & lefts. Two seconds before the bell, he was curled up on the canvas for a count of ten.

Heartbroken, despite the $77,000 he had earned, young Conn sobbed: "I lost my head and a million bucks."

STREAK ENDED: As it must to all streaks, an end came at JULY 28 last to Joe Di Maggio's batting spree. In a night game in Cleveland's vast Municipal Stadium, just two months and two days after starting the longest batting streak in the history of major-league baseball, Joe went hitless.

In 56 successive games, the crack Yankee Clipper had gone

Record-breaker Joe DiMaggio with his wife Dorothy Arnold. For 45 consecutive games he has made a hit. Now he will try for 56.

to bat 223 times, had made 91 hits (including 15 homers, four triples, 16 doubles) for a total of 160 bases. Against 42 pitchers, he had struck out only five times.

Said Joe, expelling his long-held breath: "I'm tickled to death it's all over."

SEPT. 29 **BLACK MOSES:** Next Monday night, 27-year-old Joe Louis is to defend his Heavyweight Championship—for the 19th and maybe the last time.

This time the challenger for Joe Louis' crown is a student of yoga, 26-year-old Lou Nova who has boasted that he is a Man of Destiny, that he will knock out the Champion with his "cosmic punch."

Probably about 50,000,000 radio-fight fans will listen in for good reason. (Except for President Roosevelt's last two broadcasts, Joe Louis' prize fights have attracted the largest audiences in U.S. radio history.) Not only is Lou Nova about as likely to beat Joe Louis as any challenger now afoot, but even if Joe Louis wins—it may be Joe's last fight. Recently re-classified 1-A by a Chicago draft board, the Brown Bomber will probably join the Army next month. [Louis enlisted as a private in 1942. He held his title until his retirement from the ring in 1948.]

If Joe Louis' fistic career terminates next week, ten fabulous years of a big, coffee-colored boy's life will end. Ten years ago, Joe Louis Barrow was a Detroit ragamuffin, toting ice for fly-by-night ice-men to earn a few pennies to keep his feet in shoes. Transplanted from an Alabama cotton patch at the age of 12, the strapping, slow-thinking boy, only two generations away from slavery, had found himself a misfit in city schools where his classmates were nearly half his age. He never got beyond the fifth grade.

On city streets, Joe got along better. When his gang started something, Joe finished it. One day in 1931, one of his pals persuaded him to go to the Brewster St. Recreation Center (a settlement house in the heart of Detroit's "black bottom"). There Joe learned to box. At first, he disliked it, but within a year, Joe Barrow was the best fighter in the Center.

Two years later Joe reached the finals in the light-heavyweight division of the National Amateur boxing championships at Boston. By that time Joe had come to the attention of dignified, college-bred John Roxborough (later indicted and charged with connections with the numbers racket). "What's your name, boy?" he asked the shy, shambling kid. "Joe Louis Barrow," the kid replied. "That's too long, I'll just call you Joe Louis."

Roxborough gave Julian Black, Chicago ex-gambling-house operator, a half-interest in Joe. Roxborough grew fond of the good-natured, easy-going lad, took him home, taught him to brush his teeth, take a bath, eat with a knife & fork. He got Joe a job as an unskilled laborer at the Ford Motor plant, dressed him in castoffs, gave him $5 a week for spending money.

By the time Louis climbed into the ring for his first big fight, against giant Primo Carnera, he was a living legend to his people: a black Moses leading the children of Ham out of bondage. Today, after four years of monopolizing the world's heavy-weight championship, he is not only the idol of his race but one of the most respectable prize-fighters of all time. He restored the world's championship to the gate and almost the vigor that it had in Dempsey's day.

He did other notable things: he took on all comers, fought 20 fights in four years, was never accused of a fixed fight, an unfair punch, a disparaging comment. "I want to fight hon-'est," he has often told newsmen, "so that the next colored boy can get the same break I got. If I 'cut the fool,' I'll let my people down."

Because of his dead-pan, most white folks assume that Joe Louis is a lugubrious fellow. Actually, he is as mischievous as a child. "When he was a kid," his mother grins, "I near wore his backside out with a strap."

SUNDAY PUNCH: If it was really Joe Louis' last fight, it was OCT. 6 fought like a summary of his ring career. He knocked out Lou Nova with a murderous right, in the sixth round, before 60,000 chilly and disappointed people in New York City's Polo Grounds. They had come, if not to see Joe licked, at least to see a fight between equals. But like 46 men before him, Nova was just a tackling dummy at the finish.

BUMS v. BOMBERS: Last Thursday, at 5:08 p.m., bedlam broke loose in Brooklyn. For 21 long years, Brooklynites had waited for this moment. Their beloved Dodgers ("Our Bums") had just clinched the National League pennant in Boston. Bookies last week quoted odds of 2-to-1 on the Yankees to win the World Series for the fifth time in six years.

OCT. 13 **THERE GOES THE SERIES:** Brooklyn fans will never forget the scene. In the ninth inning of the fourth game of last week's World Series, with Brooklyn leading 4 to 3 and two Yankees already out, Dodger Catcher Mickey Owen muffed the ball with which Hugh Casey had just struck out Tommy Henrich. Before Owen recovered the ball, Henrich reached first. Before Casey recovered his composure, the Yankees scored four runs to win, 7 to 4. In the wrought-up crowd fans fainted, some wept.

Next day, leading three games to one, the Yankees mopped up the disheartened Dodgers, 3 to 1, won the championship for the fifth time in six years.

BOOGIE-WOOGIE BOMBER: The sporting press has found "little Joe Louis," lightweight Ray Robinson. Young Robinson, a Harlem "hep-cat" just a half-inch under six feet tall, is neither little nor does he bear much resemblance to the world's heavyweight champion. But the way the skinny 139-pounder brushed off onetime Welterweight Champion Fritzie Zivic in a ten-round match at Manhattan's Madison Square Garden last week showed that another Negro was punching his way to ring history. In 115 fights, amateur and professional, Robinson has never been licked. [When Robinson retired in 1965, after losing a title fight by decision to Joey Archer, he had won 173 fights, lost 19, been middleweight champion five times.]

NOV. 24 **MOST VALUABLE:** Second-generation Italians made a clean sweep of U.S. baseball honors in the season just past. Joe Di Maggio, native of San Francisco's Fisherman's Wharf, was voted the American League's Most Valuable Player. Dolph Camilli, another San Franciscan, was voted Most Valuable in the National League. Phil Rizzuto, New York Yankee shortstop, was the outstanding rookie of the year.

$$\boxed{\text{ART}}$$

MOUNTAIN CARVER: Last week fog swirled over the Black Hills of South Dakota; over the sides of Mount Rushmore, ice formed a dripping glaze over four gigantic stone faces. Mount Rushmore had been finished long ago, but the granite visages carved out of its granite made it look unfinished: under their chins the mountainside fell away in a gigantic dribble of scree. And now the figures of these four great U.S. Presidents—Washington, Jefferson, Lincoln and Theodore Roosevelt—would never be finished by their creator. For the man who had devoted nearly a quarter of his life to the task of hewing them from the mountainside, Gutzon Borglum, lay dead of a heart attack in a Chicago hospital.

Together, these faces, 60 feet high, were the largest piece of sculpture ever wrought in the Christian era. For 14 years a crew of workmen, with dynamite, steam shovels and compressed-air drills, had patiently chipped their features, removing 400,000 tons of granite in the process. It would take 108 million years before wind, rain, freezes and thaws could wear them back into the stone from which they emerged.

AMERICAN LOUVRE: This week the U.S. Government got a present: the largest marble building in the world. The building, which cost $15,000,000, was the National Gallery of Art. The masterpieces that went with it were valued at $50,000,000. The donor was the late Andrew W. Mellon, onetime Secretary of the Treasury. To Collector Mellon's pictures and sculptures, 5-10-25-cent Storeman Samuel Henry Kress two years ago had added another $30,000,000 worth. Even the addition of the Widener Collection (12 to 50 million dollars worth) by Philadelphia's Horse-racing Joseph E. Widener, would leave plenty of room for future donations.

Like the Louvre in Paris, Washington's National Gallery was intended to include only the works of the past. A rigid rule excluding the work of all artists who had not been dead for 20 years tabooed all moderns. Biggest contribution ever made to a government by a private individual, Andrew Mellon's marble treasure house might well grow some day into one of the world's greatest national museums.

APRIL 14 **BENTON HATES MUSEUMS:** Art museums last week caught an egg squarely on the ear. It was hurled with a will by tough, swart little Missouri Painter Thomas Hart Benton. Growled he: the average museum was "a graveyard run by a pretty boy with delicate wrists and a swing in his gait. . . . Do you want to know what's the matter with the art business in America? It's the third sex and the museums. Even in Missouri we're full of 'em. . . . I'd have people buy the paintings and hang them in privies or anywhere anybody had time to look at 'em. . . . Nobody goes to museums. I'd like to sell mine to saloons, bawdy houses, Kiwanis and Rotary Clubs and Chambers of Commerce—even women's clubs."

JUNE 9 **MAROONED ON THE LEFT BANK:** In France, awaiting papers and passage to the U.S., were 74-year-old Abstractionist Wassily Kandinsky, Surrealist Marc Chagall. Caught by the German invasion of The Netherlands was Max Beckmann. In London, Austrian Expressionist Oskar Kokoschka was trying to find a boat that would take him to the U.S. Making the best of it in Unoccupied France were Painters Raoul Dufy and Jean Lurçat. Henri Matisse was in seclusion in his studio at Nice. Still sticking to their beloved Paris, Hitler or no, were Pablo Picasso, Georges Braque, Georges Rouault, Marcel Duchamp. To them the German army of occupation had extended special privileges, including an extra ration of coal. Though Nazi Propaganda Minister Goebbels still frowned officially on "degenerate art," German officers were reported buying up all the French modern art they could lay hands on. [Duchamp came to the U.S. in 1942.]

JUNE 16 **DEAR OLD DADDY:** Whistler's famed *Portrait of the Artist's Mother* has canonized Mother; but what about Father? The National Father's Day Committee has searched for two years for a painting that would bring Father out of the nowhere and into the here. The committee checked over 3,000 paintings by artists from Giotto to Grant Wood, last week—with

Father's Day just ahead—gave up the search. "It appears," said the committee, "that the father as a subject for great art has been completely overlooked or suppressed by every great painter in the modern art world."

MURAL PICKETED: Cheyenne Indians, in complete tribal re- JUNE 23
galia, picketed the U.S. post office at Watonga, Okla. Inside was a mural depicting their ancestors under the reign of
Chief Roman Nose. Explained 71-year-old Chief Red Bird:
"Breech clout too short, look like Navajo. Roman Nose's
baby look like stumpy pig. No good. It stinks."

SAINTS AND DEMONS: The most degenerate of all degen- NOV. 10
erate European artists (according to Hitler) is having his
biggest exhibition in the U.S. A one-man show of Oskar
Kokoschka opened last week in Manhattan—full of pictures of the Freudian subconscious which Nazi officials have
condemned and exiled as politically dangerous.

In Vienna collectors paid as high as $8,000 for his grim
portraits and angrily smudged landscapes. When Hitler invaded Czechoslovakia, Kokoschka, caught in Prague, flew to
England. From his English patrons, he still gets £300 ($1,200)
a canvas.

Moody, restless and erratic, Painter Kokoschka continu-
ally complains that he can't find attractive women models
who have souls. Once in the early '20s, he was so discouraged
trying to find a woman he liked that he commissioned a manufacturer to make him a life-size doll, giving exact specifi-
cations as to form, color of hair, eyes, etc. When the doll
arrived, Expressionist Kokoschka was so disappointed he
took it out into the back yard and burned it, meanwhile
fending off a squad of policemen who were convinced he was
removing traces of a murder.

ARTISTS' RATIONS: Painters, like other businessmen, now DEC. 1
face priorities. Foreseeing virtual confiscation of certain key
materials like cadmium and chromium pigments, Manhattan's American Artists' Professional League (2,200 members)
recently petitioned Washington for cooperation in keeping
artists supplied with their annual ration of paint (about a
gallon apiece).

Canvas, always imported from Ireland and Belgium, is the biggest problem. With Belgian linen cut off, most artists are making shift with domestic cotton substitutes. (The U.S. does not grow the right kind of flax for high-grade linen canvas.) Brushes made from soft Russian sable bristles are plentiful. But stiff German-dressed South American ox bristles and "camel hair" (obtained not from camels but from Russian squirrels) are practically unobtainable.

U.S. artists have already begun hoarding against impending shortages. Most practical plan for saving: to economize on variety by reducing the artist's palette from a possible maximum of 400 colors to 13 basic pigments. Sculptors at first were smug: no one expects a shortage in stone, wood or plaster. But last fortnight they got a jolt: a Government order specifying that after Jan. 1 U.S. foundries could cast no more sculpture in bronze.

MILESTONES

DIED: Henri Bergson, 81, French philosopher, member of the French Academy, Nobel prizewinner; in Paris. A month before his death Professor Bergson, whose philosophy of "creative evolution" had an enormous vogue before World War I, rose from his bed, declining the Vichy Government's offered exemption, renounced his honors and posts, went to register as a Jew.

SUED FOR DIVORCE: Harry Bouton ("Blackstone the Magician"), 56; by Mildred Rose Phinney Bouton, 34, assistant whom he had often sawed in halves; in Centerville, Mich.

BORN: To Yankee outfielder Joe Di Maggio and ex-Cinemactress Dorothy Arnold Di Maggio; a son, Joe III, 7 lb. 11 oz.; in Manhattan.

DIED: Simon Guggenheim, 73, head of the Guggenheim mining interests, of pneumonia; in Manhattan. With his wife he established the John Simon Guggenheim Memorial Foundation with a $3,000,000 gift in 1925 as a memorial to a dead son, gave it another $1,000,000 in 1936.

MISCELLANY

PARTYLINE: In Manorville, L.I., static on a party line was eliminated when telephone company investigators persuaded a woman to stop using her receiver as a darning egg.

APPEAL: From the North Adams (Mass.) *Transcript*: "Betsy Earle's parents wish to announce that she is suffering from worms, and they urgently urge that, in the interest of her continued good health, the townspeople discontinue the practice of feeding her candy."

YOU CAN'T MISS IT: In Boston, a motorist followed a stranger's directions, wound up driving in a subway tunnel.

$$\text{SCIENCE}$$

GLACIAL CALLING CARDS: Last fortnight and again last week JAN. 6 earthquakes shook the northeastern U.S., from Canada to Philadelphia. As quakes go, they did not amount to much, but near the epicenters (about 100 miles north of Boston) they were the most violent ever recorded with modern instruments in solid old New England. Chimneys tumbled, dishes and canned goods fell from shelves, walls cracked, furniture slid. Only one person was killed and little serious damage was done.

Quakes of last fortnight's kind are calling cards left by the huge ice masses which covered parts of the U.S. in the last Glacial Age. That ice was half a mile to two miles thick, weighed two to eight billion tons per square mile. The great weight squeezed the land below, pressed it down. Since the ice retreated northward 15,000 to 25,000 years ago, the ground once under it had been springing back upward, like a dry sponge after a weight on top of it is taken away. This recovery takes place as a series of intermittent jerks; when one occurs it makes a minor quake.

PRAISE FOR THE EARTHWORM: A onetime Texas physician and surgeon named George Sheffield Oliver is the author of a three-volume treatise on earthworms, a subject on which he is acknowledged to be the world's No. 1 authority. His story was told last week in *Nature Magazine*. Constantly and voraciously, earthworms eat earth, dead leaves, decaying organic material of all sorts. The waste material they throw off is one of the richest of all plant foods. Moreover, their tunnels air the soil and make fine watering tubes. After reading in Darwin that a healthy English acre ought to have about 2,500,000 earthworms, Dr. Oliver started propagating them, colonizing his grounds.

His trees, flowers and garden prospered. Neighbors asked him for his secret, but Oliver would not tell. Wealthy people began paying him big money to beautify their estates, pep up their gardens. They cared not how he did it. Oliver branched out to public parks, eventually to $10,000-and-up jobs for cinema stars in Hollywood, and rolled up a tidy fortune.

He is still a big worm operator. Worms are hermaphrodites; all healthy adults lay eggs by the score, and Oliver gathers them by the million. Packed in damp peat moss, they can be shipped any distance. Oliver is the only man who has successfully crossbred any of the 1,100 species of earthworms. For feeding chickens, frogs, etc., he produced a meaty hybrid ten inches long.

MARCH 10   **UNSECRET WEAPON:** Last December, as London lay almost helpless under Nazi air attacks by night, Air Chief Marshal Sir Hugh ("Stuffy") Dowding predicted with mysterious confidence, "Night bombing will be greatly reduced by spring." Since then repeated reports have come from England of Nazi raiders brought down in full darkness. Last week a clue to this amazing prediction and promise of fulfillment was provided by the U.S. Patent Office.

It granted to Joseph Lyman of Huntington, N.Y. a patent for a machine which uses radio beams to locate a plane in darkness or fog, plot its course through the skies on an indicator like a television screen. Anti-aircraft fire can thus be directed, it is thought, with even more accuracy than in present daylight firing.

Joseph Lyman's invention was supposed to be a big secret. But details were still available to anyone at the U.S. Patent Office this week. [The invention was radar, which was developed originally in Britain.]

MAY 5   **A LOOK AT A MOLECULE:** The first clear picture ever made of a molecule was last week shown on a lantern slide. Some of the ablest U.S. scientists—members of the American Philosophical Society—gaped in awe, for they were seeing something never before distinctly seen by man.

The slide was shown by Wendell Meredith Stanley of the Rockefeller Institute for Medical Research. It was a picture of the virus which causes the mosaic disease of tobacco plants, one of the largest molecules known to chemists. It is a rod-shaped structure, about 40,000,000 times the size of the hydrogen atom (basic unit of atomic and molecular weight). But even at this size it could be photographed only with the recently developed electron microscope, which by using electron beams instead of light can magnify images 50 times greater than the best light microscopes.

FOLKLORE MAN: In Cambridge, England, last week died an MAY 19 old man whose work had left a lasting mark on science, literature and the history of Western thought. It had been Sir James Frazer's lifelong task to collect the magic, myth and folklore of all peoples and times into a tumultuous, enthralling encyclopedia. *The Golden Bough* is one of the 20th Century's most influential books.

Frazer demolished the Rousseauist notion that primitive man was blithe and free. Harassed by taboos at every hand, besieged by demons, snarled in ritual, the savage was far more vexed than civilized man with his traffic lights, time clocks, income taxes.

WAR IN THE LABORATORIES: "In modern warfare, one hun- MAY 26 dred trained physicists may be more valuable than one million infantrymen." This week not 100 but some 1,500 U.S. physicists—one out of every four—are absorbed with problems of defense. Last week the National Defense Research Committee released a few cautious details on what it was up to.

Luridest field of NDRC work is atomic power—smashing of atoms to release the locked-up voltages which hold them together. NDRC's Chairman Vannevar Bush expects nothing to come of this work, but there is a slight chance—and that chance has such terrifying industrial and military implications that no nation can risk neglect of the problem. "I hope they never succeed in tapping atomic power," says Bush. "It will be a hell of a thing for civilization."

OUT OF THIN AIR: Literally out of thin air, the turbo-super- AUG. 18 charger emerged last week as a menace to Hitler's power. It emerged too from 22 years of dusty neglect as a belated triumph for its inventor, Dr. Sanford Alexander Moss, 68, who developed the turbo long ago to help beat the Kaiser.

As flyers in World War I reached for higher & higher altitudes, they found their engines losing power. Reason: atmos-

Inventor Moss and part of his turbo-supercharger for aircraft. The next high-altitude problem is to supercharge the pilots.

pheric oxygen is as vital an aviation fuel as gasoline. Fox-bearded Dr. Moss's idea: to harness energy which would otherwise be wasted—the engine's flaming exhaust gases.

When Moss introduced his turbo in 1918, he met the "glassy eye," as he recalls, of skeptical industrialists and Army brass hats. He took them to the top of Pikes Peak, where a 350 h.p. Liberty motor gave only 230 h.p. in the thin air at 14,000 feet. When Moss cut in his supercharger, the motor roared at 356 h.p. Then came the Armistice. Moss's supercharger was forgotten by almost everyone.

Last week, G.E. was completing a windowless, $5,000,000 supercharger plant at Everett, Mass. and announced plans for a similar $20,000,000 plant at Fort Wayne, Ind. This device explains the R.A.F.'s admiration for its lend-leased Flying Fortress, since it helps keep them on top of their enemies. Next problem is to supercharge the pilots.

SEPT. 15 **PEOPLE, GOLDFISH:** Last week U.S. psychologists reported:
❡ Goldfish remember better in cold water than in warm water.
❡ Young children grow faster mentally in the cool fall and winter months than in the warmer seasons.
❡ Man's intellect is at its sharpest between 35 and 40, according to Professor Harvey Christian Lehman, 52.

RADIO

CROSSLEY LOOKS AT 1940: The critical standards of radio JAN. 27
are as simple as a stone ax. The program that attracts the
biggest audience is the best program. The highest accolade
that radio can offer is conferred on aerial shows by a statisti-
cal research organization, Crossley.

New to the big ten for 1940 (announced last week) were
the deftly written serial *The Aldrich Family* (sixth), the
schmalz of Band Leader Kay Kyser (ninth), the soap-opera
One Man's Family (tenth). Beating the graven image Charlie
McCarthy by a whisker, Jack Benny led the pack for 1940.

Others in Crossley's peerage: *Fibber McGee & Molly*,
the *Lux Radio Theater*, Bob Hope, Kate Smith, Major
Bowes.

SPEECHLESS SKIER: Last week with a good deal of hoopla MARCH 3
NBC announced that Champion skier Torger Tokle had
agreed to broadcast his sensations while jumping at Lake
Placid. Earnestly an announcer described how he was being
fitted out with a 15-lb. transmitter, a mike in a mask. Then
Torger swished away. There was a faint crunch of snow and
nothing more. The champion, it seemed, forgot to talk.

DEATH OF THE LONE RANGER: One dawning last week a APRIL 21
tired, chubby suburbanite was driving home through the outskirts of Detroit. In front of the Methodist Church at Farm-
ington his eyelids dropped, the front wheels fluttered, the
car curved, careened, crashed into the back of a parked truck.
So died a rootin', tootin', shootin', hell-for-leather buckaroo
—radio's Lone Ranger.

All over the U.S. that night hundreds of thousands of children to whom the Ranger had sent toy lariats, six-shooters,
ten-gallon hats and bristling wild west mustaches, mourned
the most adored character ever to be created on the U.S. air.
In real life, the Ranger was Earle Graser, who liked to garden

and play badminton and didn't learn to ride a horse until a couple of years ago. He was 32 years old.

JUNE 16 **LAST TELEPHONE CALL:** The most elementary radio program ever devised in the U.S. vacated the airwaves last week. It was NBC's *Pot o' Gold,* which in its heyday a year ago kept 15,000,000 listeners at home each Tuesday night, hoping that a telephone call would net them $1,000.

JUNE 23 **THE INESCAPABLE GOLDBERGS:** This week Mrs. Gertrude Berg, authoress and leading lady of *The Goldbergs,* becomes practically inescapable. Her program, which originated in 1929, is already being heard over 23 CBS stations and MBS's WOR. The foam of her soapy masterwork for Procter & Gamble will henceforth pour from 30 stations of NBC's Red Network. The Goldbergs will be on the air morning, noon and night: first with NBC at 11:30 a.m., then with CBS at 5:15, and finally via transcription with WOR next dawning. No other radio show has ever had such a thorough airing.

JULY 14 **TELEVISION GOES COMMERCIAL:** Television broke out of its experimental hobbles last week. NBC celebrated its commercial tag by telecasting a Brooklyn-Philadelphia ball game from Ebbets Field. Bulova Watch Co. paid $4 for a time signal before the game, $8 for another in the evening. Sponsorship was not television's main worry. The big problem is that priorities for television equipment are so low that there is not much chance that many sets will be added to the estimated 4,500 now in operation.

OCT. 20 **ELOQUENT COWGIRL:** At Manhattan's Rodeo, Cowgirl Alice Greenough took a WOR mike along on a straightbucking bronco to describe her sensations to the radio audience. Alice's description was brief: "Ooph . . . ooph . . . ooph!"

NOV. 3 **HEIRDOM:** The *Are You a Missing Heir?* program, which for nearly two years has been dramatizing each week over CBS true tales of estranged souls whose deaths—and estates —were unknown to their presumptive heirs, last week turned up its luckiest missing heir so far: a quiet, 40-year-old, much buffeted Chicagoan named Rawlins Phillips.

Rawlins' father, a dining-car steward, dropped dead in Kansas City last May. He had invested his earnings to good purpose. Fortnight ago his story was broadcast. Son Phillips and his wife had heard all but one of the *Missing Heir* programs. That evening they were—for the second time in two years—not listening. But friends told them about it. Last week they claimed their estate: $85,000.

U.S. RADIO AT WAR: At 2:25 p.m. the news tickers clanged, DEC. 15 hammered out seven words: "White House says Japs attack Pearl Harbor." Within a few moments the networks crackled with the news. By 3 p.m. all the networks were in action—and in a turmoil.

The news was beyond the grasp of some listeners. WOR, butting into its football broadcast, got furious phone calls from people too excited about the game to become excited about anything else. In Denver, when a religious hour was canceled, one man called station KFEL to ask if it considered war news more important than the gospel. Nowhere did the straight radio reports of terrific bombing at Honolulu create anything resembling the panic created three years ago by Orson Welles's famed faking of a Martian invasion.

MILESTONES

BIRTHDAY: Winston Churchill, 67; working at No. 10 Downing Street, London. Among his "birthday presents": planes from South America, tanks from The British West Indies, tanks and Bren gun carriers from The Netherlands Indies.

ENGAGED: Cinemadolescent Mickey Rooney, 21; and Actress Ava Gardner, 18, Hollywood newcomer.

DIED: Dr. Henry Winters Luce, 73, retired Presbyterian Missionary to China, father of TIME Editor Henry R. Luce; in Haverford, Pa. Lifelong friend of China, largely responsible for the establishment of Shantung's first Christian University and Peking's Yenching University, he was a dynamic worker for the political, cultural and religious education of the Chinese. He died in his sleep on the day the U.S. and China became allies against Japan.

MISCELLANY

AID: In Mexico, Mo., passing motorists pulled an injured man from a wrecked car, carefully laid him in a bed of poison ivy.

SPORT: In Birmingham, England, police arrested a drunk. He was at the bottom of a crater, wrestling with a time bomb.

ENTERPRISE: In the Bronx, N.Y., five children with one nickel tried to pass through one turnstile all at once. Police pried them out with a crowbar.

RELIGION

MARCH 3 **OBSOLETE KISS:** Passed last week by the North Carolina Legislature was a law excusing persons taking oaths from kissing the Bible. Reason: "obsolete and unsanitary."

MARCH 24 **SIN REDISCOVERED:** The religious book-of-the-year was published last week, and it puts sin right back in the spotlight. Its author: Union Theological Seminary's Dr. Reinhold Niebuhr, high priest of Protestantism's young intellectuals. Its title: *The Nature and Destiny of Man: Volume 1.* Its significance: that America's most influential theologian is reversing the optimistic and rationalistic trend of Christian liberalism to lead his legions back to an almost medieval emphasis on the basic sinfulness of man.

The book is doubly interesting because 15 years ago Dr. Niebuhr was himself an outstanding exponent of the liberal credo he now seeks to discredit as opportunism. In the light of history, especially from 1920 to 1940, he finds liberal optimism about the goodness of man untenable.

Protestant liberalism is not alone in feeling the lash of its former leader. He also makes out a vigorous case against Catholicism, denounces Marxism as the false religion of the lower classes, Freudianism as the false religion of the upper crust, and Nietzschean fascism as the false religion of the lower middle classes.

MARCH 31 **BIBLICAL BOTANY:** Adam & Eve fell, not through eating an apple, but an apricot. The "rose" of the Bible is perhaps an oleander, perhaps a narcissus, certainly not a rose. The locusts John the Baptist ate are not bugs, but the flat seed pods of the carob tree. They can now be bought in the markets of Manhattan's lower East Side as "St. John's Bread."

Thousands of fascinated spectators learned all this and many another bit of Biblical botany at the International Flower Show in Manhattan last week, where the most popular single exhibit was the New York Botanical Garden's show of some 75 plants mentioned in the Bible.

JONAH VINDICATED: To vindicate the story of Jonah and the MAY 26 whale, Chicago's Pharmacology Professor Eugene Maximillian Karl Geiling crawled through the gullet of a dead cetacean to prove it could be done. "It was a pretty slimy trip," he said, "but there was plenty of room."

KARL BARTH DECLARES WAR: "We Christians do not accept this war as a necessary evil. We approve it as a righteous war, which God commands us to wage ardently."

So last week declared the world's most influential Protestant theologian, Swiss Calvinist Karl Barth. So saying, he reversed his pre-war stand that Christianity need not concern itself with such mundane struggles, that war never solves anything.

German Bishop von Galen denounces the Nazis three times from his pulpit.   *Gestapo Chief Heinrich Himmler urges Hitler to have the bishop shot.*

CATHOLIC NIEMOELLER: Another Niemoeller [Lutheran OCT. 6 minister Martin Niemoeller was imprisoned by the Nazis in 1938 for his opposition to Hitler] has arisen in Germany— this time a Roman Catholic, Count Clemens August von Galen, Bishop of Muenster in Westphalia. In August he denounced Nazism three times from his pulpit so vigorously that, according to news which percolated to the U.S., Gestapo Chief Heinrich Himmler has urged Hitler to have him shot.

To date he has not been touched, for his influence on the workers of Westphalia is so great, and the news of his resistance has grapevined so rapidly throughout the Reich, that the Nazis fear there would be a major work stoppage if they harmed him. Bishop von Galen's sermons followed two attacks: one by British bombers which gave Muenster one of the worst poundings any German city has ever suffered; the other from the Nazis, who suppressed all Catholic religious orders in Westphalia and imprisoned many prominent Catholics. The attack from the "inner enemy," Bishop von Galen said, was spiritually the more dangerous.

"No German citizen," he added, "has any longer any security, and justice has come to be a thing of the past. If the Church is accused of disputing the unity of the nation, the reply must be that the secret police is disrupting that unity in a way which concerns all Christians." He denounced Nazi use of euthanasia, revealing that many patients in his diocese had been taken away from asylums and put to death.

DEC. 8 **GRANDEST VISTA:** The largest Gothic church in the world was opened to its full length Sunday. When the great grey curtains separating the new nave from the older crossing and choir were dramatically drawn back, the congregation of 10,000 in New York's Cathedral of St. John the Divine saw an unbroken 520-ft. vista grander than that of any medieval cathedral.

Though nearly $20,000,000 has been spent since its cornerstone was laid in 1892, St. John's is still far from finished. But for a cathedral 49-year-old St. John's has made rapid progress. St. Peter's in Rome, the only larger church, took 177 years to build. Chartres and Cologne, pride of France and Germany, each took over 300 years.

DEC. 15 **WANDERING JEWS:** Some highlights of a 151-page report, *Jews in Nazi Europe*, released last week by Manhattan's Institute of Jewish Affairs:

¶ Not a Jew is left in Danzig.

¶ The number of Jews in Greater Germany has dropped

from 760,000 to about 250,000 since the Nazis came to power.

¶ Warsaw's ghetto had more than ten times as many deaths (4,290) as births (396) last June. In all Poland Jewish deaths have been five times the normal rate—300,000 in two years.

¶ The Nazis boast that some 20,000 Jewish enterprises are already under Aryan control in The Netherlands.

¶ Nearly a million European Jews had to flee their homes between 1933 and 1940. Principal havens: 330,000 to Russia; 150,000 to England, France, Belgium and The Netherlands (the Nazis caught up with them again in the last three); 135,000 to the U.S.

MILESTONES

MARRIED: James Roosevelt, 33, U.S. Marine captain on leave from his job as motion-picture producer; and Nurse Romelle Theresa Schneider, 25, who attended him after his ulcers operation at Rochester, Minn. in 1938; one month after the divorce of Betsy Cushing Roosevelt, surgeon's daughter, became final, and two days after Catholic nurse Schneider had finished observing Lent; in Los Angeles. The five Roosevelt siblings have now been married a total of eight times. [In 1967 the total was 15.]

DIED: Lou Gehrig, 38, "Iron Man of Baseball"; in Manhattan. Stricken two years ago with amyotrophic lateral sclerosis (hardening of the spinal cord), the great, clean-living, slugging Yankee first baseman, son of a German-born janitor, had hung up the all-round record of baseball: 2,130 consecutive games (for 14 years he played in every Yankee game); more than 100 runs a year; a lifetime batting average of .341.

BIRTHDAYS: Henry Ford, 78. He predicted that "the job of getting our subsistence will eventually take so little time that we will not pay much attention to it." Queen Elizabeth of England, 41. She spent the day quietly in the country.

SUED FOR DIVORCE: Sinclair Lewis, 56; by Columnist Dorothy Thompson, 47. Grounds: willful desertion.

MISCELLANY

RIDER: Near Barcelona, a peasant hitched a ride on a truck carrying an empty coffin. As it was raining, he crawled inside the coffin. Soon, the truck took two more passengers aboard. As they drove on, the peasant raised the lid, ejaculated: "It's stopped raining." Over the side went the other riders in terror. One was killed, the second badly hurt.

DEFERRED: In New Britain, Conn., a man obtained draft deferment because his occupation was investigating applications for occupational deferment.

ARMY WIFE: In Atlanta, an enterprising lawyer turned up an 1864 statute specifying as adequate grounds for divorce: "that the husband is in the military service of the U.S."

MUSIC

JAN. 13 **"DOWN BEAT" POLL:** Every year *Down Beat*, jazzmen's magazine, polls the trade for its opinions, which are downright. This year's opinions:

¶ Best swing band: Benny Goodman with 2,130 votes to Duke Ellington's 1,841.

¶ Best sweet band: Glenn Miller nosing out Tommy Dorsey, 2,605 to 2,427.

¶ Favorite soloist: Clarinetist Goodman. Next: Trumpeter Harry James, Clarinetist Artie Shaw.

¶ Best small combination: Goodman's sextet.

¶ "King of Corn": Guy Lombardo.

¶ Best vocalists: Bing Crosby, Helen O'Connell. Blonde, dimpled singer O'Connell, 20, has never studied singing, learns songs and perfects her whiskey-voiced style while lying in bed. Her best-seller of the year: *Six Lessons from Madame LaZonga*.

MARCH 31 **STOKOWSKI QUITS:** Last fortnight Maestro Leopold Stokowski, in firm, rayon tones announced his resignation as conductor of the Philadelphia Orchestra. It appeared that next season, for the first time in 29 years, Stokowski really would not wave pale hands over the orchestra which he had made one of the two or three plushiest-sounding in the world.

In recent years, Stokowski has been Philadelphia's conductor more in name than in fact. While he gadded, the orchestra's responsibilities fell upon the dependable shoulders of Hungarian-born Eugene Ormandy. Now Ormandy has a five-year contract as full conductor.

MAY 5 **CAFÉ SOCIETY CONCERT:** Nightclubs do not usually hire other people's halls to give public concerts, but last week one of them—Manhattan's "Café Society"—did exactly that. The concert's most musicianly talent was half-blind Art Tatum, who long ago achieved a safe middle ground between

Bach and Boogie-woogie. The evening ended in the loudest jam session ever heard in the hall, or perhaps anywhere. There were three bands—33 men in all, including nine pianists scrambling for places at three baby grands. The composition was announced as *One O'Clock Jump*, may well have been.

HUT-SUT SONG: Thirteen recorded versions of this pandemic JUNE 16 double-talk ballad are now available. The refrain—*Hut-Sut Rawlson on the rillerah and a brawla, brawla, soo-it*—is not Swedish, as its composers mischievously would lead their public to believe. At its present rate it may well top the nut songs it succeeds: 1936's *The Music Goes 'Round and 'Round* and 1939's *Three Little Fishies*.

DEATH OF PADEREWSKI: Death's final cadence this week JULY 7 closed the long career of a frail, wispy-haired Pole, the greatest pianist of his time, and one of the greatest who ever lived. Only the late, mighty Liszt and Rubinstein ever equaled him at a piano. Patriot, man of affairs, *bon vivant*, philanthropist, Ignace Jan Paderewski had not played publicly since Poland fell. "I could not stand it," he said.

But to the last he had labored for his beloved Poland. Poland's Premier after World War I, he was now the figurehead

Singer Helen O'Connell perfects her voice while lying in bed. Page 191.

The late Ignace Paderewski. He fought to the end for Poland.

President of its parliament in exile. Last November, on his 80th birthday, he arrived in the U.S. Since then, Paderewski spent himself making public appeals for money for starving Poles. Last week, against his doctor's orders he made one more appearance in New Jersey. As a result he contracted pneumonia and two days later, in his Manhattan hotel, he died.

JULY 14 **CONDUCTOR, 11:** The orchestra looked at him—plump, mop-haired, about the size of a cello and eleven years old. And *this* was to be the conductor of the NBC Summer Symphony—the same orchestra which veteran Arturo Toscanini had whipped into one of the world's finest. Before their first rehearsal under Lorin Maazel, the NBC players gagged about bringing lollipops along.

But with precocious composure, Conductor Maazel called his tough situation to order. He chided a clarinetist for an altered beat. Gently he pronounced the NBC strings "messy," then "much better." All this he did without consulting a score; Lorin Maazel knows 22 symphonic works by heart. When the first rehearsal was over, the NBC Symphony was with him. Conductor Maazel had acted the terrible child just a trifle, but so do many full-sized conductors.

Conductor Maazel is much better than good-for-a-kid. Articulate beyond his years, Lorin Maazel says: "I still have a lot of hard work ahead of me. I have yet to prove my mettle." [In 1965, at age 35, Maazel became musical director of the West Berlin Deutsche Oper.]

JULY 28 **HOT SHOT AND HUT-SUT:**

> *Hot Shot Dawson on a river boat*
> *With his brawlin', sprawlin' sweetie. . . .*
> *Hot Shot is an Irish pug,*
> *The river boat is the Queen,*
> *His brawlin' lass is Bridget Cass*
> *And Hot Shot is her dream.*

That snatch of a song had numerous song collectors and Mississippi river folk scratching their heads last week. The lines had been sent to a Los Angeles *Times* columnist by a friend who remembered hearing them many years ago in St. Louis. The *Times* printed the song, remarked its similarity to the current No. 1 sheet-music seller, *The Hut-Sut Song*. (. . . *Now the Rawlson is a Swedish town,/ the rillerah is a stream. . . ./ The brawla is the boy and girl/ The Hut-Sut is their dream.*)

Apparently the *Hot Shot* song was never published, but Cincinnati rivermen remembered it, and two Memphis experts narrowed the authorship of the song down to a blind Missouri Negro who sang at boat landings around 1914. Of the music, nobody remembered a note.

The authors of *The Hut-Sut Song*—to whose bouncing tune the lyrics of *Hot Shot Dawson* can easily be sung—last week kept silent as soo-it, mum as a rillerah.

5¢ CONCERTO: Many a concert classic has been swung higher than Obadiah, but last week a Tchaikovsky theme was swung five different ways at once. The Tchaikovsky *Piano Concerto in B Flat Minor*, played straight, had its popular start in the movies last spring; Mary Astor's make-believe pounding of it in *The Great Lie* got it widely known as "the Mary Astor Concerto." Freddie Martin recorded it, but neglected to give it lyrics which could be copyrighted. So by last week there were four competing versions: OCT. 6

¶ Woody Herman gave his the most accurate title: *Concerto No. 1, B Flat Minor*.

¶ Guy Lombardo called his version *Concerto*.

¶ Tony Martin's was a song, *Tonight We Love*.

¶ Best record of the lot was *Concerto for Two*, in a subtle arrangement by the fine new band led by piano-playing Claude Thornhill.

From many a U.S. jukebox, in strict dance time, in moody thumps, Freddie Martin's record, *Piano Concerto in B Flat*, had moved in among the ten best nickel pullers.

OCCUPATIONAL HAZARD: If you are a member of a swing band, one of the gravest risks you run is being killed in an automobile accident. With the death last week of Leon ("Chu") Berry, one of the best hot saxophonists in the business, the toll of bandsmen fatalities reached more than 100 this year. The musicians' union recently tried to reduce casualties by limiting jumps between dates to 400 miles a day. The hazard is not just a matter of long drives between en- NOV. 10

gagements—it is multiplied by drink, fatigue, recklessness and special indulgence by the police.

DEC. 1 **JUKEBOX DIVAS:** Three singing sisters from Minneapolis made another 2¢ last week. The Andrews Sisters had sold the 8,000,000th of the discs for which Decca Records pays them 2¢ apiece. The Andrews girls are the first sister act to owe fame & fortune to the jukebox alone. The Andrews Sisters make $5,000 a week.

Only one Andrews sister (LaVerne) reads music. Once they took singing lessons, but apoplectic Manager Lou Levy stopped that, pronto, for fear they would be ruined.

MILESTONES

BIRTHDAY: John Pierpont Morgan, 74; at his estate near Glen Cove, L.I. Said he to reporters: "Will you just leave me alone today?"

DIED: Louis Chevrolet, 62, the old-time racing driver the car is named for; in Detroit. Backed by W.C. Durant, he started making Chevrolets in 1911, lost faith in the car's future, stepped out of Chevrolet Motor Co. three years later and then sold all his holdings.

BORN: To Singer Mary (*My Heart Belongs to Daddy*) Martin Halliday: a 7-lb, 13-oz. daughter, her second child; in Hollywood. Name: Heller. Said scandalized Weatherford, Tex. townsfolk: "It's not a very nice name for a girl to have."

MISCELLANY

PAPER HANGER: In Pasadena, Calif., Paul Cardinal, onetime trapezist, rounded out his eighth year (not too busy) as a one-armed paper hanger.

CURIOUS: In Los Angeles, Calif., Charles F. Ellis, who is almost 103, declared that he wanted to live two years more "just to see what this man Roosevelt's going to do."

WARRIOR: In Hot Springs, S. Dak., a summons to a year's military service was dispatched to Tribesman Hobert Shot-to-Pieces, of Wounded Knee.

MAN: In Manhattan, a man was committed for observation who allowed he had never heard of Hitler.

COLOR: In London, a girl filing her A.T.S. (Auxiliary Territorial Service) registration blank stated that the color of her hair was "temporary."

RING: In Washington, an early-morning motorist happened on a girl standing under a street light. All she wore was an engagement ring. Her story: when she refused to give back his ring, her boy friend took everything else.

(8): In Fort Worth, Tex., Cowboy Kid Fletcher walked off with the Stock Show's prize for best bowed legs. His winning span (knee-to-knee): 8 in.

MOBILIZED: In Wilmington, Del., a 15-year-old was found counterfeiting nickels by remolding his lead soldiers.

MEDICINE

PERMANENT CURE: Scientists Earl Ralph Norris and James FEB. 24 Hauschildt, of the University of Washington, announced discovery of a new vitamin, found in yeast and liver, that prevents baldness. They dubbed it "inositol." The vitamin, said bald Dr. Norris, worked beautifully on mice. But it killed them.

BETWEEN THE LINES: A British surgeon recently did a mas- MARCH 1 toid operation on a middle-aged man who had once been a sailor. He decided to graft some skin from elsewhere on the patient's body to the site of the operation behind his ear. When the surgeon viewed the patient's body, he found it almost completely covered with tattooed images of naked women and erotic designs. The surgeon finally decided to take a number of small pieces of skin from between the lines of the tattooing, leaving the designs intact.

BANTING: Just before dark, one evening last week, in Toronto, a big, camouflaged bomber swooped in from the east. From it were taken the mortal remains of Major Sir Frederick Grant Banting, world-famed discoverer of insulin, dead at 49 after a bomber in which he was flying to England crashed in Newfoundland.

Next day the body of the man who made life livable for diabetics lay in state at the University of Toronto, while colleagues recalled some episodes of Sir Frederick's turbulent career. He was a stubborn man of strong feelings, sudden temper, trenchant speech. After insulin was discovered in 1921, Biochemist James Bertram Collip was called in to polish up the glandular extraction technique. The stuff began to be called "Collip's extract." Banting leaped on Collip in the university halls, threw him down, banged his head on the floor, bellowed: "So, you will call this 'Collip's extract,' will you!"

Fame and the Nobel Prize did not make Banting a happy man. When World War II broke out, he was too old to fight but he wanted to help. Rumor had it that he was working on ways to prevent "blackouts" (brief losses of consciousness) in fighter pilots pulling out of steep dives. It was known last week that Dr. Banting was not immediately killed in the crash, but was able to bandage the injuries of Captain Joseph Mackey, the only survivor. When he had done that, he lay down on a bed of broken branches, covered himself with his overcoat, and stopped being stubborn.

APRIL 7 **THE CAPITAL OF ILL HEALTH:** One of the worst pestholes in the nation is its proud white capital. The worst health menace is overcrowding—since last spring the population of Washington, D.C. increased from 663,000 to 735,000.

One of the barometers of a city's bad health is its tuberculosis rate. Of every 100,000 Washingtonians, 89 died of tuberculosis last year (national rate: 47 per 100,000). Washington's 177,000 Negroes live mostly in condemned alley buildings. Six Negroes die of t.b. every year to one white person.

In the last few weeks Washington streetwalkers have lowered their prices from $3 to $2 to accommodate $21-a-month soldiers. In 1940 Washington had over 10,000 reported cases of venereal diseases, had a higher rate of syphilis than any of the ten larger U.S. cities.

MAY 12 **UNFIT FOR SERVICE:** "We are faced with the cold fact that about 40% of the young men of our country at ages 21 to 35 are either considered physically unfit to enter training for military service or are fit for limited service only." Thus last week spoke Dr. George Canby Robinson, chairman of a conference on national-defense health problems sponsored by Manhattan's Milbank Memorial Fund. Most rejections are for bad teeth. Other defects, in order of prevalence: poor eyesight, diseases of the heart and circulation, deformities of arms and legs, genito-urinary and venereal disease, mental and nervous disorders.

MAY 19 **WHISKEY FOR PAIN:** "Whiskey is one of the cheapest and best painkillers known to man." So reported Dr. Harold

George Wolff of Cornell last week. Two ounces of 90-proof whiskey in a glass of ginger ale raises the "threshold" of pain 45% in two hours. Said Dr. Wolff, "It is cheaper than morphine. . . . Of course alcohol is habit-forming but an alcohol habit is less difficult to deal with than a morphine habit."

PSYCHIATRISTS ON HESS: U.S. psychiatrists had a field day MAY 26 last week explaining the method and madness of Nazi Rudolf Hess [who had flown suddenly from Germany to Britain; see page 124]. Some of their remarks:

¶ Dr. Foster Kennedy of Cornell: "Hess may have set out for the Duke of Hamilton because he thought a duke could do what Churchill could not—bring about peace. The Germans are such snobs. . . . His activities must be considered as those of a perfectly sane man."

¶ Dr. Gregory Zilboorg of Manhattan: "Hess may have a megalomanic-paranoiac trend. His profound devotion to Hitler over so many years was semi-pathologic and he may have been suffering from a homosexual panic when he ran away."

¶ Dr. Karl Murdock Bowman of Manhattan's Bellevue Hospital: "I am not a good enough psychiatrist to speculate a diagnosis on a patient in Scotland."

YOU'LL CATCH YOUR DEATH!: U.S. medicine (as represent- JUNE 9 ed by the American Laryngological Association) last week caught up with grandma. After years of trying to change the subject, the scientists finally broke down and admitted that colds are caused by a draft. Their language, however, was somewhat different from grandma's. Said Dr. Irwin Gabriel Spiesman, making a clean breast of it: "Rapid cooling of most cutaneous surfaces produces a reflex vasoconstriction (tightening of blood vessels) and ischemia (lack of blood) leading to lowered mucous membrane temperature of the upper respiratory tract."

The specialists made it clear that medicine only partly agrees with grandma: doctors still believe that colds are carried by a virus. Drafts, as well as heavy drinking, emotional upsets, constipation, weaken the body's resistance, make it easy for the cold virus to enter.

Sister Kenny develops a revolutionary new treatment for polio.

A mother at eight considers her two-year-old son her brother. Page 200.

JUNE 23 **SISTER KENNY'S TREATMENT:** A new and apparently successful treatment for infantile paralysis—reversing all accepted methods of treating the disease—was last week described to U.S. doctors. Instead of immobilizing paralyzed limbs by strapping them to splints, the new treatment calls for patiently flexing a victim's useless limbs while he is still sick in bed. No doctor invented this method, but a nurse in the Australian bush named Sister Elizabeth Kenny. (In England and Australia experienced graduate nurses are called Sister.)

Sister Kenny places a patient flat on a firm mattress which does not quite reach to the footboard of his bed. The patient's feet, with heels and toes stretching beyond the mattress, are set squarely against the footboard. Thus he exercises the muscular reflexes used for standing up. Hot packs made of pieces of blanket wrung out of boiling water are laid on his paralyzed limbs. Several times a day Sister Kenny flexes the patient's arm or leg. As pain is reduced, the exercises are increased. By the time the first, contagious stage of the disease is over, all pain and stiffness are usually relieved. [Sister Kenny's treatment caused a good deal of controversy in U.S. medical circles. But the National Foundation for Infantile Paralysis endorsed her revolutionary treatment, and Sister Kenny was portrayed in a movie by Rosalind Russell.]

BIRTHDAY PARTY: Next to the Dionnes [the Canadian OCT. 6 quintuplets born May 28, 1934] this family is one of the wonders of nature: the world's youngest mother and her child: Lina Medina of Lima, Peru, who last week celebrated her eighth birthday, with her two-year-old son Gerardo.

Unlike the Dionnes, who last week were to leave their private home under the care of Dr. Dafoe to go back to their family, Lina and her son last month left her own folks to live with the family of Surgeon Alejandro Vargas Morales. She now reads, writes, considers Gerardo her brother.

RED PLAGUE: The biggest killer of children between the ages NOV. 10 of five and 15 is rheumatic heart disease. In one year it claims almost twice as many victims as infantile paralysis does in ten years. Today, about 1,000,000 people have been left crippled by this insidious, recurring malady.

Rheumatic fever, which smolders in slum districts and over-crowded tenements, usually occurs after a streptococcal infection of the nose or throat. It is not caused directly by streptococci but seems to be an allergic response to their activity. Early symptoms are a tired feeling, loss of weight, rapid breathing, fast heart action, vague pains in the joints. The disease usually attacks the heart muscles, lining, or valves, often deforming them permanently, cutting down the power of the heart to withstand the strain of daily life.

During the fever, some drugs are useful. Chief thing to do: keep the child in bed. This may be for as long as a year. Children with rheumatic hearts have to learn to walk, not run, to go upstairs one step at a time, play gentle games.

WAR & SANITY: The British people, too busy to worry about DEC. 1 personal troubles, have so few neuroses in World War II that psychiatrists have less work than they expected. Said Dr. Robert Dick Gillespie, psychiatric specialist of the Royal Air Force, as he arrived in Manhattan last week: "In 30 years I have never been more idle than when serving in the R.A.F." Some of his data:

¶ On the whole, poor people bear up far better under strain than those in the upper income groups. Reason: they don't suffer from competition, don't worry about appearances when everything is gone.

¶ Most normal children play air-raid games, sometimes enjoy the excitement. Only four per cent of 8,000 Bristol school children showed symptoms of terror after air raids. What bothers children more than bombs is disrupted family life.

¶ Best way to prevent mental breakdown after tragic experiences is to keep people occupied. In one survey, everyone seemed quite well after the raids; several weeks later, almost one-third of the victims came down with various kinds of hysteria. Said Dr. Gillespie: "It was only after they had finished rearranging themselves and their affairs and had time to sit down and consider the situation that the symptoms appeared. It is disorganization rather than fright that is the causal factor here."

DEC. 29 **F IS FOR FIRST AID:** All over the U.S. last week, as the news of Pearl Harbor sank in, 30,000 volunteer Red Cross teachers called a roll of 1,000,000 pupils who had registered for a 20-hour course in First Aid. The first lesson was the same everywhere; as an outline of the course, the teacher dictated the nine basic principles of First Aids, starting with F, ending with S. The acrostic:

F is for fear. "Allay it! Tell the victim he will be all right, even if you know he is doomed. Turn his head so he won't see his mangled limbs."

I is for information, injuries. Find out what organs are injured before you act.

R is for reclining position. Keep a victim lying down.

S is for shock. If a victim turns white, has a lifeless expression, he must be covered up immediately, kept warm.

T is for transportation. Don't move a victim unless he is in a burning building.

A is for air. Be sure the victim gets plenty. If a crowd has gathered, pick two big men to push them back.

I is for immediate treatment of bleeding, asphyxia, poisoning.

D is for drink. Water, tea or coffee may be given people who are conscious.

S is send for the doctor.

BUSINESS & FINANCE

MAJOR LIQUIDATION: For decades the art market had its JAN. 6
ever-normal granary and his name was William Randolph
Hearst. Until 1937 when he stepped out of the market for
keeps he had purchased better than a million dollars worth
of art treasures a year. He stopped buying because he was
broke. The income of his 25 newspapers, the profits of the
mines he had inherited from his prospector father, were no
longer big enough to pay the interest on their debts and his.
By 1939 he was in hock to the banks, and employed as editorial director of his own newspapers at a yearly salary of
$100,000. For Mr. Hearst that was chicken feed.

To get $600,000 for spending money, Hearst had mort-
gaged San Simeon, his vast California estate. In 1938 it was
announced that part of his $50,000,000-or-so accumulation
of art objects would be offered for sale. But the art market
couldn't take it back. Dealers were afraid their price structure would collapse under the weight. Another market had
to be found.

Last week a deal was made. Bernard Gimbel, of Gimbel
Brothers, and Adam Gimbel, of Saks Fifth Avenue, signed
a contract to offer the bulk of Hearst's collection to the public
over the bargain counters of Manhattan's Gimbel Bros. department store and its swank subsidiary, Saks. Whether
housewives will plank down their money for medieval cannon or Egyptian mummies is a merchandising unknown.
[Most of the collection was sold during the year.]

PACKARD TO MATCH: To a Manhattan automobile dealer, JAN. 20
Mrs. Elizabeth R. Fajardo of Puerto Rico sent a bottle of
the fuchsia polish she uses on her nails. The dealer sent her a
Packard to match.

LESSON IN SPEED: Bald, tight-lipped Henry J. Kaiser is one MARCH 3
of those American industrial geniuses that average Americans

are prone to take for granted until the country gets in a jam. A fabulously successful engineer, he refuses to believe in clocks or calendars. When he turned 50, he started counting his birthdays backwards; outside of his own family, no one knows how old he is now. Within the limits of the day's 24 hours, he manages to be president of 15 companies and director of 20 more.

Dynamic Engineer Kaiser does not recognize nature's other obstacles any more than he kowtows to time. He has headed companies which helped build the Grand Coulee Dam (largest in the world), the San Francisco-Oakland Bridge (longest in the world). When slides threatened to hold up work at Coulee, he froze a hillside solid to keep it in place.

Under the defense program, busy Mr. Kaiser has been busier than ever. He is helping build 60 cargo ships for Britain, 87 freighters, a fleet of destroyers for the Navy. Now he is hard at work building a plant to produce badly needed magnesium at the rate of 12,000 to 15,000 tons within a year. Since total U.S. production last year was only 6,500 tons, the proposal sounded fantastic. But now Kaiser hopes to get the plant into operation inside of six months instead of the year it ought to take.

MARCH 17 **EXIT BOY WONDER:** William McChesney Martin Jr. became first paid president of the Stock Exchange (salary: $48,000) after the Richard Whitney scandal in 1938. [Whitney, five times President of the New York Stock Exchange, was expelled from the exchange in 1938 on charges of grand larceny. He was convicted and served a term in Sing Sing.] Bachelor Martin, 31, was a New Dealish, sobersided, optimistic mathematics whiz who ate in the Automat, wore no hat and dabbled at writing plays.

From the beginning Bill Martin was pulled one way by the Old Guard, another by the Young Turks, a third by the SEC, several ways at once by public opinion. He had no talent for playing politics, soon found that by trying to please everybody he was pleasing nobody. As the Exchange's business slumped from bad to worse, Martin was bound to be the scapegoat. But fate had provided Bill Martin with a face-saving exit. He is prepared to be drafted as soon as his number comes up. Wall Street's Boy Wonder of 1938 is

1941's most willing draftee. [In 1951, Martin became Chairman of the Federal Reserve Board, for many years after-
ward helped direct U.S. monetary policy.]

SHOALS AHEAD IN SHIPPING: This year Nazi ship sinkings MARCH 24
have averaged 350,000 tons a month. Ships are being torpedoed much faster than new ones are launched. Although
ship-building is booming in the U.S. all the way from New
England to the West Coast, no more than 1,000,000 tons
can be launched this year. A real squeeze in ships was in
the making.

Last week the Maritime Commission received from the
Office of Production Management a list of "essential" and
"non-essential" imports which soon will be translated into
cargo priorities. Classed as essential were strategic and critical materials like rubber, tin, etc., plus such civilian musts as
leather, wool, coffee, sugar, cocoa. On the nonessential list
were frillier items: spices, wine, tea, palm oil and burlap. By
rationing shipping space, the U.S. hoped to make every
ship that sails the seas work at 100% efficiency for defense.

THE FEED BAG: Harry Hopkins' report to the President on MARCH 31
Prime Minister Churchill's immediate wants can be summed
up in two words: food and ships. Neither was surprising.
Britain's hunger is conditioned by two things: 1) the scarcity
of refrigerator cargo space; 2) the constant bombing of gas
mains, which puts a premium on food that does not have to
be cooked. The British also want the maximum of food in
the minimum of space. This means they want as much of
their meat as possible in tins, which is not the way the U.S.
is accustomed to packing it. The British are interested in proc-
essed and packaged foods of all sorts, especially condensed
or powdered milk, cheese, dried and frozen eggs, canned and
dried fruits and vegetables.

WRIGLEY'S WRAPPERS: Well aware was Philip K. Wrigley APRIL 14
that priorities would allow him no more aluminum for foil
to wrap his chewing gum. So last week smart Phil Wrigley
sold his remaining 500,000 lb. of the metal to OPM (Office
of Production Management), thus simultaneously 1) struck
a blow for national defense, 2) pulled his neatest publicity

coup since he bought famed Pitcher Dizzy Dean for his Chicago Cubs in 1938.

APRIL 21 **BIG STICK:** "If we are to keep this a New Deal war, we have got to keep prices from skyrocketing the way they did in the last war." Well over a year has passed since the President laid down that basic principle to the inner circle of his advisors. Last week, price-conscious Franklin Delano Roosevelt created a new defense agency to control prices with more potential power than previous agencies had ever held. He called it the Office of Price Administration and Civilian Supply: OPACS.

At the head of it he placed burly Leon Henderson, most dynamic and executive of the New Deal coterie. Into Henderson's hands he placed authority to fix priorities on all civilian supplies, to withhold supplies from offending industries, to use priorities on transportation, to fix and publish maximum price schedules—and to advise the President to commandeer plants which fail to cooperate.

Price Tsar Henderson laid hands on his new job with the gusto of a man who has starved for months for just such power. "You can name anything," he told his first press conference, "and I would say that prices are already too high. . . . All prices ought to come down."

MAY 19 **TOO MUCH BUILD-UP:** Plastics men, meeting last week to discuss the role of their industry in defense, had a strange problem: their reputation was too good. Wherever a shortage has arisen—in aluminum, zinc, nickel—someone has stepped up to say that the nation would use plastics instead. Many a citizen, after watching a series of plastic miracles in fountain pens, steering wheels, etc. has come to think of plastics as the national Handy Andy. But there are some things even plastics can't do, and when rushed into new uses without proper advance research, plastics sometimes have failed as spectacularly as they have succeeded elsewhere.

Since the industry's basic raw materials are found everywhere (air, wood, coal, petroleum, soybeans, milk), it can eventually overcome any shortages. Right now expansion of plastics capacity is hampered by shortages of metals required for molds. Already the industry is producing washing-machine parts and thermos-bottle caps which take the place of aluminum, refrigerator panels which take the place of steel. This week the Army tested a plastic fuse cap. But plastics men are wary of the too-enthusiastic demand. Said one manufacturer last week:

"We're like a zoo keeper with a lot of big and hungry animals to feed. . . . If they wake up one at a time our job will be easy. If they all wake up at once we'll be in a hell of a fix."

GONE FOR THE DURATION: The spice industry is the No. 1 MAY 26 example of a business where shortages will soon be complete. Some examples:

¶ Before the war, sage was plucked by Greek and Yugoslav goatherders. When spice-grinders tried to use wild California sage, it could not be sold because it smacked of turpentine.

¶ Thyme came from France.

¶ Best paprika came from Hungary. A little still arrives from Portugal and Spain.

¶ Spanish saffron is almost impossible to get. Because it takes 14,000 tiny flower stigmata to make an ounce, U.S. growers will not even try to produce it.

LEON'S WORST WEEK: Last week was bad for Price Admin- JULY 7 istrator Leon Henderson. Cotton crossed 15¢ a lb. for the first time since 1930. Chrysler, Ford, Hudson, Nash, Studebaker had all announced price increases ranging from $10 to $53 a car. The faster prices have risen, the faster has Leon brandished his only effective weapon over them—his jawbone.

Last week Leon needed to have his wits about him. Instead he got into a tiff with Chrysler, infuriated cotton Congressmen, got a bad press and wound up with a price-fixing law which Congress promptly tore to pieces.

Henderson wired the automakers to rescind their increase; Chrysler refused. So Leon let Chrysler have it. If everybody were as uncooperative as Chrysler, he said, the whole country's price stability would be undermined. In this tiff, Henderson chose to occupy an unpopular salient. He picked on Chrysler's profits. Said the *Wall Street Journal*: "Profits . . . are not the business of Mr. Henderson." "The honeymoon is over," Henderson told a Congressional committee.

Industrialist Henry Kaiser is busy building ships for Britain. Page 203. *Price Boss Leon Henderson. His best weapon is his jawbone.*

JULY 28 **OIL FAMINE CLOSER:** Petroleum Coordinator Harold Ickes sent oilmen reeling this week. He asked them to turn over 100 more tankers to the British, 25 of them immediately. With 50 tankers already turned over, that will cut the U.S. coastwise tanker fleet by 40% to 200 vessels. It means the Atlantic seaboard gasoline famine is closer and graver than ever.

AUG. 11 **SILK CURTAIN:** In its boldest move to date, OPM last week marched into the U.S. silk industry, became sole holder, buyer and seller of raw silk. Reason for this extreme action was to hoard all U.S. silk supplies for military use (chiefly powder bags and parachutes).

SCRAP SQUEEZE: Shortage of scrap put the screws on the whole U.S. steel industry last week. *Iron Age* made a somber prediction at week's end: steel production would drop to 90% of capacity by fall unless more scrap was found. One reason for the shortage is that the U.S. shipped 8,222,259 tons of scrap to Japan from 1936 to 1940 (when exports were finally prohibited). That scrap is gone forever.

AUG. 18 **AT LAST:** Jeremiahs had predicted it. Last week they turned out to be right. Steel, the No. 1 defense metal, was slapped under 100% mandatory priorities. Nobody can buy steel now without government priorities. And for the first time, steel companies must accept all defense orders. The Government's control of steel was virtually complete.

TROUBLE IN PARADISE: Radio manufacturing has looked SEPT. 1 like the first U.S. consumer industry to take the guns-*v.*-butter dilemma in stride. Although it faced a 75% cut in its normal business and felt the metals shortage, the industry said it had "no squawks." But last week it was squawking as hard as the rest. As long ago as last April, OPM told radio manufacturers not to count on scarce materials. Their own leaders said the same, warned them to "get out and dig" for defense business to survive. The radio-makers paid good heed. Already they are about 25% engaged in defense work (ammunition and machine-gun parts and the wartime "walky-talky," a two-way battery set for field use).

Last week a bomb dropped on this comparative industrial paradise. OPACS was now, according to one radio bigwig, "a bunch of goddam, nit-witted, half-baked college graduates." Reason: a new allocation order for plastics which eliminated their use for radio cabinets. If the order sticks, radio manufacturers face a painful, costly switch to wood cabinets to house even the 2,500,000 sets they were planning to make next year (*v.* 11,600,000 in 1940). It would also mean a 20% jump in radio prices, additional layoffs, and a possibly ruinous scramble for lumber.

GET THE JUNK MAN: U.S. housewives wondered last week SEPT. 8 why their aluminum pots and pans, given to their Government weeks ago, were still stacked high around courthouses and fire stations. The reason: New York's bustle-bottomed Mayor Fiorello H. LaGuardia, who had waddled into the aluminum drive as head of the Office of Civilian Defense, did not trust the junk dealers who were to buy the local scrap and sell it to smelters. Too many already were bootlegging aluminum utensil scrap for as high as 40¢ a pound (Leon Henderson's ceiling: 12¢).

MEADVILLE *v.* THE U.S.: One city where the effect of priori- SEPT. 15 ties was likely to hurt the most was Meadville, Pa., the home of Talon, Inc., zipper manufacturers. Talon had been unable to buy any metal since Aug. 1, had laid off 800 workers, had only enough inventories to keep going until next month. Talon, which furnishes 5,219 of the city's 9,000 industrial jobs, means as much to Meadville as auto plants to Detroit.

Talon, Inc. began with the harebrained idea of Inventor Whitcomb L. Judson, who had trouble lacing his shoes and decided that there must be an easier way. Not until 1914 did the company turn out a really successful product. But in 1923 Goodrich Rubber gave it a big contract to make zippers for galoshes and the company jumped into the big money. To replace all Talon fasteners now, the company estimates, would take 1,300,000,000 buttons a year—and many firms were having trouble getting buttons. Washington was sympathetic. To make Meadville a ghost town for lack of 6,300 tons of copper for zippers seemed like junking an automobile for lack of a spark plug. But that is sometimes necessary on the battlefield.

SEPT. 22 **THE RUINS OF BRISTOL:** Part of the foundation for Manhattan's new East River Drive is provided by rubble from Bristol, England. Rubble for fill is hard to get in Manhattan. But in Bristol, Nazi bombs have made plenty of it. The debris also makes excellent ballast for British ships coming to the U.S. partly empty to load up with war supplies.

OCT. 13 **PATRIOTIC DISTILLERS:** The U.S. liquor industry turned up as a helper in a critical sector of the munitions industry. From 20,000,000 bushels of Government-owned surplus corn, the distillers will run off 40-50,000,000 gallons of ethyl alcohol. The U.S. needs this alcohol. Each time a 16-inch naval gun is fired, 1,500 lb. of smokeless powder, which took 60 gallons of alcohol to manufacture, is blasted into air. Even a rifle shot blows up enough alcohol to make a cocktail.

OCT. 27 **THE PRESIDENT CAN REQUISITION:** The President of the U.S. can now requisition private property needed for defense. Until he signed the bitterly fought bill last week, his power to do this was vague and general. Now it is definite and specific. The new Presidential power is not as complete as he asked for. Dictator-fearing Congressmen limited it so that the act automatically expires June 3, 1943, or when the emergency ends, whichever comes first. And the Government must pay "fair market value" of the property.

The President got the power just in time. Priorities Chief Donald Nelson last week told a Congressional committee that 1,378,000 lb. of copper, some of it "undoubtedly Axis-owned," lay in U.S. warehouses, untouchable despite the acute shortage. Not only will that copper now be requisitioned, but also carloads of machinery, steel, silk, rubber, tin plate, manganese and other hoarded, hidden and frozen inventories.

DON'T PHONE—WRITE: New York Telephone Co., largest NOV. 17 unit in the Bell System, told its employes not to make long-distance calls except in dire emergency, and then only in off-peak hours. Reason: national defense is straining the wires.

KILLING TWO BIRDS: In England arrived a ship whose en- DEC. 1 tire hold had been turned into an icebox by insulating it with boxes of frozen lard, filling with frozen meat, covering with more lard. U.S. meat packers had solved the problem of scarce refrigerator space. They had also killed two birds with one stone, since England needs both meat and lard.

CONSERVATION: To boost pulp paper supplies WPA is man- DEC. 8 gling 25,000,000 folders of World War I draft records, baling the shreds. But, complained the Conservation Division, the equivalent of 400 Army tanks is being thrown away in used razor blades annually—not, unfortunately, into any one place.

ALARMS AND EXCURSIONS: The New York Stock Exchange DEC. 22 was sagging gently along early last week, when suddenly the news ticker flashed: "Unidentified planes two hours away. . . ." Later, a huge siren right across the street went off with an awful wail. On the trading floor men wheeled, dashed for the trading posts, frantically dumped thousands of shares of stock for whatever they would bring. This done, many of them high-tailed for office or home. When the all-clear sounded 17 minutes later, leading stocks had lost 2 to 10 points, the market was at a new four-year low.

Next day brokers kicked themselves for getting the jitters, sheepishly started buying stocks back. At week's end they had recovered most of their losses.

THE BIGGEST JOB BEGINS: "Your Government has decided on two broad policies. The first is . . . a seven-day week for every war industry. The second . . . rush additions to capacity by building more new plants, adding to old plants and using the many smaller plants."

Thus last week did President Roosevelt thumbnail the biggest industrial job ever tackled by the U.S. It meant that the U.S. economy was to be turned on its ear. That vast, delicate, intermeshed mechanism has been producing about 15% war goods, 85% peacetime goods. To reach the President's goal, it will have to be put on a 50% war-50% peace basis.

Last week the first steps were taken. OPM ordered capacity production at once in planes, ships, anti-aircraft guns, ammunition, tanks. Copper mines jumped from a six- to a seven-day week so that the mines are never idle. And in Detroit the automakers suddenly stopped every non-defense production line, told 300,000 autoworkers to stay at home. The industry's engineers will this week re-examine the dead assembly lines for possible conversion to war work.

WAR-CLAUSES: U.S. life insurance firms, their best crop of prospects now earmarked for military service, last week broke out in a rash of war-risk clauses in all new policies. Anything but uniform, the clauses all produced the same net result: no payment for death due to war. (Policies already in effect are not affected.) No companies are anxious for soldier-&-sailor business. They discourage all such applicants, suggest they let the U.S. insure them. The U.S. will.

DEC. 29 **BROTHERS, WE'RE RETREADING:** The rationing of new tires announced by OPA last week was a blessing and a boon to some 4,500 little businessmen. For years the poor relation and black sheep of the U.S. rubber industry, the retreading business had suddenly become the white hope of U.S. car owners. Said Cleveland's Roy Snyder, 15 years a retreader: "The rush is on. It's like the Klondike. No use answering my phone. I can't handle the business."

CINEMA

"THE PHILADELPHIA STORY"—Critics have long noticed that JAN. 20
Katharine Hepburn's popularity waxed and waned in direct
proportion to the similarity of her roles with her own per-
sonality. In *Little Women*, she was full of the eager, well-
bred enthusiasm she absorbed in her free-thinking but social-
ly impeccable Hartford, Conn. family. Then she slid into in-
terpretations as heavy and lifeless as plum duff. Two years
ago, she and Hollywood called it quits.

Finally she found herself with just what she wanted—a
sophisticated play about high life in Philadelphia's Main
Line society with a glamorous, smart-talking leading role
especially stitched to her lovely measurements by her friend,
playwright Philip Barry. With the backing of a onetime
suitor, Aviator Howard Hughes, she bought herself an interest in the play. Hollywood was interested and Owner
Hepburn could write her own ticket. She demanded two
leading male stars, an all-out production, $175,000 for the
screen rights, $75,000 for her services as an actress. M.G.M.
ponied up that amiably stringy young man, James Stewart,
plus Cary Grant, whose $137,500 fee was paid directly to
British war relief.

The result of all this is terribly funny, terribly upper class.
The Philadelphia Story lifts the daily drudge into a charming
never-never land and is a good, entertaining show.

CITIZEN WELLES RAISES KANE: Louella Parsons nearly fell JAN. 27
out of her chair. On the preview screen before her, Orson
Welles was playing Citizen Kane, a corrupt newspaper publisher, in a way that reminded Cinecolumnist Parsons irre-
sistibly of her boss, William Randolph Hearst. She thought
she detected some glaring similarities between the picture's
plot and the career of her boss. It was a picture lush with
the leggy beauty of Publisher Kane's teeming love life, gro-
tesque with his wholesale grabs of Europe's artistic off-

James Stewart, Cary Grant and Katharine Hepburn in "The Philadelphia Story." It is terribly funny; terribly upper class.

scourings. Columnist Parsons got up from her seat. She rose like a geyser. As the lights came on she and two lawyers who had accompanied her steamed out. Only her chauffeur had enjoyed the picture.

First result was that no more mention of R.K.O. pictures appeared in Hearst papers. Next Lolly Parsons phoned R.K.O. Headman George Shaefer in Manhattan, appealed to him to stop *Citizen Kane*. R.K.O. officials decided to release the picture anyway. Would Citizen Hearst sue? R.K.O. lawyers decided he had no case. [Hearst did not sue. R.K.O. had trouble at first finding theaters willing to dare Hearst's wrath by showing the film. But it received rave reviews and was named Best Picture of the Year.]

MARCH 3   **COOP:** In the movie *Meet John Doe* Gary Cooper plays a gawkingly uncouth but handsome bush-league baseball pitcher who is out of work. A newspaper hires him and interviews him daily to deliver naive but manly sermons on the subject of Love Thy Neighbor. When his sermons touch local and then national hearts, John Doe makes a nationwide tour, falls in love with the girl reporter (Barbara Stanwyck), acquires such a nationwide reputation that his face appears on the cover of TIME.

Both the sentimentality and the rhetoric of *Meet John Doe*

profit greatly by its star. Tens of thousands of fans know that Gary Cooper (his friends call him "Coop") is 6 feet 2³/₄ inches tall, 175 pounds heavy, 40 years old. Though special tributes are often paid him where young women gather, he escapes such masculine calumny as sometimes finds its way toward the ears of Clark Gable. Boy friends and husbands watch him without defensive squirming.

Gary (christened Frank James) Cooper was born in Helena, Mont. in 1901. Like all healthy Montanans he learned to fish, shoot, ride horses. After leaving Grinnell College in 1924, he tried free-lance cartooning, punched cows on his father's ranch. He used up his funds getting to Hollywood, got fired from his job selling electric signs for not selling any.

For a year Coop was a cowboy extra. Then Sam Goldwyn saw him in a bit part, gave him the second male lead with Vilma Banky and Ronald Colman in *The Winning of Barbara Worth*. He soon won a long-term contract. Eventually his roles included *A Farewell to Arms, Lives of a Bengal Lancer, Mr. Deeds Goes to Town*. Coop considered his acting more & more. But even when he was "acting to beat hell" his fans praised him for his indestructible naturalness. It is this quality, which almost every American likes to identify with himself, that accounts for Cooper's tremendous appeal to all kinds of Americans.

THE GROANER: Out of the Paramount Studio last week came some of the most uninhibited, daffy nonsense to hit the U.S. screen since the heyday of Harold Lloyd. It was *Road to Zanzibar,* and its principal assets were two recruits from radio who bounced gaily through its inanities like a pair of playful puppies. For one of them, Bob Hope, it was the tenth film in a new and rapidly rising movie career; for the other, Bing Crosby, a dulcet, broken-toned singer who has confounded all the rules of show business for more than ten years, it was his 24th feature-length picture.

Road to Zanzibar, part radio, part vaudeville, part lunacy, is not a 100% movie. That is as it should be, for Crosby, its star, is not a 100% movie star. He is a law student who turned to singing as a gag. He has never studied music or voice; yet jobs kept turning up—each a little better than the last. He

APRIL 7

always falls uphill. Once on a vacation trip to Los Angeles, Bing and his friend from Spokane, Al Rinker, ran out of money. They polished up a couple of tunes, landed a job in a local theater. Al played the piano and Bing stood by, tapping a cymbal while they harmonized on some speedy ditties like *Paddlin' Madeline Home* and *Five Foot Two, Eyes of Blue*. Paul Whiteman heard them, offered them $150 a week to join his show.

That was Bing's start. From then on he violated the strictest tenets of success. Whiteman let him go because he was lazy. He immediately landed a better job at Los Angeles' Cocoanut Grove—which fired him for disappearing on long weekends. Mack Sennett hired him to act in some movie shorts. Prohibition booze gave him laryngitis, and he received a $3,500-a-week radio contract.

Like Babe Ruth, Jack Dempsey and Bill Tilden, who thrilled the fans of the '20s, Bing knows how to please the crowd. That "The Groaner's" voice is America's voice depends upon the fact that Crosby sings every song—whether *Mexicali Rose* or *Silent Night*—as though he felt it was the best song ever written.

JUNE 2 **"MAJOR BARBARA"**—George Bernard Shaw, 84 and the world's No. 1 living dramatist, did everything but grind the camera in this second authorized screen version of one of his plays. He wrote its scenario and dialogue, brought the 36-year-old drama up to date with some 30 new scenes, supervised its direction, dominated its production. The result, starring Wendy Hiller, Rex Harrison, Robert Morley and Robert Newton, is a cinema treat.

Fate can be as capriciously cruel to the movies as to any other business. Work on the script began two weeks before hostilities began. Then there was a shortage of lumber for sets. Half the picture was finished when the bombing of London began. For months, bomb bursts, air-raid sirens and anti-aircraft fire made it impossible to make more than a few brief shots a day. Some of the cast lived on the set, passed much of the day in air-raid shelters and the night in rescue work. Once, when the company returned to complete a sequence begun on a street in London's East End, the houses had disappeared.

"SERGEANT YORK"—Twenty-three years ago a good-natured, AUG. 4
redheaded, gangling young hillbilly from Tennessee headed
for Europe with the A.E.F. His name was Alvin Cullum
York, and the way he could handle a Springfield was a caution. At the height of the Battle of the Meuse-Argonne,
Corporal York, his sergeant and 15 men were ordered to
wipe out a hillful of German machine-gun nests. The corporal thereupon, singlehanded, picked off 20 machine-gun-
ners—enough to persuade the entire salient to surrender.

Lionized, feted, decorated when he got back from France,
modest Sergeant York, the No. 1 U.S. war hero, quietly
passed up a fortune in commercial ventures. One of them
was an offer from Jesse L. Lasky to make a picture. The
hero's flat refusal stuck hard in Producer Lasky's craw. Last
year he finally persuaded the Hero York that it had become
a patriotic duty to film his life.

Alvin York, now 53, made three stipulations before sur-
rendering to Hollywood: 1) that Gary Cooper impersonate
him; 2) that no oomphy girl portray his wife; 3) that the
picture be an honest account. Result: one of the cinema's
most memorable screen biographies.

Gary Cooper, the cinema's epitome of a natural American, plays Alvin York to perfection. Joan Leslie plays his
sweetheart. *Sergeant York* does not glorify war, does not try
to horn in on World War II. It stays scrupulously within the
bounds of one man's part in another war. But by showing
what he found in the U.S. worth fighting for, it becomes
Hollywood's first solid contribution to national defense.

"THE LITTLE FOXES" is a blue-ribbon adaptation of Play- SEPT. 1
wright Lillian Hellman's bitter Broadway drama of a rapa-
cious Southern family hell-bent for power and money at the
turn of the century. So completely conceived was the stage
play that its leading character, heartless, ambitious Regina
Giddens, is played by Tragedian Bette Davis with scarcely
an accent's difference from gruff Tallulah Bankhead's inter-
pretation of the original role. This was not Miss Davis' idea.
She quarreled with gap-toothed Director William Wyler
(*Jezebel, Dead End*) for her own version. He—or the play—
won. Result: the films' foremost dramatic actress not only
acts like Tallulah but looks like her.

OCT. 20 **"THE MALTESE FALCON"** is frighteningly good evidence that the British have no monopoly on mystery films. A remake of Dashiell Hammett's hard-boiled mystery, it is rich raw beef right off the U.S. range. The dramatic suspense is heightened by some practically perfect performances by a slick cast. As sly Sam Spade, a hot & cold detective, Humphrey Bogart gives the performance of his career. Close behind him is an aging (61), solid (280 lb.), crackerjack Broadway actor (Sydney Greenstreet) making his first movie a shivery success. Making a trio with this pair is slight, saccharine, sinister Peter Lorre, whose mere presence would turn a bedtime story macabre.

Director John Huston accepted only a slight assist from his father in his new venture: as an unlisted bit player, Walter Huston, sieved with bullet holes, appears long enough to deliver the falcon to Sam Spade, mumble a word or two, and fall dead.

OCT. 27 **"ONE FOOT IN HEAVEN"**—They have just put the "old preacher" on the morning local when the Rev. William Spence (Fredric March) and his pretty bride (Martha Scott) arrive to take over their first parish. To the ardent young pastor, brimful of Methodism, the whistle-stop town looks ripe for good works. For the first time Hollywood has created a U.S. pastor with marrow in his bones. Human and humorous, *Heaven* is a bracing pastor's-eye-view of the Midwest U.S. of two wars ago.

First lesson the parson's wife learns is that the parsonage belongs to the ladies of the congregation. She cannot so much as remove a boar's head from the livingroom wall without causing talk. No prude, the parson wisely reinterprets the Methodist Discipline to fit changing times. Discovering that his son has been to a movie (forbidden), he takes him to another, to point out what there is in the picture that is bad for him to see. The picture (a 24-year-old William S. Hart film, *The Silent Man*) so thoroughly wows the pastor that he uses it as a text for his Sunday sermon.

Fredric March poses, postures, struts his Shakespearean dignity to his heart's sweet content. It is a first-rate job—possibly because in many a good minister there is a forgivable touch of theatrics.

"**DUMBO**" takes Walt Disney back to the animals. His fifth full-length cartoon movie, profiting from the shortcomings of its predecessors, is notable for its freedom from the puppeteering of *Snow White*, the savage satire of *Pinocchio*, the artiness of *Fantasia*, and the woolgathering of *The Reluctant Dragon*. Like *Three Little Pigs*, *Dumbo* (a taupe-colored, blue-eyed baby elephant) is a catchy fable with a moral.

Its craftsmanship is far beyond that of *Snow White*. And seldom has Disney articulated his characters so aptly. Dumbo is a most human little fellow, not bright, but willing. The elephant ladies' aid society ("Girls! Have I got a trunkful of dirt!") is artful satire. Five black crows are to *Dumbo* what the Seven Dwarfs were to *Snow White*. Their burlesque song-and-dance routine, hilarious, eminently crowish, is typical of the good circus humor that bubbles through the picture.

CALIFORNIA CARMEN: It was news in Hollywood that a new NOV. 10 star had been made. But it was news throughout the U.S. that the best tap dancer in the world, Fred Astaire, had a new dancing partner. A partner for Astaire is a Hollywood problem. She has to be good-looking, since he himself is no beauty, and she has to match his humming-bird agility. In *You'll Never Get Rich*, Astaire has the right girl: Rita Hayworth.

Carmen was a justifiable middle name for Eduardo Cansino to give his first child. He named her Margarita Carmen Cansino. He always called her Carmen. He wept when (for Hollywood purposes) she took her Irish mother's name (Hayworth) and shortened her own first name to Rita.

In 1935 Fox signed Rita for a dancing bit in *Dante's Inferno*, one of the worst big-budget movies ever made. Rita played in 14 cheap B pictures for Columbia. Then she set her sights on a part in an A production called *Only Angels Have Wings*. Squandering $500 on a lush evening outfit, she got a table in a nightclub in full view of sulfurous Harry Cohn, Columbia president, and Director Howard Hawks, and let nature take its course. After the ecstatic male huzzas that greeted her in *Only Angels*, Rita set out to train herself for stardom. She had never got beyond first-year high school, but she barged into lessons in voice, drama and other useful things, changed her name, dyed her hair, slowly sloughed her Spanish looks and pounds.

One of her prime functions, Rita thinks, is to be glamorous. Says she:"After all, a girl is—well, a girl. It's nice to be told you're successful at it."

NOV. 24 **"HOW GREEN WAS MY VALLEY"** is Hollywood's answer to Wordsworth's definition of poetry: emotion recollected in tranquillity. Although it is as dramatically incoherent as life itself—for the most part the actors are silent, as befits inarticulate people—*How Green* is a radiant idyll of the dignity and charm of honest, simple working people. Well acted (the cast includes Roddy McDowall, Maureen O'Hara, Donald Crisp, Walter Pidgeon), the picture is a credit to Director John Ford, who has a talent for turning out superb pictures (*The Informer, Grapes of Wrath, Stagecoach*). It is also his last picture—for the present. Ford is now on active duty with the U.S. Navy.

Dumbo, Time*'s "Mammal of the Year." Among all the grim and forbidding visages shines the face of a true man of good will.*

MAMMAL-OF-THE-YEAR: Last week Dumbo, the lovable DEC. 29 little baby elephant with blue eyes and a winning manner, seemed to be all over the place. His name was up in lights on some 200 cinemansions. He was getting a big play in big-city department stores. Toyland was his without a struggle. He was selling giant green peas and bottles of ink, gasoline and women's collars. As a children's book, he was sensational—50,000 copies at $1 each. The tunes from his picture were everywhere.

Dumbo could only have happened here. Among all the grim and forbidding visages of A.D. 1941, his guileless, homely face is the face of a true man of good will. He may not become a U.S. folk hero, but he is certainly the mammal-of-the-year.

MILESTONES

DIED: Sara Delano Roosevelt, 86, mother of Franklin Delano Roosevelt; at Hyde Park, N.Y.

BIRTHDAY: General John Joseph Pershing, 81; in Walter Reed General Hospital, Washington.

MARRIED: Deanna Durbin, 19, blue-eyed cinema lark; and Vaughn Paul, 25, associate producer, her only beau; in Los Angeles' Wilshire Methodist Episcopal Church, with 900 screen folk looking on.

MARRIED: Donald Budge, 25, national professional tennis champion; and Deirdre Conselman, 18; in Chicago's swank St. Chrysostom's.

DIED: Joe Penner (real name: Joseph Pinter), 36, Hungarian-born radio, stage and screen comic who gained fame a few years ago by his inane radululations ("Wanna buy a duck?" "You nasty man!"), of heart disease.

MISCELLANY

BOY: In Bisbee, Ariz., Officer A.S. Orton caught a small boy making off with assorted loot from a store. "Just what," asked he, "did you intend to do with the brassière?" Said the boy: "Make a blindfold for my burro."

RENTED: In Los Angeles, Insurance Salesman Samuel Brummel, 56, sued his wife for half of the $10,000 fee he says she got by renting him for a year to another woman.

HANDLE: In Chicago, Butcher Louis Harris found his Greek customers could never remember his name, changed it back to Elias Haralampopoulas.

FIDELITY: In Medford, Ore., a hunter found his missing bird dogs in the parlor, pointing an owl.

SPADE AID: In Memphis, local grave diggers organized, joined the C.I.O. canners and packers union.

KID PRO QUO: At an East St. Louis School while members of the Parent-Teachers Association discussed "Children in a Changing World" some children stole the adults' lunch and locked them in the building.

EDUCATION

APRIL 28 **MODERN DISCOVERY:** An addition to the sum of human knowledge reported last week by the American Oriental Society: In ancient China, books were written on vertical bamboo slats. Significance of this finding: it probably explains why the Chinese write up & down instead of across the page.

JULY 28 **LYNCHING IN GEORGIA:** "There was a lynching in . . . Georgia Monday," said the Atlanta *Journal* describing the ouster of Walter Dewey Cocking as dean of University of Georgia's College of Education. At week's end Georgia's cigar-chewing, red-suspendered Gene Talmadge had knocked out two more important Georgia educators and provoked serious retaliation.

Dean Cocking, a "furriner" born in Iowa, had been accused of proposing a graduate school where Negroes and whites might study together. He had also been messing around with a "subversive" organization—the Julius Rosenwald Fund (which has spent some $15,000,000 supporting education of Negroes and whites in the South).

Last week, in a packed hall in the Capitol, the Board of Regents held a hearing. The Governor, himself a regent, was there, munching his lunch and prompting his fellow board members. Said Talmadge to Regent James S. Peters: "Hit the chair and holler." Peters hit, hollered. Cried he: "Negroes will ride in the same railroad cars, sit in the same schools, go to the same lavatories as white men."

"They won't do it," shouted Talmadge.

Hearing over, the board voted 10-to-5 to fire not only Dean Cocking but "Furriner" (Mississippi-born) Marvin S. Pittman, president of Georgia State Teachers College and Georgia-born J. Curtis Dixon, vice chancellor of the State University system.

Educators, North and South, lost no time in rebuking Talmadge. The Southern Association of Colleges & Secondary

Schools began an investigation of "political interference" in the university. If the association dropped Georgia from its accredited list, its degrees would not be recognized in other States and enrollment would decline.

Unruffled, Governor Talmadge retorted: "We credit our own schools down here." At week's end he was in hot pursuit of "furrin" textbooks.

KITTY'S LAST EXIT: Professor George Lyman Kittredge's AUG. 4 last exit was unstagy. But when he died last week, at 81, peacefully in his bed, part of Harvard died with him. For 48 years he was Kittredge of Harvard, Shakespearean and Chaucerian scholar, one of the last Victorians. Harvard men will remember "Kitty" for his studied, perfectly timed classroom entrances and exits, his imperious walking stick, his snowy beard (which he kept so, according to legend, by dippings in laundry bluing). One day (also according to legend) he presented himself, magnificently dressed and bearded, at a Beacon Hill mansion for tea. The girl who opened the door exclaimed: "Jesus Christ." "Not at all," snapped Kitty, "I am George Lyman Kittredge."

Kitty's English 2 was one of Harvard's hardest courses and its best show. Kitty tolerated no coughing or sniffling during his lecture. Once, halfway through, he coughed himself. He pulled himself together, said, "I am sorry, gentlemen, I cannot go on," and marched out. To pedants surprised at his lack of a Ph.D., he retorted: "Who would examine me?"

Kitty's death was almost the end of a great chapter in Harvard scholarship. At his last lecture, in May 1936, the room was crowded with reverent visitors. Kitty lectured as usual on *The Winter's Tale*. But he did not end his lecture as usual by marching up the aisle and uttering his last sentence at the door as the bell tolled the hour. Instead, he stood on the platform and said quietly, "We'll stop here." A roar of applause roared over his bowed head. Then Kitty silently waved his students from the aisle and went out.

EDUCATION FOR DEATH: Adolf Hitler's plans for America NOV. 3 are no secret in his schools. Every young Nazi is taught to hate the U.S., knows that some day he will have to fight it. This week an educator who had heard Hitler's plans from the mouths of Nazi babes told what he had heard:

❡ In a Nazi school, Michigan-born Educator Gregor Zie-mer heard a geography lesson for nine-year-olds. Teacher: "The U.S. has a low type of government, a democracy. What is a democracy?" Pupils: "A government by rich Jews . . . that will be defeated by the Fuehrer."

❡ Excerpts from a favorite song of Berlin University students (tune: *O Tannenbaum*):

America, America,
Oh, Jewish land, America.
You certainly conceited are;
A big fat pig, that's what you are.

NOV. 10 **PROGRESSIVES' VICTORY:** Progressive Education won a thumping victory over traditional education last week in the nation's largest city school system. The biggest Progressive experiment ever conducted involving 65,000 of New York City's 600,000 elementary school children, was officially pronounced a success.

The experimental schools scrapped their formal curriculum and educated their pupils by "activities," *e.g.*, keeping store, building a post office, taking an imaginary trip to California.

DEC. 15 **GEORGIA VERDICT:** Last week, despite a penitent appeal by Georgia's Board of Regents, the Southern Association of Colleges & Secondary Schools decided to black-list ten colleges in Georgia's University System. It ruled that students' credits at University of Georgia, Georgia Tech and eight other State colleges would not be recognized by other universities after next Sept. 1. [The black-listing lasted three months, was lifted on December 1, 1942, when newly-elected Governor Ellis Arnall promised legislative action to protect the State's Board of Regents from political interference.]

DEC. 29 **SHORT CUT:** U.S. colleges took a step last week that they thought would enable them to weather World War II better than they did World War I. Instead of making things easier for their students, they decided to let them work harder. Yale, Harvard and Princeton jointly launched a scheme to cut their course from four to less than three years by staying in session all year round.

BOOKS

In addition to reviewing the latest books, TIME'S *book section in 1941 also reported on a remarkable and tragic coincidence— the deaths within six months of four great authors: F. Scott Fitzgerald, James Joyce, Sherwood Anderson and Virginia Woolf.*

"OUT OF THE NIGHT"—Jan Valtin. In the plain, unvarnished JAN. 20 days of the Russian Revolution, the Chekists used to keep batteries of automobile engines constantly running to drown out the human and mechanical sounds from the execution cellars. Few of the men & women who might tell how Communism really works ever escaped to tell. This week a deserter stepped out of the night and spoke his piece. He had no face and no identity. He called himself Jan Valtin. He claimed that he was 1) an ex-German Communist; 2) an ex-agent of the Communist International; 3) an ex-co-worker of the OGPU [Soviet secret police]; 4) an escaped prisoner of the Gestapo; 5) an escaped prisoner of the OGPU; 6) a man wanted dead or alive by both. What he had to tell seemed pretty well to substantiate his claims.

Part of this book's peculiar power comes from its casual reporting of weird, harrowing, unfamiliar things. But its real power comes from something else. Communism in its heyday was a materialist religion for which its believers were ready to die. Valtin's book is a clinical record of the moral disintegration of that religion. The ultimate horror in reading it is less its portrait of violence, of crimes, of vague or too real terrors, than the sense it gives of the soft, slow collapse of civilized men into total depravity.

FITZGERALD UNFINISHED: In Hollywood one day last JAN. 27 month, Francis Scott Key Fitzgerald phoned the doctor to put off his visit until the next day. Fitzgerald was writing,

The late F. Scott Fitzgerald. The "lost generation" died with him.

The late James Joyce, with Stephen, who was his chief solace. Page 227.

did not want to be disturbed. He kept on writing the next morning, too. When the doctor got there a little later, Novelist Fitzgerald's heart had stopped.

Nostalgic Fitzgerald fans realized that the "lost generation" had died with him. And they wondered what he had been racing death to write. Last week they penetrated several wrappings of reticence to find out. Fitzgerald was writing a novel about Hollywood. As a "gag title," he called it *The Love of the Last Tycoon—A Western*, expected it to run a little longer than *The Great Gatsby* (218 pages). Friends were sure that it would be published in some form, perhaps under some other title. Others thought that after the typical Fitzgerald ending of Fitzgerald's life, a Fitzgerald novel reworked by somebody else might come as something of an anti-climax.

Fitzgerald was the last survivor of a generation that never grew up—or rather of its period of hectic arrested development. This period he had fixed memorably in a series of remarkable prose movies: *This Side of Paradise, The Beautiful and Damned, Tales of the Jazz Age, The Great Gatsby, All the Sad Young Men.*

When the jazzed arteries had begun to calcify, and the bravely broken hearts began to miss a beat, Fitzgerald slowed down too. For the last three years he lived in Hollywood, tranquilly, soberly (friends claimed that he had not had a drink for years), but also somewhat like the last passenger pigeon in the Cincinnati zoo.

SILENCE, EXILE AND DEATH: Last week a little group of peo-   FEB. 10
ple got together in Manhattan in an atmosphere of unaccustomed awe. They were friends of James Joyce. Fortnight before, a terse cable had announced that the author of *Ulysses* and *Finnegans Wake* was dead in Zurich. To many a baffled reader, the death of Joyce meant merely that the "cult of unintelligibility" had lost its chief prophet. To his admirers, it meant the loss of the greatest figure in European letters since Marcel Proust. To his friends Joyce's death seemed like some simple lapse in nature, grandly tragic and fitting.

Bit by bit, his friends in Manhattan pieced together a picture of his last months. It was a picture of monstrous ironies. Joyce, the young man who fled from Ireland to live by "silence, exile and cunning," died a destitute refugee from Paris. The mind that thought history "a nightmare to which I hope never to awaken," was caught in the fall of France. The mind that created the Miltonic rhetoric, the subtle architecture of *Ulysses* and *Finnegans Wake*, found its last peace in talking to an eight-year-old child.

The Joyces (wife Nora, son Giorgio) lived in Paris. His daughter Lucia, who suffered from a nervous disorder, was in a sanitorium near St. Nazaire. Joyce's grandson Stephen (son of Giorgio) was in school at St. Gérand-le-Puy, near Vichy. The Joyces were invited there for Christmas in 1939, had a big party. Even then Joyce was suffering a good deal of pain. For ten or twelve years he had had a mysterious intestinal ailment which caused him agony whenever life did not go smoothly.

After Christmas the Joyces rushed back to Paris. He could not stand the tranquility of village life. But shortly before the Nazis moved to Norway in April 1940, the Joyces moved to Vichy. Forced out of Vichy when the army took over, the Joyces arrived at 8 a.m. at St. Gérand-le-Puy. Joyce was indignant; he was not in the habit of going out before 11.

He made frantic efforts to get an exit visa so that he could take his family to Switzerland, birthplace of *Ulysses*. Thanks to influential friends, he finally procured a visa from Vichy.

But the Swiss government was fussier. At one point it re-fused to admit Joyce on the fantastic claim that he was a Jew. Then it demanded a $7,000 bond. The mayor of Zurich got the sum reduced to $3,500 which some Swiss friends got together. But on the day the Swiss entrance visa arrived, the French exit permit expired.

When Vichy finally granted a second visa, there was no gasoline for the drive to the train. Defying police regulations, Giorgio Joyce bicycled to Vichy, begged a gallon of gas. In Zurich the Joyces put up at a small pension. They had al-most no money. Moreover, the Germans canceled the per-mission to remove Lucia from occupied France. Friends say that the thought of his daughter's remaining in a bombed area intensified Joyce's intestinal pains.

More and more his bitter day dreams took on the pro-longed, chaotic misery of the night dreams in his last great book *Finnegans Wake.* (*A hundred cares, a tithe of troubles and is there one who understands me? One in a thousand of years of the nights?*) And as the voices of the awakening children humanize the nightmare in *Finnegans Wake,* the voice of his eight-year-old grandson Stephen became Joyce's chief solace. All day he would sit telling the boy (*the child we all love to place our hope in for ever*) stories from Greek and Roman mythology, the Norse sagas, Shakespeare. But when only a small sum of money arrived from the U.S., scarcely enough to pay a part of their debts, Joyce collapsed from worry.

An X-ray showed a malignant ulcer on his duodenum. After the operation, he had to have two blood transfusions. He tossed around, worrying about Lucia. Then he had a last brief talk alone with his wife. During the night he began to lose consciousness. (*My ho head halls. I feel as heavy as yon-der stone. . . . Night now! Tell me, tell me, tell me, elm! Night night! Telmetale of stem or stone. Beside the rivering waters of, hitherandthithering waters of. Night!*) Unlike the Finne-gans, Joyce never woke up.

APRIL 7 **DARK AND LONELY:** Last week in the Blue Ridge foothills at Marion, Va., a coffin was lowered into a grave. In it was the burly body and curious brain of Sherwood Anderson, paint manufacturer, ad writer, editor, short story teller, novelist, poet, American. The grave had had to wait more than two weeks. Anderson died at Colón, Panama Canal Zone, last month. He had sailed from Manhattan and fell ill at sea. He had to be carried ashore at Colón 48 hours later on a stretcher. Three days later he died of an abdominal obstruction and peritonitis—"right on schedule," said one of the hospital men, explaining that people with such trouble usually live just five days.

Anderson the artist, too, died about on time. Critics had begun to point at the mediocrity of his recent work. It didn't matter, for his job was done. If an American writer's job is to reveal Americans to themselves, Anderson had done his greatly. With a boy's keen eyes he had seen the hates, passions and queer lives that lie just behind the drab façade of the small U.S. town where he grew up (Clyde, Ohio). As a man he set down what he saw in a series of great short stories —*Winesburg, Ohio*; *The Triumph of the Egg*; *Horses and Men*, and half-great novels—*Windy McPherson's Son*; *Poor White*; *Dark Laughter*.

Few U.S. writers have been so conscious of the physical body of mid-American earth, the chokingly hot or numbingly cold prairies whose distance envelops the lonely villages and their lonely people at night. On that lonely darkness he tried all his life to shed light. When Sherwood Anderson had written his way out of his own loneliness, he found he had nothing more to say.

AN ARTIST VANISHES: One morning last month British Novelist Virginia Woolf sat down at her desk as usual, but instead of revising her new novel, she wrote a note to her sister saying: "Farewell to the world." She also left a note for her husband. Then she took a walking stick and went across the rolling Sussex Downs to the River Ouse. When her husband, following her footprints across the fields, rushed up in panic, only her stick was lying on the bank. Searchers dragged the Ouse, but found no body. APRIL 14

All her family was inclined to think that Virginia Woolf was a suicide. But they did not think that it had been brought on by the war. When German airplanes roared overhead, dropping incendiaries, Virginia helped to give first aid. When a bomb demolished her London home, destroying valuable murals, she observed: "Every beautiful thing will soon be destroyed." More unsettling than the war had been her literary worries. Three weeks ago Virginia Woolf finished a short novel, *Between the Acts*. She felt that the end of her book was not up to the exacting Woolf standard.

The late Sherwood Anderson. He saw hates, passions and queer lives.   *The late Virginia Woolf: "The whole world was clamouring: Kill yourself."*

She had always been morbidly self-critical, sometimes suffered a complete nervous collapse. In 1922 she published *Jacob's Room*; in 1925 *Mrs. Dalloway*; in 1927 *To the Lighthouse*. All three were stream-of-consciousness novels. To some readers they didn't always make sense, but they made her name and parts of them almost made music. Perhaps, as World War II and the war's changes closed over her, Virginia Woolf came to feel at last like war-shocked Septimus Smith, whose suicide she had described in *Mrs. Dalloway*: "Human nature, in short, was on him—the repulsive brute with blood-red nostrils. . . . The whole world was clamouring: Kill yourself, kill yourself. . . ."

MAY 5 **SUICIDE NOTE:** Last fortnight the note that Virginia Woolf left her husband was read at the coroner's inquest which pronounced her death a suicide: "I have a feeling that I shall go mad and cannot go on any longer in these terrible times. I hear voices and cannot concentrate on my work. I have fought against it, but cannot fight any longer. I owe all my happiness in life to you. You have been so perfectly good. I cannot go on and spoil your life."

"DARKNESS AT NOON"—Arthur Koestler. Of Author Ar- MAY 26
thur Koestler little is definitely known. But he has written the most exciting novel of the season. And it is obvious from *Darkness at Noon* that he knows Russia and the deep places of the human mind.

The book begins with the clang of a cell door closing in a GPU prison. It ends with a shot in the back of the head in a murky passageway of the prison cellar. It moves with the speed, directness, precision and some of the impact of a bullet.

"BERLIN DIARY"—William L. Shirer. This diary is the most JUNE 23
complete news report yet to come out of wartime Germany. When Shirer went to Berlin in 1934 to report Nazi doings, most people outside Germany were convinced that the Nazis were crazy and would soon be turned out by a popular uprising. Goering was an overblown playboy who liked to dress up like Lohengrin. Hitler was a mad man and a paper hanger to boot. Before Shirer left in 1940 he had reported the destruction of European civilization from the center of the destroying whirlwind.

In Godesberg, during the Czech crisis, Shirer had a glimpse of Adolf Hitler: "I was having breakfast . . . when the great man suddenly appeared. . . . X, one of Germany's leading editors, who secretly despises the regime, nudged me: 'Look at his walk!' On inspection it was a very curious walk indeed. In the first place, it was very ladylike. Dainty little steps. In the second place, every few steps he cocked his shoulder nervously, his left leg snapping up as he did so. . . . And now I understand the meaning of an expression the party hacks were using when we sat around drinking . . . last night. They kept talking about 'the carpet-eater.' . . . They said Hitler has been having some of his nervous crises lately and that in recent days they've taken a strange form . . . he flings himself to the floor and chews the edges of the carpet." Shirer saw Hitler again right after Munich: his nervousness was gone.

Arthur Koestler. His "Darkness at Noon" has the impact of a bullet.   *Gypsy Rose Lee wrote "The G-String Murders" herself. Page 232.*

JULY 21 **"THE KEYS OF THE KINGDOM"**—A.J. Cronin. Last week advance sales of this book passed 250,000 copies, the biggest since *For Whom the Bell Tolls*. The first novel A.J. Cronin has written since *The Citadel* is a reverent piece of hagiography about a Catholic priest, Father Chisholm, who is spiritually a good deal wiser, intellectually not quite so bright as most of the people around him. His keys are humility and kindness. The kingdom they unlock for him is a religious commonplace: the kingdom of God is within you. Its outward manifestation is tolerance.

Chief difficulty in writing about Christian goodness is that almost nobody believes it is possible. Next difficulty is that few people find it exciting. In *Les Misérables* Victor Hugo succeeded in making goodness exciting by free flourishes of his supercolossal, Wagnerian style. His Bishop Myriel is Christian virtue carried to the point of elephantiasis. Author Cronin succeeds by exactly the opposite means—by simplicity, artful artlessness, complete sincerity.

SEPT. 29 **"MILDRED PIERCE"**—James M. Cain. James Mallahan Cain's first novel (*The Postman Always Rings Twice*) was a tawdry, expert shocker. His second (*Serenade*) was a highly spiced account of singing and sex in Mexico. His third (*Mildred Pierce*) is the most interesting of the three. It is about a

Glendale, Calif. housewife, her husband, her two lovers, her pie-bakery business, her daughter.

James Cain has a cold authority about suburban vice. His trouble is not knowing when to stop. His money gets so cold, his sex so hot, his snobbery so snakelike that their victims are scarcely more than caricatures. But the drugstore-library sensationalism that overhangs Cain's work does not stop him from being one of the most readable storytellers in the U.S.

"THE G-STRING MURDERS"—Gypsy Rose Lee. When H.L. OCT. 13 Mencken called stripteaser Gypsy Rose Lee an ecdysiast (from a Greek root meaning one who sheds) ten years ago, Gypsy—whose finale at the time consisted in dropping her garter belt in the tuba—accused Mencken bitterly of reading books. Now Gypsy has written one herself. It is a lurid, witty and highly competent detective story.

Gypsy wrote every word herself, between shows. Nobody else could have. Two bitchy strip queens are murdered with their own G-strings in a Manhattan burlesque house. Agatha Christie herself could not have contrived the tag line of the book. After it is all solved, a haunting little G-string peddler remarks: "You know, me bein' in the G-string business, I was afraid the cops'd think I done it for the publicity."

"THE LAST TYCOON"—F. Scott Fitzgerald. When Francis NOV. 3 Scott Key Fitzgerald, aged 44, died of heart disease in Hollywood last winter, he left part of a novel and a voluminous pile of notes on the unwritten part of the story. There was some talk, then, of having another writer complete the novel from the notes.

But Critic Edmund Wilson, friend of Fitzgerald and his "intellectual conscience," chose another way to get this truncated work before the public. *The Last Tycoon* contains 128 pages of completed manuscript, covering a little more than half the story; a synopsis of the rest; a selection from the notes; some fragmentary scenes. In his foreword, Critic Wilson states his belief that *The Last Tycoon* is Fitzgerald's "most mature" work, that Hero Monroe Stahr, a "boy wonder" movie executive, was the most thoroughly explored of all Fitzgerald characters.

Numerals in italics indicate a picture of subject mentioned.

PICTURE CREDITS

XX

PRODUCTION STAFF FOR TIME INCORPORATED
John L. Hallenbeck (Vice President and Director of Production),
Robert E. Foy and Caroline Ferri
Text photocomposed under the direction of Albert J. Dunn and Arthur J. Dunn

QUOTES OF THE YEAR

President Roosevelt *(quoting Abraham Lincoln to describe the world crisis three months before Pearl Harbor—p. 20):* "I have no word of encouragement to give. The military situation is far from bright; and the country knows it as well as I do."

Prime Minister Winston Churchill *(on Mussolini, whose troops the British were fighting in Greece—p. 123):* "This whipped jackal comes frisking up at the side of the German tiger with yelpings not only of appetite but even of triumph."

Joseph Stalin *(while directing dinner guests out of the Kremlin—p. 135):* "The lavatory is on the left."

A German officer *(to a Greek woman whose only food he was requisitioning—p. 150):* "I am sorry, but you must realize there are at present twice as many Greeks as we need here. Half must die."

Mrs. Lily Barrow *(of her son, Joe Louis—p. 174):* "When he was a kid, I near wore his backside out with a strap."

Gangster Al Capone *(as a marshal served him with papers involving a suit for tax evasion—p. 160):* "This won't make me feel very good."

Winthrop Rockefeller *(as a corporal in the U.S. Army—p. 161):* "The best investment I ever made was not learning how to play craps or poker."

ANSWERS TO PICTURE QUIZ—1: Winston Churchill; 2: Secretary of Commerce Jesse Jones; 3: Labor Leader Philip Murray; 4: Gary Cooper; 5: Henry Ford; 6: Bing Crosby; 7: Adolf Hitler; 8: OPA Boss Leon Henderson; 9: Benito Mussolini; 10: German Field Marshal Keitel; 11: General Charles de Gaulle; 12: Secretary of War Henry L. Stimson; 13: Interior Secretary Harold Ickes; 14: Soviet Marshal Budenny; 15: Japanese Premier Tojo; 16: Rita Hayworth.